Dave Bricker offers a new and powerful approach to storytelling. Whether you're working on a marketing campaign, a business strategy, or a novel, you'll find useful tools and perspectives in *The Story Story* that will help your messages connect.

—Houston Gibson King, Ph.D.
International best-selling author of *The Happiness Book*

Also by Dave Bricker

The Dance
Waves
Currents
The Writer's Guide to Powerful Prose
The Blue Monk

The Story Story

A VOYAGE

THROUGH THE ISLANDS OF CONNECTION
AND ENGAGEMENT FOR WRITERS, SPEAKERS,
PROFESSIONALS, AND VISIONARIES

BY

DAVID E. BRICKER

PERSPECTIVES ON STORYTELLING

EXPLAINED THROUGH STORYTELLING

ESSENTIAL ABSURDITIES PRESS

All rights reserved. No part of this book may be reproduced or transmitted in any form or by any means, electronic or mechanical, including photocopying, recording, or by an information storage and retrieval system — except by a reviewer who may quote brief passages in a review to be printed in a magazine or newspaper — without permission in writing from the publisher.

Though the island settings in this book are based on actual places, the narrative is a work of fiction. Characters, names, businesses, places, and events are wholly fictitious. Any resemblance to actual persons, living or dead, or to actual events is purely coincidental.

The schooner illustration on the front cover of "The Ship We're Here," was rendered by I.W. Tabor for the original 1896 edition of *Captains Courageous* by Rudyard Kipling.

Copyright 2017 Essential Absurdities Press
Book design and production by Dave Bricker
Edited by Steven Bauer

ESSENTIAL ABSURDITIES PRESS

ISBN: 978-0-9862960-2-4

For Eva

Dave Bricker

Introduction

The rationale behind *The Story Story* is simple: Too many books explain *why* stories are powerful tools for engagement, and *how* to use storytelling techniques to forge stronger connections with colleagues, clients, friends, and family members. But these books are *about* stories. As insightful as some of them may be, few of them are stories unto themselves—an oversight this book aims to remedy.

The Story Story reads like a novel. The narrative—a Socratic dialogue of sorts—describes a group of diverse characters who encounter an unlikely teacher in a remote and beautiful wilderness. Together, they look into the sea, out into space, and deep within themselves to discover what stories are, why they're important, and how they work.

The Story Story is a non-fiction book wrapped in a novel, a literary anomaly that will surely have the librarians out marching in the streets with torches and pitchforks! You'll encounter practical storytelling advice and techniques, explore the thinking and feeling behind stories, learn how stories flow through your psyche like blood through your veins, and find inspiration to rewrite the stories of your life and business. Hopefully, you'll enjoy a few smiles along the way.

If you're a writer or speaker, you'll find ideas in this book you can use. If your language is business or marketing or science, you may be surprised to find that your stories follow the same rules as those of your literary colleagues. The same is true if you're a visual, musical, or technological storyteller—or even a cook or a dancer. Though our individual stories are as unique as fingerprints, those magic swirls are found at the ends of fingers that share a common purpose—to touch and be touched.

The Happiness Congress

*T*he Happiness Congress was off to a less than ideal start.

The setting was inspiring enough. The tiny island of Moraine Cay[1] in the northernmost reaches of the Bahamas offered a pristine white beach any postcard would covet. If those sands had ever been walked on, the wind and tide had long since erased any footprints. The clear, shallow waters of the Little Bahama Bank glowed as a stripe of vivid turquoise and aquamarine patches between the shore and the reef, a band of coral that extended from the seaward edge of the island like an encircling arm around a shallow, seagrass-bottomed anchorage where a lone sailboat bobbed gently. Beyond it, waves from the deep Atlantic driven by a brisk northeasterly wind exploded against the outer, barrier reef, sending spray high into the air. The pines of Little Abaco Island nine miles away—the "mainland"—and the radio tower at Foxtown rose at the far side of the glittering blue Sea of Abaco.

Small twin-engine planes from the South Florida coast had carried this year's Happiness Congress participants—seven lucky

---

1. A cay is a small, tropical island — pronounced "key" like in the Florida Keys.

strangers—over freighters and cruise ships in the Gulf Stream; across a surreal tapestry of submarine colors and shapes dotted with green, sand-rimmed islands; over a patchwork of shoals and shallows on the backside of Abaco; and down onto a tiny airstrip in the pines on Great Abaco Island.

Three overpriced minivan taxis—*three!*—piloted by dark men chattering in marginally understandable Caribbean patois had carried the seven-member group a quarter-mile down the S.C. Bootle highway to the ferry dock where Charlie Albury waited with his outboard-powered launch.

Mr. Albury, with his Bahamian lilt, had been kind and encouraging as he'd answered questions about their tropical surroundings. He'd apologized for the spray as they set out against the wind across the Sea of Abaco, and he'd helped carry their bags down the dock to the beach on Moraine Cay when they'd reached their destination.

Charlie had sounded confident when he'd assured his passengers that Mr. King, their mentor and teacher for the ten-day retreat, would be delivered to the island within an hour or so. He'd suggested they walk around the quarter-mile-long island, enjoy the beach, perhaps take a swim, and explore their surroundings until King arrived. Everything about the trip up to that point had screamed "joyful island adventure!"

The Happiness Congress

But that was four hours ago. The sun was setting behind the tops of the Abaco pines across the bay, and an incongruously chill February wind had stolen the romance from the setting.

Moraine Cay was not without shelter. A yellow and white wooden villa with a screened wrap-around porch stood not far off the beach. It was all quite charming except for the locked doors and the oversized "NO TRESPASSING" signs, subtitled "Seriously! This Means You!"

As the light faded, the Happiness Congress discussed whether "trespassing" included the invasion of the screened porch on the side of the house opposite the wind, especially if stranded visitors needed shelter from the elements. Micky Tomm argued that the goal of the owners of the house and the sign was to prevent intrusion and damage—which would only be a minor problem if they broke a screen and spent the night on the porch. They could always leave some money behind to cover repairs. Audrey argued that it was the owners' prerogative to define the terms and boundaries—not the visitors' to interpret them; the sign offered no caveats or exceptions.

Several of the castaways were able to raise a signal on their cellphones, but nobody quite knew who to call or what to say the problem was. They had food—snack food, but at least it was food—enough to get through the night, nobody was sick or injured, and they had all been delivered to exactly where they'd asked to be. The phone at the Happiness Congress office back in Orlando rang continuously through to voicemail. The prospects of anyone sending a boat out on a windy night to navigate through the coral heads and rescue them seemed remote. And where would they go once they got back to the mainland? Hopes for a comfortable evening rested on the elusive Mr. King turning up soon with the keys to the house and a compelling excuse.

They decided to hunt for driftwood. If enough could be found to make a suitable fire, they might stay warm on the beach. Barring that, Plan B would be to camp on the porch.

They found weathered planks and branches along with a few coconuts and a piece of blue sea glass. The scavenging operation was beginning to look as if it might produce sufficient fuel for a good-sized fire when Vincent, a young man who had arrived with a backpack and a guitar, asked if anyone had matches or a lighter. That scuttled plans for fire-building and dropped morale another notch.

As the temperature dropped, Micky Tomm grew frustrated. "You guys can freeze if you want, but I'm going to break through one of those porch screens and get some shelter from this wind. I'm cold enough already, and without a fire…"

He paused and pointed out at the anchorage. A lone, lanky, sandy-haired figure clambered over the side of the schooner[2] into a dinghy and began to row toward the dock.

A few minutes later, a shirtless middle-aged man with bronzed skin clad in a pair of zebra print exercise pants—his smile missing one front tooth—stared up from his small boat at the Happiness Congress's welcoming committee on the rickety pier. "Howdy," he said. "I'm Strider. I have a hot grouper stew on the stove if anyone is interested—and I'm guessing you all will probably appreciate some warm bunks once the temperature drops tonight."

"You're not Mr. King, are you?" asked Micky Tomm.

Strider laughed. "Nope. Just Strider."

The castaways searched one another's eyes.

Strider read their hesitation. "This isn't the United States," he assured them. "Nobody's going to hold you up or push you under. And it's … what? Seven against one? You can spend the night on the beach if you want, but you'll sleep better aboard *The Metaphor*."

"You guys can do what you want," Audrey told the others as she handed her bag down to the mysterious boatman and began to descend the ladder between his stabilizing arms, "but a hot stew and a warm bunk sound a lot better to me than freezing on a beach all night and feeling like a dumbass in the morning."

Strider advised her to keep her weight low and centered until she was seated safely in the stern. "Anyone else? I can carry two at a time, plus bags."

A half-hour and several trips later, the Happiness Congress and way too much luggage had been ferried out to the anchorage,

2. Schooner: A sailboat with two or more masts, the tallest of which is in back.

over the rope railing, and onto the wooden deck of *The Metaphor*. Down below, the travelers arranged themselves on settees on either side of the main cabin. The promised fish stew and a few bottles of wine quickly restored their spirits.

"Before we get to introductions," Strider said, "will someone enlighten me as to how you ended up stranded on an island in the middle of the Bahamian wilderness? It's not often that…"

Micky Tomm volunteered an explanation. "We come from all walks of life—I'm a pharmaceutical company executive; we have a musician and a teacher, a scientist, a writer, and a few others in our group. We're all here for the Happiness Congress; we've taken time off to spend ten days talking about and studying the nature of happiness."

Strider raised an eyebrow. "So you guys paid some serious money—I assume—to get marooned on an island in the Bahamas so you could study…"

"Getting stranded wasn't part of the plan," Walter, a tall man propped up in the forward corner of the settee assured him. He absentmindedly fingered his empty plastic wineglass. "We were expecting ten days' accommodations and a well-respected teacher as part of the deal. I'm embarrassed to admit we all paid $5000 in tuition plus travel expenses for this little adventure to nowhere."

Strider twisted his chin and closed his eyes. After a long moment, he spoke. "Well … you're certainly not nowhere. In fact, if there ever was a *somewhere,* you're smack dab in the middle of it. But there's no way you can know that yet.

"I have a suggestion — an offer to make — and if my instincts are right, you're all going to take me up on it. Why don't you spend the next ten days sailing on *The Metaphor* with me? I can't think of a better way to study happiness, and if anyone wants to jump ship, we'll be here in the Abacos — only a quick ferry hop and a short, overpriced taxi ride from the airport."

Micky Tomm looked Strider in the eye. "That's a kind offer," he said, "but I'm not sure why you're making it. What's in this for you?"

"Curiosity … intuition … a feeling. I was minding my own business out here in what you call 'the middle of nowhere,' and I suddenly found myself with an islandload of interesting folks aboard. The romantic, silly, or stupid part of me wants to find out why you landed on my deck. Maybe the answer to that question is 'happenstance,' but I can't resist the potential for this to turn into a story. The play has begun. I want to see how it ends."

"What about money?" asked Walter.

"Buy the groceries and be good company," said Strider. "I'm not here to prey on your misfortune. I'm going to go topside and check the anchor lines. You folks discuss it. I'll drop anyone who wants to bail out at the Green Turtle Cay ferry dock tomorrow."

Strider rose, offered a gentle bow to his guests, and ascended the companionway ladder.

Deliberations among the Happiness Congress were short. Strider seemed pleasant enough if a bit quirky. And if he was going to murder or rob them, he would have done so already. At sixty-two feet, the sailboat offered ample room and comfortable quarters. Ten days in the Bahamas aboard a classic wooden schooner certainly beat retreating to the airport and slogging home defeated.

Strider returned to the cabin. "Anyone leaving tomorrow?" he asked, grinning.

"We're all in," said Audrey. "But why were you so sure we'd accept your invitation? We don't know anything about you. And I'm not convinced you don't think we're a bunch of bozos for dropping five grand on a ten-day workshop to study happiness."

"I'm not convinced I don't, either," Strider confided. "I can't think of a bigger oxymoron than 'Happiness Congress,' but there's one thing I know for sure: You are all invested in your stories … and stories are what happiness and the rest of the Essential Absurdities are all about."

We Are All Salesmen

Strider retrieved a stack of blankets from a locker and suggested everyone retire to the deck of the schooner. He handed out the blankets as his guests climbed through the companionway. "Now that you've settled into your cabins, grab a cushion and a blanket and stake your claim on a piece of deck or cabin top.

"You'll have to excuse me," Strider continued, "but it may take me a few tries to remember all your names. A round of introductions will at least help me get started."

Audrey sat to Strider's left and spoke first. "We're all just getting to know one another, too. We landed on the island and got caught up in playing *Robinson Crusoe*. I think we pulled together pretty well, but we never got past superficial greetings."

Strider looked Audrey in the eyes. "Why don't you start off, then? Tell us your name, what you're passionate about, and what message you'd like to share with the world. Then we'll go clockwise around the deck and come back to me." Strider grinned comically. "We'll save the best for last."

"Okay, so I'm Audrey. I'm a counselor and a non-denominational minister. I have a Master's degree in social work and a Ph.D. in psychology. I offer couples therapy, conflict resolution, grief counseling…"

"May I interrupt you?" interrupted Strider.

Audrey cocked her head. "Uh … I suppose. Was my introduction not up to your standards, Captain?"

The happiness delegates chuckled over Audrey's lighthearted challenge to Strider's authority.

"I'm sorry to drop anchor while your sails are up, love, but you're a lousy salesman. Tell you what; hold that thought. Let's move on and we'll come back to you. I suspect our friend sitting next to you will make my point. You are…?"

Walter bowed his head to his colleagues, made eye contact with each of them, and took a deep breath. "I can't promise to know myself any better than Audrey knows herself, but I'm Walter. I'm a bestselling author, a two-time cancer survivor, and a motivational speaker. I offer workshops, coaching, and seminars on…"

"No, you don't." Strider pointed a finger and directed a stern gaze at his guest.

The thought occurred to several of the happiness delegates that a trip to the airport in the morning might not be a bad option after all, but then Strider's features softened and he began to laugh. "I'm sorry," he wheezed. "I'm having a bit of fun at your expense.

You probably think I'm woggly in the flooglebumpkin." Strider circled a finger around his ear. "But if you'll allow me, I'd like to test myself, here. You see, I live on a classic wooden boat in the Bahamas. I like to think of myself as happy—happiness being the magic sprinkles on the ice cream of life that you all came halfway around the world to learn more about. With your kind permission, in the absence of the venerable Mr. King, I'd like to take a stab at presiding over your Happiness Congress.

"But before you vote me off the island, I'll share a little secret about teaching. I know I just kicked your introductions into the scuppers, but we'll get right back to that. Do we have any teachers aboard?" Audrey nodded. Walter extended an index finger and Doug waved a tentative hand from across the circle. "Every good teacher learns as much from the students as the students learn from the teacher. I do *not* want to be a stuffy professor who feeds data to ignorant pupils. I want to be the *agent provocateur* who keeps the conversation off-balance and focused on the Essential Absurdities. You're free to put me in my place ...

"And sooner or later—probably sooner—I'll say or do something stupid. I'm extremely thick-skinned and you shouldn't waste an opportunity to have a laugh on me—laughter, of course, having plenty to do with happiness.

"So who here wants to push forward with the Happiness Congress under the misguided, irreverent, and nautically themed guidance of Captain Strider ... and who wants to walk the plank? All who like pirate noises say, 'aye' and all who like horse noises say 'nay.'"

The deck of a wooden schooner anchored in the lee of a sheltering reef in crystal waters adjacent to a tropical island is no place to be disagreeable, especially after a hot bowl of fresh fish stew and a few glasses of wine—and especially after a stressful afternoon spent marooned in paradise. Applause and a chorus of approving *ayes*—and a piratical *aarrgh* or two—celebrated Captain Strider's ascension to the throne of the Happiness Congress.

After an exaggerated bow, Strider raised his palm to his circle of guests strewn about the deck. "With the ceremonies behind us, let me circle back to Audrey and Walter—and indirectly to all of you. It may be that some of you voted me in due to the lack of other candidates and not due to any great faith in my leadership. Let's rewind.

"I'm Strider. I'm forty-six years old. My blood type is O-positive. My shoe size is 11. I was born in Saint Anthony's hospital in Oklahoma City. My eyes are gray." Strider clasped his hands under his chin in mock swoon. "I like candle-lit dinners and walks on the beach ... but nobody cares about *any* of those forgettable factoids.

"Audrey, you offered me a story about what you *do*. That story may work in a world of concrete and glass office buildings and competitive corporate politics and societal pageantry, but it makes no sense here. Your *real* story is far more valuable and beautiful; let's figure it out so you can carry it back to the land of clocks and calendars with you.

"Walter, you did the same thing; you told me what you *do* — seminars and coaching and the rest of your services.

"Audrey, with your permission, I'm going to pick on you because I stepped on you the hardest.…"

Audrey smiled. "Thanks, Captain. Shall I go fetch the cat-o-nine-tails for you?"

"There'll be no flogging here," Strider assured her, "just playful banter. If you're not laughing, you're not learning — another important piece of teaching wisdom that's too often overlooked.

"So, Audrey, let me rephrase my original question. *How would you describe yourself — as a person?*"

Audrey closed her eyes and gathered her thoughts. "I'm 45 years old. I'm single and amicably divorced, and 15 frustrating pounds overweight. I love the outdoors; I hike in the mountains and ride my bike. I like to read fiction and I love to travel. I own a house in Colorado where it's currently a lot colder than it is here. I have two dogs — both rescues and both mutts — and I keep a vegetable garden when it's not ski season. My daughter is in her first year of college … I can go on if you want more."

"No, that's perfect," said Strider. "But notice how *different* your two stories were. When you thought I wanted an introduction, you talked about your academic and professional qualifications;

I didn't get to know *you* at all. When you described your *self,* you talked about the place you chose to live and the things you love to do. You gave me ways to *connect* with you—human connection being one of the most powerful and important of the Essential Absurdities.

"So I ask all of you, how can anyone be *happy* if you have two or more completely different stories about who you are—and you don't know which one to use when?"

"Strider," Walter said, "you accused Audrey of being a poor salesman. What did you mean by that?"

"I wondered when that bubble would break the surface." Strider crossed his arms behind his head and lay back against a sail bag propped against the mainmast. "We are all salesmen—or sales*women* if gender equality in language is important to you. Some of us sell products; some of us sell services—and that's part of our business, which is part of how we survive in the urban world. That's probably why the 'what we do' story is the first thing to pop out of our mouths; survival is a big priority.

"But we are all driven to *connect* with other people. That's hardwired into who we are. We want to be loved and trusted. We want to be listened to. We want to be understood. We want to share our ideas and dreams and philosophies and stories. We are all selling our *selves,* but we can't do that when we wear the 'cloak of respectability' story we're *told* will impress others. That story tells us to cover up who we really are with degrees and qualifications and achievements. Those things can be meaningful, too, but why present them in any context other than what we are passionate about? I don't care if you have a law degree, but I care if you're passionate about justice and fairness. I don't care if Audrey's a Ph.D. psychologist, but I do care if she's passionate about exploring how people behave and communicate. I don't care if Walter is a motivational speaker, but I do care if he's passionate about connecting with people and making them feel better about their lives and work."

Doug joined in from his perch on the aft cabin top. "So I could tell you I'm a high school art teacher, but that would just describe my function within society? If I tell you instead that I love painting and drawing and sculpting and I love teaching young people how to express themselves in creative… "

"Exactly!" Strider sat up straight. "Sell the benefits, not the features."

Strider allowed his audience a moment of silent contemplation and then continued. "Take a sailing trip aboard this boat as an example. The *features* of my ship include the number of bunks, the configuration of the sails, the fact that she's a traditional boat built in the 1930s, the horsepower rating of her engine, her eccentric captain, et cetera, et cetera. Those details may or may not be of interest to various people, depending on whether they like boats or are shopping for an excursion.

"So what are some of the benefits?"

"She can carry a lot of people?" responded a voice from under the shadow of the main boom.

"No, that's a feature, but we can turn it around and make it a benefit. What is the *value* to the prospective passenger—the customer—of *The Metaphor* being able to sleep eight guests?"

"You can bring your whole family on a cruise?" suggested Doug.

"You can have a meeting or a corporate retreat?" offered Walter.

Audrey smiled. "I think I'm getting this; there's room aboard for more people to connect and share."

"Exactly," shouted Strider. "Hoist the ship's colors to the masthead for Audrey! Those are all good answers. People don't care about what you *do*; they care about *who you are*; they care about what you have to *offer* them. They care about connecting with their families, colleagues, and communities. Sure, they want a board-certified dentist when their tooth hurts, but they also want a dentist who empathizes—one who understands that needles and drills are scary things. They want to *connect* with someone who can deliver a painless, fearless experience that delivers the functional results they need.

"How can we sell ourselves, and how valuable it will be for others to connect with us if the story we tell about ourselves has *nothing to do with our real worth?*

"What about the name of this ship—*The Metaphor?* I could have called her *Aquatic Wooden Passenger Carrier*. That would have explained her function…"

"But it wouldn't have explained anything about what she *offers*," added Audrey.

Strider smiled. "Now you're sailing in blue water. Good! What this ship is about will be revealed in time, but does anyone remember the two questions I asked when I kicked off our short-lived round of introductions?"

A 30-ish woman with her hair in braids spoke up. "I'm Kaitlin and I love to write—more details when it's my turn—but I think one of the questions you wanted us to answer was what we were passionate about."

Strider offered an upturned thumb of approval. "Good. And the other question?"

Doug jumped in. "What message do we want to share with the world?"

"Does everyone understand why I asked those *particular* questions?"

"Because you wanted us to share what we love and what we have to offer?" suggested Walter.

"An extra ration of grog and hard tack for you, Walter. We are all salesmen. What we are selling is that message we want to share with the world. What motivates us to share that message is our passion.

"What conveys our value to others is the *story* we choose to wrap our passion and our message in. Everything you know and think you know is wrapped in story. The story of our degrees and achievements is so much peacock tail-fanning. Those *features* are small details in the larger story of our *benefits* — of what we have to offer. Too many of us get sold on the ridiculous notion that a weak and poorly crafted story is the best way to describe who we are and what we're all about. How does a résumé describe a person in any way that helps an employer decide whether or not they're worth sharing forty hours a week of life with? Yes, qualifications are important, but hiring someone without bothering to learn what they find meaningful sounds like a recipe for unhappiness if I've ever heard one."

Strider uncorked another bottle of wine and filled a few empty glasses before refilling his own. "It's getting late and I'm an early riser. I'm getting a bit gibblywobbled. Let's coil this cable and move on to other topics. Did we get past grounds for mutiny?"

Kaitlin switched on her smartphone. "I'm a writer. I hope nobody thinks I'm too much of a geek for taking notes, but here's what I got:

"We're all salesmen, but too many of us sell the features and not the benefits — what we do instead of what we offer. People want to connect with us because they *relate* to us, and they can't do that unless we tell them who we are and establish why we're valuable to them. The closing of the deal is all about that connection, and I'm guessing that means in a practical, business sense, that the transaction shouldn't be the goal; it's a by-product of the relationship."

"You *are* a writer," encouraged Strider. "And a good one, too. Do continue."

"You also said that we wrap *everything* in a story—even the things we don't know—which doesn't make sense to me yet, but I imagine we'll get there. A story can be a narrative or a single word we use to label something, but … and let me think about this for a moment … a story is more than just a functional description; a powerful story conveys meaning and value. If it's about you, it conveys *your* meaning and value."

Strider raised his wineglass. "The student becomes the master. Will you write my book for me, dear?"

Kaitlin's blush was visible even in the starlight. "So the story we write about who we are has important consequences. If we're not telling people what our passion is and what our purpose is, our connections will be superficial. We might close a few transactions but we'll never get to what you call…"

"The Essential Absurdities," said Strider. "There's nothing quite so deep, wonderful, magical, and mysterious as the Essential Absurdities—especially when, as their name implies, they're *essential*.

"But we still have introductions to get through and warm bunks are waiting. Let's get to know each other and save that topic for later."

Who Are You?

"Back to introductions," suggested Strider. "Name, location, passion, and purpose. Take a few moments to think about it if you need to; it's not a test."

"I'm Audrey from Boulder, Colorado. I love exploring the relationships between thinking and feeling, and the relationship between spirituality and rational thought. My message revolves around encouraging people to think, feel, and act broadly, deeply, purposefully, and meaningfully."

"Now that's an introduction!" said Strider, "Walter, you've got a tough act to follow."

"I'm Walter from Boston—and as I said, a cancer survivor. I love the mind-body connection. I love the idea that a positive attitude can have physiological, healing effects on the body and that a healthy body is part of a healthy outlook. The message I share in my keynote speeches is tied to that. I encourage people to think of mental health and physical health as flipsides of the same coin."

"I'm Vincent from Austin, Texas and I love playing music—mostly guitar—in a variety of styles: jazz, blues, rock, classical, folk. I love the idea that I can connect musically with people who don't share my spoken language and with people who don't know anything about music except that it makes them move their feet. My mission is to encourage people to listen deeply and experience the joy of playing an instrument."

"My name is Micky Tommaczinsky—which is unpronounceable and unspellable so people call me Micky Tomm. I'm vice-president of a large pharmaceutical company in Chicago. My passions are both selfish and caring. On one hand, I love making decisions that combine billions of dollars with the skills and talents of thousands of people to keep an enormous business enterprise profitable and healthy. I get a thrill out of having my hands on the wheel of an aircraft carrier-sized company. It's like being the benevolent dictator of a small country. But I also like that the products we make cure diseases. The end result of our efforts is comfort and hope for a lot of people. I sleep well at night knowing that's where our profit comes from.

"As for my message for the world, I'm not sure what that should be. I could give you all some corporate cloudtalk about leadership, but I don't think everyone can or should experience running a 150,000-employee public corporation. Maybe you all will help me figure that out on this trip."

Strider nodded. "That's okay, Micky. I'd rather hear an incomplete story that's honest. When we answer life's 'fill-in-the-blank' questions with fluffy filling, we prevent ourselves from discovering who we really are; we become the fluff we use to define our destinies, and spend our lives playing video games and watching reruns of *I Love Lucy*."

A sprinkle of laughter followed Strider's remarks. "I've been 'off the grid' for a while," he apologized. "I live on a wooden boat in a blue wilderness. I don't have a television … and let me know if any of you come across that fancy phone I'm supposed to be able to get on the Internet with while you're climbing around the boat. I'm not engaged with the media and electronic distractions that run through your lives—and that puts me out of touch with a lot of things and *in* touch with a lot of others. If you hear me get cynical about business and technology and city life, understand that I'm just like you. I'm invested in my story—and part of what I love about my story is that it's not like *everybody else's* story. Like all good storybook characters, I'm human, flawed, and fraught with contradiction."

"So what about you, Captain Strider?" asked Micky Tomm. "What's *your* story?" He looked around the circle at the guests who hadn't yet introduced themselves. "I don't mean to go out of order. It's just that he got started and I wanted to…"

"Hear the rest of the story? Yes. That's one of the peculiar things about stories; we naturally hate incomplete ones. Have you ever sat through a bad movie or read a lousy book because you had to find out how it ended?" Strider smiled at his audience who responded with nods of agreement. "Well, here's another one....

"I grew up in a small town in Oklahoma where I lived a fairly typical white middle-class suburban existence. My father sold real estate. My mother was a poet and a very bad housewife. But as a poet she found beauty and comedy and tragedy in all of life's mundane and meaningless people, places, and tasks. She inspired my two brothers and me to love books and language and to dig deeper into the world around us.

"I went to college and majored in English, though I found the program a bit too regimented and structured for my taste; it focused too much on writing eloquent prose and not enough on writing meaningful messages. I got As and Bs, drank a bit, chased some pretty girls, married one, and got a job as a high school college counselor.

"That was supposed to be it. I had the college degree and the job and the pretty wife and the Chevrolet. If you'd asked Betty, she would have told you the 2.7 children were waiting on the other side of the white picket fence I was about to hammer into the perimeter of the yard of the tidy white house we were about to get financing for.

"My job as a guidance counselor got me in touch with all sorts of things that people study and how those things led to various jobs people ultimately do to buy milk and Cheerios and lawn mowers and barbecue grills, but something about it didn't feel right. I didn't realize it consciously at the time, but I was helping young people write stories about what they were going to *do* instead of what they wanted to *stand for*. As a guidance counselor, I didn't feel I was offering very good guidance—and when I did start offering what I considered 'good guidance,' the school administration didn't think too highly of it." Strider raised an administrative eyebrow.

"And then my Aunt Freddie died. Betty and I got on a jet and went out to Kennebunk, Maine one cool New England March weekend for the funeral, and there she was—a wooden John Alden schooner up on blocks in a boatyard with a 'For Sale' sign on her. She'd had a lot of work done on her—and she certainly needed some more—but spring was coming and she was ready to drop in the water.

"I didn't think about it much at first because it seemed like an unobtainable and frivolous fantasy, but I had always loved adventures at sea—pirates and wooden ships and swords and cannons. All those old Herman Melville and Joseph Conrad books and those Sterling Hayden movies I'd loved in my childhood kept bubbling up in my mind.

"Then they read the will. Turns out my tough old Aunt Freddie had been hoarding cash since the Great Depression and a chunk of that went to me. She kicked over the house of excuse cards I'd been living in and I found myself at a very important crossroads in my life.

"That evening after the funeral, Betty starting talking about good neighborhoods to buy a house in and what names we'd give our first child if it turned out to be a boy or a girl. I just broke down at the table—I'm sure the other restaurant patrons got treated to quite a sideshow that night.

"I don't remember a word I said to her. I'm pretty sure I begged her to come with me, but at the end of the evening, she got our savings account and the car and the furniture and all the rest of our stuff, plus half of Aunt Freddie's inheritance money and a broken heart. I left with enough money to buy the schooner and pay for repairs, updates, and supplies.

"I could spend the rest of the night telling you stories about boats and boatyards and how a 62-foot schooner on the ocean is a different beast altogether than a 12-foot Sunfish on a lake at Camp Winnetonka, but the divorce and my decision to become a boat bum happened seven years ago. The important thing is not what all those stories are about, but that I have them. My life is richer because I stopped myself from writing the typical, boring life story that had been prescribed as a cure for my 'imaginative curiosity disorder' and chose to write an exciting one ... and here we sit talking about stories.

"So to complete the introduction: I'm Strider. I live on a sailboat currently located in the Bahamas. I'm passionate about stories and sailing and how the latter provides a perfect metaphor for the former. And my message for the world is that a life well-lived is full of meaningful stories that bring us closer to the Mystery."

Doug clapped and that sent a ripple of light applause around the circle of guests. "That's a great story!"

"Marvelous!" agreed Micky Tomm.

"You're not the first people to tell me that," said Strider. "The story doesn't necessarily make *me* great, but after we get past the Essential Absurdities, I'll share some thoughts on what *does* make a story great.

"But we're still not finished with introductions and I'm not the only one yawning."

Strider gestured at the next guest.

"I sort of introduced myself earlier, but I'm Doug from Miami — which means I probably had a shorter trip to get here than the rest of you. I'm an art teacher because — well, because I love art. I'm also a graphic designer, which means I find ways to put art to work for people. My message to the world is that creativity is important and valuable, even when you can't measure its worth on a spreadsheet." Doug nodded to his left.

"I'm Kaitlin from Seattle. I love the idea that you can take something abstract like an idea or an experience and convert it into squiggly marks on a page. If you do it artfully, others can decode those marks and understand your experience or idea. I guess my message to the world—in light of the discussions we've already had—is that literacy is an important vehicle for connection. The better people become at reading and writing, and the more they do, the better able we are to share what we see and learn.

"And if no one objects, I'll be our self-appointed note-taker and secretary."

"That's cool," said Vincent. "I think a lot of what you just said about letters on a page can also be said about *notes* on a page."

"*Click* — another connection," observed Strider. "But if Kaitlin will make a note to pick up that thread later, we'll finish up the intros."

"Aye, Captain," replied Kaitlin. "One more to go."

"I'm Lenore from New Mexico," offered the last guest. "I'm an astrophysicist and a mathematician at Los Alamos labs. I get to be the exception to all those jokes; what I do literally *is* rocket science. My passion is expanding what we know about the Universe and what's in it and the rules it abides by. My mission—which I haven't thought much about before tonight—would be to encourage people to explore the world with an open mind. Too many people grab onto a 'fluffy' story—to use your word, Strider—that makes it easy and safe and comfortable to explain the unknown. I doubt science will ever explain everything, but the more we learn, the more we're *able* to learn. My message is 'learn, explore, and grow.'"

"The butcher, the baker, and the candlestick maker have spoken," announced Strider in a deep, deliberate, story-telling voice.

"Now take a moment and look around the circle of Happiness Delegates trying not to fall asleep on the deck. I'll bet everyone here remembers everyone else's name. Try it."

After a pause, everyone laughed with surprise. "Yeah, I remember everyone," said Micky Tomm. "Me, too," said Audrey. "I'm pretty sure I've got all the names," added Vincent. The rest of the group nodded and smiled.

Strider continued. "As I said when we first started introducing ourselves, nobody cares what your degrees are or what school you went to or what your blood type is, what hospital you were born in, or what you do. People care about your *story*—about what you're passionate about—about what you have to share with *them*. When you shared your passion and your mission instead of your qualifications, everyone here *connected* with you and what you care about. That's why they remember your name.

"And collectively, we're writing a story about *eight* characters off on a sailing adventure. Those characters had better be memorable or our readers are going to wander off. Even *Gilligan's Island* only had seven castaways — though I bet anyone here who's over 45 can name them all."

"This is great stuff!" said Audrey. "I love it, but how do you put your story on a business card?"

"Make a note of that, Kaitlin," suggested Strider. "Doug the designer is here, and I suspect he'll have some suggestions to make about branding.

"Tomorrow morning, we'll get into some diving and sailing, and then tomorrow after we're anchored up at Green Turtle Cay, we'll get into the Essential Absurdities."

Watercolors

Light streamed through *The Metaphor's* ports and deck prisms. Bleary-eyed passengers followed the smell of pancakes and coffee to the main cabin. Lenore and Walter arrived first. Kaitlin only wandered in after her colleagues' laughter roused her from her bunk.

"How'd everyone sleep?" inquired Strider as he flipped another pancake.

Vincent raised his coffee cup. "I was out *cold!*"

"Me, too," said Audrey. "I haven't slept that well in years."

Walter smiled contentedly and offered a simple, "Mmmmm."

"Anyone need a refill on coffee?" asked Strider. "I can make another pot."

Micky Tomm and Kaitlin raised empty mugs.

Strider held up his spatula. "Today's storytelling topic is 'water.' You're going to spend the next ten days living and traveling in it and on it. In fact, you're about 80% water yourselves—physically *and* mentally. You've already experienced the benefits of sleeping on it while it rocks you gently and gurgles past the hull.

"Since you're my captive audience, I'm going to force a short geography lesson on you to start your day." Strider handed out a nautical chart and a cruising guide for his guests to pass around and then continued.

"Think of the Bahamas as a small continent adjacent to North America. Most of that land is submerged; the water's about ten feet deep. The name 'Bahama' comes from the Spanish *baja mar* which means 'shallow sea.'

The Abacos—the northernmost Bahamas—consist of a 112-mile-long 'mainland island' that's really the two islands of Great Abaco and Little Abaco separated by a small tidal creek. To the north and east of that lies the Sea of Abaco, a shallow bay with a sand and seagrass bottom. Beyond that lie the 'out-islands.' Some of these are tiny green jewels like the one I rescued you from yesterday. We'll visit others that have had settlements on them for over two hundred years. Shallow water extends about a mile beyond the islands—mostly sand patches, seagrass, and scattered coral heads, and then you get to the drop-off. The third largest barrier reef in the world rises to the surface there from about twenty-five feet of water to where it plunges to thousands of feet. That's where you saw all that spray blasting up off the horizon if you were looking out to sea yesterday. After that you'll find miles and miles and more miles of deep, cobalt blue North Atlantic Ocean.

"That barrier reef is a beautiful place to snorkel and explore, but with eight people aboard and only one of my two small rowing dinghies currently in the water, the story of us all getting out to that reef and back is one I'm—shall we say—unwilling to invest in. But Moraine Cay—the *one* island we happen to be anchored off of—provides a unique opportunity for us to explore what's happening *in* the water. Just to windward of us is a coral strip that extends from the tip of the island out about a quarter-mile. It's within easy swimming distance and the tide is nearly slack—which means we're all going in the water.

"Put on your bathing suits and we'll meet on deck in ten minutes. In the *aft* locker—the one in the back end of the boat which you newly nautically initiated types will henceforth refer to as the 'lazarette'—you'll find a big bag of masks and fins and snorkels. Find some gear that fits and jump in. It's winter and it's going to be *cold* until you get used to it, so the faster you get in, the faster you'll get acclimated and start having fun."

"Aren't we supposed to wait an hour after eating before we get in the water?" asked Kaitlin.

"Ah ... and here we see the dark side of stories," replied Strider. "Long ago—probably back in the '30s or '40s—some mommy reasoned that if little Johnny was full of Oscar Meyer wieners and Fritos and chocolate cupcakes, his body must be diverting its resources to converting all that food into energy and poop—and therefore he'd have fewer resources to devote to the muscles in his arms and legs—the muscles he'd need for swimming. This theory sounded plausible and oh so deliciously erudite so she shared it with the other women in her mahjong group and they agreed it made perfect sense. The next thing you know, they were all sharing this fabrication at the hair salon, and in the checkout line at the Safeway—the end-result being that millions of children who were amped up on sugary foods that were far more damaging than a dunk in the pool on a full stomach had to writhe and whine and convulse and cry while their mommies forced them to wait out their sugar blasts on *terra firma*.

"A plausible story—or even worse, an *im*plausible story—can spread like measles if enough people are willing to believe it without question—and this is where evils like wars and racism and the notion that you actually get better deals on Black Friday come from."

The happiness delegates responded with a round of hearty applause.

Strider bowed. "I went off on a rant, didn't I?"

Kaitlin giggled. "I guess I'll go put my swimsuit on."

Twenty minutes later, the group had suited up, finished screaming hyperbole about the cold water, adjusted masks and snorkels,

Watercolors

and made their way to the reef. Strider swam with the dinghy in tow and anchored it just behind the coral. Removing his snorkel mouthpiece, he said, "Float on the surface or dive down and explore. Keep track of how you feel and what you see."

When confronted by the captivating array of sea life, the swimmers soon forgot about the cold. Living things of every conceivable shape and color entertained the happiness delegates for the next hour. Vincent swam down under a coral arch. Doug and Lenore marveled when Strider pointed out a paisley peacock flounder camouflaging itself on a coral head. As his guests grew more confident, they spread out. Walter spotted an octopus slinking through the coral. Micky Tomm rose to the surface over a grass patch with a large, weed-covered conch shell in each hand. Strider retrieved a spear from the dinghy and used it to procure a half-dozen lobster and a small collection of fish.

After the crew had ascended the boarding ladder and rinsed themselves and their gear with fresh water, Strider suggested a plan. "Green Turtle Cay is about 33 miles southeast of here. That's about a six-hour sail. We'll anchor up there tonight and go ashore in the morning. The old colonial settlement of New Plymouth is there along with two beautiful, protected anchorages. We'll pick up some basic food and supplies—which we need to do because I wasn't planning on having seven guests aboard—and then if the weather cooperates, we'll bang on over to Marsh Harbour the next day where they have a big grocery store and anything you forgot to pack."

In short order, Strider hauled up the big mainsail and the anchor. The jib[3] at the front of the boat followed and *The Metaphor* was under weigh.[4] Once the three sails were set to his satisfaction, Strider engaged the self-steering vane. The vessel cheerily piloted herself on a steady course across the brilliant tapestry of blues and greens, heeling gently with the dinghy charging along in her wake. Strider took a final glance at the compass, took a few visual bearings on the surrounding islands, and assembled the happy happiness delegates on deck.

"Let's tell some stories about water," suggested Strider. "How did it feel to be out on the reef this morning?"

"Exhilarating," said Audrey.

"That was gorgeous," crowed Kaitlin.

"That was one of the most beautiful places I've ever seen," offered Micky Tomm.

"Inspiring," said Lenore.

Strider adjusted the rim of his battered straw cowboy hat. "So it's safe to say that you all had a *powerful* experience this morning?"

---

3. *Jib:* The sail at the front of a boat — usually raised on a "forestay" that runs from the mainmast to the bow or bowsprit.

4. A ship was originally thought of as being under "weigh" once the anchor had cleared the sea floor. The phrase derives from "weighing anchor" and not from the common misunderstanding that the ship is making her "way" through the water.

"Absolutely," nodded Audrey and Doug in unison.

"Now what if I were to suggest a different type of swim?" continued Strider. "What if I offered to take you offshore to swim in the blue water where it's a mile deep?"

"That sounds dark and freaky to me," said Vincent.

"Yeah, I think I'd sit that one out," agreed Doug.

Strider continued. "So clear shallow water is exhilarating, but deep, dark, mysterious water is…"

Kaitlin broke in. "There could be sharks or killer whales or giant squid or God-knows-what down there. I'm not swimming in *that!*"

"No worries," assured Strider. "If we see any deep water on this trip, we'll stay aboard the ship. But since we have our psychologist, Audrey, with us, let's see if she and Carl Jung can offer insights into your reactions to water of different depths.

"Audrey, can you enlighten us about archetypal symbols and about the significance of water in dreams and stories?"

Audrey gathered her thoughts and took a deep breath. "Certain symbols are common to all people — or at least common to people of particular cultures. For example, sand probably has a different symbolic meaning to Bedouins who live in the desert than it does to you and me. A car would probably not appear in a Bedouin's dreams, but in urban industrialized society, a car in a dream can be assumed to be symbolic of 'your way of getting around in the world.' Shortly after I finished my studies and moved to Colorado, I had a dream that I was driving my old car around in my new town, and that I was having trouble finding my way. This was my subconscious expressing anxiety over the contrast between my old, academic life and my new, natural, small town, mountain lifestyle.

"So an archetypal symbol is one that's shared by most members of a society. If you look at fairy tales, you'll find symbols like treasure maps, golden keys, dragons, princes and princesses—the list is endless—and these symbols are part of the psycho-spiritual fabric of our culture.

"In isolated tribal cultures, symbols from the environment like mountains and owls and foxes and rivers seep into the collective unconscious and assume the roles of deities or spirits that deliver messages through dreams. In industrial culture, we end up with cars that represent our perspectives, audio and video discs that represent memories and choices, et cetera. But because our society changes so rapidly and because our experiences with the surrounding environment, culture, and technology are so varied, our symbolic language is a bit jumbled up. People like me help sort out the psychic mess."

Strider checked the compass and walked to the windward side of the deck so he could scan the horizon ahead of the ship before returning to his sailbag throne. "Excellent. So what is water in the language of symbols?"

"Water is symbolic of the unconscious. If you dream about water, you're usually dreaming about feeling or thinking. Have any of you ever had a dream where you can breathe underwater?"

Most of the happiness delegates nodded.

"That's usually you getting in touch with your *sub*conscious. Something 'below the surface' is being revealed."

"Good," said Strider. "So if you were to dream about clear, clean water with beautiful living things and vivid colors in it where you could easily see the bottom, what would that mean?"

Audrey smiled. "That dream would be about clarity. If you could see into your subconscious mind and find that it was beautiful, and if you could see the metaphorical bottom and know there was nothing dangerous or threatening there, I imagine you'd wake up feeling pretty confident and complete."

"And what if you dreamed you were far out to sea swimming in deep water? Kaitlin was less than thrilled about that idea."

"That's the nature of the subconscious, isn't it? We aren't in complete control of ourselves. Because of those fifteen pounds I mentioned, I know I shouldn't eat chocolate cake but when it's in front of me, I find it hard to resist. People lose their temper and say things in anger. Sometimes we speak or act without any conscious awareness of the conflicts or problems that motivate our behavior. All those sharks and sea monsters down there in that black void can come up and bite you at any moment...."

"... even if the odds of it happening in the actual, physical ocean are remote," interrupted Strider. "More people are killed by vending machines every year than by sharks. The story of the infinitely deep, dark, dangerous ocean is a reflection of the *internal* world more than it is a picture of the *external* world. Deep ocean water is just as clear as that gin we swam in on the reef this morning. We even use adjectives like 'deep' and 'shallow' to describe ideas and experiences. Where do you think words like that come from, and what does this tell us about stories?"

Micky Tomm spoke up. "I guess we experience things on two levels, even when we don't know it. There's the literal level and there's the symbolic level. We can enter a situation and use our senses to evaluate what it *is,* but without being aware of it, we may react more to what it *means.* Also, the physical world gives us things like cars and keys and sea bottoms that our subconscious 'borrows' so it can map meanings onto them. These two worlds are reflected onto one another."

"You know what's cool?" offered Vincent. "I like the idea that this could be a two-way street. The conscious mind can be influenced by the subconscious mind, but if I surround myself with clear water and white sand beaches and green islands and blue

Watercolors

sky, doesn't that have a positive effect on parts of my psyche that I can't access with my rational mind? If the subconscious creates symbols and archetypes out of things it borrows from the physical world, why not give it beautiful things to borrow?"

Strider clapped slowly in approval. "…Which is why you feel so much better when you're on a beach or mountain top or blasting across the Sea of Abaco in a wooden boat with the wind pushing you past a string of beautiful islands. I doubt anybody ever had a peak experience while they were stuck in traffic or waiting in a checkout line to pay for their groceries.

"And we use this dual consciousness for effective storytelling." Strider opened his arms. "It's related to 'selling the benefits, not the features,' which we spoke about last night. So many advertisements and sales pitches — and introductions — talk about what the product or service or person *is* or *does*. That's all literal stuff. When we speak about what the product or service or person *means,* and how that meaning is relevant to what our listener naturally finds meaningful, we engage them at a much deeper level.

"Meaning is one of the Essential Absurdities. We'll get deeper into that, but though meaning can't be measured, it's like love, God, and pornography; you know it when you see it — or feel it. In fact, though it can't be defined or calculated or examined in a test tube, some philosophers argue that the one, single, overarching theme in all of human literature and endeavor is the search for meaning. Whether Kaitlin is writing a poem or Lenore is calculating the orbit of a comet or Walter is encouraging an audience to live a healthier lifestyle or I'm sailing around proselytizing to a band of abandoned happiness seekers, we are all engaged in finding and creating meaning."

Strider paused before continuing. "And this will lead shortly to something truly meaningful to all of us: With the caveat that we'll soon resupply at Green Turtle Cay and gather the resources to assemble better fare, I'll put together some peanut butter sandwiches.

"Kaitlin, you're our official ship's secretary. Give me just a minute to go below and grab some lunch-making supplies. Then you can regale us with one of your eloquent summaries."

"Aye aye, captain." Kaitlin's swinging braids followed her forward to where she stood and leaned against the foremast. "This is pretty heady stuff considering we haven't been here twenty-four hours yet, but let me see if I can put it together."

She smiled professorially. "Point number one: there is no need to wait before swimming if you've just eaten."

"Point two: there's no need to number these points so I'll stop.

"Point ... or next ... or whatever: We live in a world of *literal* people, places, things, and actions, but we also live in a world of *abstract* symbols and meanings that lie beyond our senses. We perceive these worlds in conscious and subconscious ways that overlap and communicate. The subconscious borrows literal objects from consciousness and maps meanings onto them. The conscious mind dumps an avalanche of sensory data into the subconscious—most of which, I imagine, it filters out and discards as meaningless. So if we want to connect with others, the stories we tell have to be *relevant* and *meaningful*. Otherwise our messages go in through consciousness, down into subconsciousness, and out with the psychic garbage. For a message to stand out against the cacophony of words and images, it must be relevant to your listener's personal search for meaning. Your story will be perceived on a conscious, literal level, and also on an abstract, subconscious level. If it doesn't pass the meaningfulness test, it won't hold anyone's attention for long.

"To use Audrey's example, most western people—the 'normal' ones who don't live on sailboats in the wilderness—are surrounded by cars." Kaitlin smirked playfully at Strider. "You drive around in them, shop, go to work, as part of your interaction with a literal world full of concrete objects and actions. When you dream, those same objects and actions are used as symbols that represent nonliteral feelings. Your car—or maybe your old car in your new neighborhood becomes a vehicle—pardon the pun—through which you can create a literal reflection of the abstract. If you're experiencing stress because you're adjusting to a new environment, the only way you can wrap your literal mind around that is to write a story about it. The subconscious mind does that for you.

"Meaningfulness and relevance come into play when we tell stories in the conscious world. If you tell a car story to a remote tribesman in the Andes, it won't resonate with his subconscious 'vocabulary.' If you tell a car dealer or a mechanic or a racecar driver a car story, their daily exposure to cars is different from yours; your story might not resonate with them the way you hope. If your words are not relevant and meaningful to your listener on a subconscious level, they'll be tuned out or quickly forgotten.

"Vincent suggested that it's valuable to surround ourselves with an environment that contains positive and beautiful symbolism. If everything we send 'down below' is psychic junk food, we could end up suffering from psychic malnutrition!"

Audrey chimed in. "I'm going to steal that if you'll let me."

"I'd be honored," Kaitlin said with a smile.

"*Connection* happens when we communicate an idea that is *meaningful* to everyone engaged in the interaction. Walter, you probably feel this from your audience when you give a speech. Doug, you probably get this when your class is interested in your lecture or engrossed in a creative project under your direction.

"In fact, as I think about it, the whole notion of *engagement* must run deeper than many people think. The fancy car or the low-cut dress or the slick business card are just *invitations* to engage.

They may get brief attention in the literal world, but unless the subconscious mind stops dismissing them as sensory junk, they won't be effective messages.

"If we understand the *meaningful* symbols that are shared by a society—archetypes—we find tools for connecting and engaging. This is probably why so many books and articles are called *Seven Keys to Success* or *Three Steps to Raising Happy Kids* or *The Road to a Happy Marriage*. Keys, steps, and roads imply opening locked doors, ascension, and moving forward. Their symbolic content transcends their literal meanings—nobody is going to turn a physical key or climb a physical stairway or hike down an asphalt road to accomplish those goals.

"And finally, we are all engaged in a lifelong search for meaning. Effective storytellers—whether they're artists, teachers, scientists, or businesspeople—understand this, at least intuitively. By understanding the art of connection and engagement, they create meaning in their own lives and in the lives of those they engage with. Financial success and survival in the physical, literal world are only *by-products* of engagement in the unseen world that lies beyond sense and intellect. Stories are the bridge that makes that possible."

Strider handed out sandwiches. He glanced once more at the compass, scanned the water around the ship, and laughed to himself. "Anyone want a glass of water?"

The Story Story

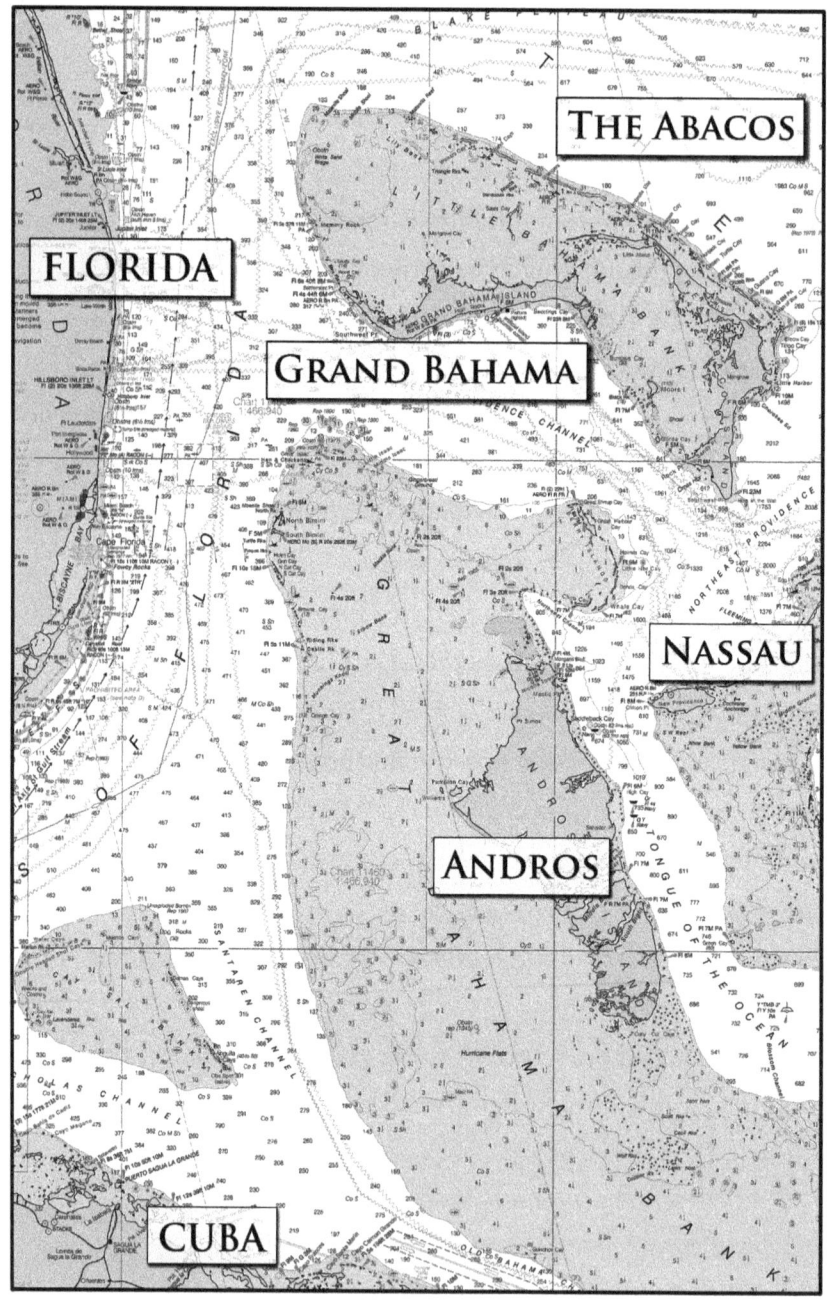

Fear

The sun arced slowly toward the Great Abaco pines. The wind had moderated throughout the afternoon and *The Metaphor* glided gently over clear sand bottom and seagrass in the lee of Green Turtle Cay. With all sails up, Strider approached the narrow channel that looped behind a shallow sand bank into White Sound, the northernmost of the island's two harbours.[5]

Doug and Vincent had been trimming[6] the sails under Strider's tutelage throughout the day. Each stood ready to adjust one of *The Metaphor's* sails at the captain's request.

Lenore approached Strider in the cockpit at the aft end of the boat. "Wouldn't it be easier to just start the engine?"

"It certainly would."

"But aren't you worried you'll run aground or have to maneuver around a crowded anchorage when you get inside?"

---

[5]. The Bahamas was a British territory until it became independent in 1973. To avoid conflict between the spellings of named places like Marsh Harbour and the various "harbors" visited in this book, the British spelling is used throughout the text.

[6]. To "trim" the sails is to adjust them to suit a vessel's course relative to the wind.

"You bet."

"You don't find this scary?"

"I don't hear the engine," called Vincent from the deck. "Is everything okay?"

Strider offered an upturned thumb and then looked at Lenore. "Every time I raise the sails on this ship, I put fifty thousand pounds of wood, steel, and canvas into motion. A lot of mass under a lot of power means enough momentum to split this hull like a walnut. If one wire goes, the whole rig—masts, sails, hundreds of feet of rope—could come crashing down. I could have a bad fastener, spring a plank, and sail this baby right down to the bottom. *Of course I find it scary.*" Strider grew animated as if succumbing to a fit of hysteria. "I could hit a coral head. We could get attacked by pirates. A line could get tangled; I could lose control of the sails and put the bowsprit right through the marina's fuel pumps. An electrical fire is always a possibility. And we could combine that with a propane leak in the galley if we want to get even more pyrotechnical.... And y' know, love, come to think of it, I've got solvents in one of the lockers—alcohol, mineral spirits, acetone. If one of my rags was to combust, the whole big top could blow; there'd be nothing but scorched cotton candy and scalded elephants and roasted clowns and..."

Lenore shook her head and smiled. There was no bitterness behind Strider's exaggerations. "I trust you're about to make a point?"

Fear

Strider dabbed at his eyes. "Actually, yes, but give me a few minutes to avoid fulfilling any unintended prophecies. As you observed, I'm not doing this the easy way; I'm doing it my way."

The Metaphor ghosted along the channel and emerged into a lagoon surrounded by low scrub-covered coral banks, mangroves, casuarina pines, docks, traditional wooden houses, and a small marina. Strider spoke deliberately and calmly. "Doug, can you lower that foresail for me—nice and gentle, please?"

As instructed, Doug let the two lines run slowly through his hands. Canvas piled up on the deck and the gaff—the boom at the top of *The Metaphor's* traditional foresail—glided down to rest on top of it. Doug gathered up the canvas and tied it out of the way.

Strider nodded. "That was pretty, Doug—mighty pretty."

The harbour was not without its obstacles. Strider coaxed his ship through a field of two-dozen fiberglass sailboats on moorings. More than once, he brought her within inches of a dinghy tied behind a yacht. Some of the sailors stood on their decks to watch *The Metaphor's* silent dance with the fading wind. A less experienced couple on a charter boat readied themselves to test their delusion that they might somehow fend off the 25-ton schooner with their hands. Strider smiled confidently and tipped his battered cowboy hat as he adjusted course and passed just behind them. "G'd afternoon to you folks."

At last, Strider chose his spot, a mooring ball just upwind of and between two expensive, high-tech European cruising boats. He rounded into the wind—what little of it there was left—toward his destination and spoke again. "Vincent, can you furl that jib for me like I showed you?"

The sound of line running through the masthead blocks and sail hanks zooming down wire cable accompanied the descent of a triangle of sail canvas at the bow. Vincent gathered the cloth and tied it out of the way.

Creaking sounds echoed through the mooring field as Strider hauled the big mainsail in tight. *The Metaphor* turned straight into the wind between the two neighboring boats and continued forward under her own momentum.

Strider stretched his arms above his head, rose from the cockpit, and walked casually and unhurriedly toward the bow. He paused to wish Micky Tomm a "Pleasant afternoon, sir," before continuing forward.

The Metaphor moved straight into the wind, gradually losing speed until she hovered a few feet behind the mooring ball. Before she could begin drifting backward, Strider reached down with a boathook, grabbed one of the mooring's pendant lines, and secured it to the bow.

"And that, my friends," Strider announced, "is how you moor a schooner. I won't bore you with why schooners are particularly suited to theatrical entrances—the sailing arcana behind that is way beneath your pay grade—but we got ourselves tied up safely, indulged ourselves in the mischief of reminding a few folks that

Paradise can be a scary place, and challenged ourselves to be *oh so elegant*. Did anyone enjoy that as much as I did?"

A chorus of "Aye, Captains" and light applause recognized the end of a successful passage and affirmed the satisfaction of The Metaphor's crew.

"Let's put this ship back together so the lounging can commence. Then I'll get myself down to the galley and assemble some sort of concoction from the fish and conch and lobster we had the good fortune to stuff in the icebox this morning."

Strider showed his crew how to 'flake' the sails in accordion pleats and tie them down neatly. Within a few minutes, the canvas was put away, lines were coiled and hung out of the way, and the deck of *The Metaphor* was ready for another session of the Happiness Congress to convene.

The light faded. The wind died altogether. The soothing calm of the anchorage and the cool air inspired all aboard to enjoy a lingering red sunset and a bowl of Strider's savory seafood rice on deck.

Not unexpectedly, Strider spoke up. "Just before I turned into White Sound channel, Lenore asked me if I planned to turn on the engine. She asked if I didn't find entering an unseen harbour under light wind without power to be *scary*.

"She appears to have forgiven my obnoxious rant of a reply — thank you — I'm sure each of you will get to do that at least once before your suitcases hit the dock — but the answer to her very reasonable question is 'yes.' *You* may have full confidence in my seamanship, but every time I pick up the anchor, I'm *scared*. Plenty of delegates from the Common Sense and Insurance Agent Congresses—not that those two groups are on speaking terms—would have found me to be reckless and irresponsible *not* to enter the anchorage under power, but wasn't there something *magical* about the way we did it? Does anyone here feel richer for the experience?"

The guests reflected for a moment, exchanged looks, and nodded.

"Within certain limits of reason, fears that begin with 'what if…' are our own creations. We sit around catastrophizing—writing silly stories about everything that could possibly go wrong—and the end result is that we stay home nice and safe until the ceiling caves in.

"Has anyone ever heard of Anne Hodges?"

The happiness delegates shook their heads.

"In 1954, in Alabama, Anne Hodges was napping on her couch when a meteorite crashed through the ceiling, bounced off the radio, and hit her. The odds against that happening are—wait for it—astronomical—but at the risk of being unfair to poor Anne who was just taking an innocent nap, the notion that inaction equates to safety is one of the most dangerous stories we can ever believe. Life—if you're actually living it—is scary. Let me offer some perspective...."

Strider paused to enjoy a few bites of rice.

"A few years back, a friend and I sailed *The Metaphor* across the Atlantic, down the coast of Africa, back across the Atlantic to the Caribbean, and then back up to here. Everyone I knew asked the same questions: 'Weren't you afraid?' 'Did you hit any storms?' *Of course* I was afraid and *of course* I hit storms. You don't spend that kind of time at sea without getting the crap scared out of you in nasty weather.

"But I asked one of the friends who had asked those questions how much time he spent on the expressway every day. An hour! An hour a day on the expressway! Now *that's* scary to me. Some of you might find that typical, but hundreds of boats successfully cross the Atlantic every year. Their odds of survival are statistically much greater than those of the average highway commuter who spends five hours a week fifty weeks a year—that's 250 hours—*ten-and-a-half days*—dodging blind, drunk, and digitally distracted drivers.

"Fear is a double-edged sword. If I see black clouds on the horizon, my healthy relationship between fear and common sense will keep me in port. But if I want to go enjoy life, if I listen to all the silly worries and warnings manufactured by the voices in my head, I'll miss out on the thrill of riding that magic edge between the wind and the water. I engaged with the world and got it to push me precisely where I wanted to go.

"Starting the engine is a strategy I could easily have built solid, rational, compelling support for. But sailing in the channel, reading the water, playing the little zephyrs and puffs of wind, navigating through the field of boats — that deepened my relationship with myself and with the Universe.

"You all came here to study happiness. Sitting around inventing new things to be afraid of is the *antithesis* of happiness."

Strider tipped his hand toward Walter who had just cleaned the last of his dinner off his plate. "Walter, you're a speaker, right? Are you still scared when you get in front of an audience?"

Walter took a deep breath. "Speaking in public is a fear many people rank higher than death. Everyone thinks an experienced speaker is immune to that fear, but every time I walk onto the platform, a part of me reminds me that I'm about to be judged. What if I fail to engage this group? What if they don't like my message? What if I get my speech tangled up or suddenly have an urgent need to go to the bathroom in the middle of my presentation? If I was half as inventive as a speechwriter as I am as a spontaneous writer of stories about things that might go wrong on stage, I'd be able to double my fee."

Fear

Strider removed his Stetson and placed it over the compass. "Vincent, you play music. Are you scared when you perform?"

"Yeah, but that's what keeps my music fresh. I might forget a chord change or blow the timing or hit a wrong note—and all those things happen—but that's part of the magic of live performance. Canned music has zero potential for error. Live musicians are tightrope walkers. Sometimes we fall but when we nail it in front of an audience, the energy in the room is indescribable. And if we successfully build rapport with the audience, they *become* our safety net. If they're loving the music, they won't even hear half the mistakes, and they'll forgive us the ones they do."

"How about you, Micky Tomm? You're a big boss man. I bet a lot of your employees think you're not afraid of anything."

"I'm sure many of them think that, but when you fly in the corporate stratosphere, the consequences of wrong decisions can cost millions of dollars. If my decision leads to 15,000 people losing their jobs—if a facility has to be closed in a town we built it in because we thought we were bringing opportunity where it didn't exist—I could single-handedly destroy a local economy. If I check the wrong box, children end up going without food. Now add a board of directors and a pack of executives who don't always see things the way I do. Or add a situation where shutting a plant down is a sad necessity because it's been losing money for years. That's enough to send anyone off to the Bahamas to study happiness!"

Micky's remark provoked the expected smiles.

"But that fear keeps me on my toes. If I let it paralyze me, I won't ever make the decisions that keep my enterprise profitable. That fear keeps me tuned into the people and communities who depend on me to succeed as the business climate changes. It's scary as hell, and every so often I make a bad call—I guess we all hit storms on long passages—but if I make the best of the leadership and don't let leadership get the best of me, my work can be pretty satisfying."

Strider raised his right hand high above his head. "Do *any* of you live a personal or professional life that's free from fear?"

All the happiness delegates shook their heads.

"Kaitlin—honorable ship's secretary—can you provide another of your delicious sum-uppances?

Kaitlin rose and took up her favorite position—leaning against the foremast. "You all have nothing on me. I have to listen to Strider's soliloquys, make sense of them, and translate them into English on the spot. *This* is scary!"

Strider placed his palm on his forehead and looked down at the deck.

Kaitlin twisted a braid across her chin and then continued. "There are two kinds of fear—fear that actually keeps you safe and fear that keeps you from enjoying life. Maybe there's a spectrum or a range rather than two well-defined categories—there's probably some overlap—but we all need to distinguish between the scary things in the world that threaten us and the scary things in our heads that we mistake for the same thing.

"Life involves risk, and that means *connection* and *engagement* involve risk. If we're afraid to meet new people or make important decisions, the irony is that we end up being dangerous to ourselves and to those around us. We have to risk being rejected to find acceptance. We have to risk making the wrong decision to make the right one. We have to risk leaving the engine off to know we're sailors.

"If I can go back to last night's discussion about symbols, *The Metaphor* is Strider's ship—it's his way of getting around in the world—and ours for the next nine days. If Strider's 'way' is expressed by using wind and wits to carry us from point A to point B, starting the engine would be like having someone carry you the last ten feet of a marathon. I'm sure there are situations where common sense would have him start the diesel without a moment's hesitation, but doing that when it isn't needed amounts to sacrilege—a lack of faith in self and a surrender to irrational voices that write stories about imaginary calamities."

Strider sighed. "You have special gift, Kaitlin. I like to pretend I'm eloquent, but this stuff that rambles and rolls out of my head—you turn it into music.

"In 1932," Strider continued, "Franklin D. Roosevelt issued his famous proclamation: 'There is nothing to fear but fear itself.' Truer words were never spoken, though I'm not sure they're as universally understood as they could be."

Kaitlin grinned. "The irony of this is that we can't be happy or successful unless we're scared out of our wits. Avoiding fear means avoiding growth, progress, confidence, and connection."

"*Happiness depends on fear* — a perfect segue!" shouted Strider as he rose to his feet. "It's Essential Absurdities time!

"Let me grab the last bottles of wine. We're going to have a perfect, dark, clear evening. I want you all to look deep into the stars. Marvel at the Milky Way. Appreciate the beauty of the heavens. Gasp at the magnitude of the Universe. Ponder your connection to it. Enjoy nature's spectacle… because for us to understand the Essential Absurdities, *I'm going to have to destroy it all.*"

The Essential Absurdities

*A*fter dinner, Strider gathered the Happiness Congress on deck. "Humor me for a few minutes. The rabbit hole I'm about to take you down is a bit convoluted but I want to put some philosophical foundations under our discussions."

"You have a captive audience," said Doug. "I don't expect many of us will be going home in the middle of your exposition."

"You can always jump overboard and swim for shore." Strider laughed. "But hopefully you'll find my ideas interesting and maybe even enjoyable."

"Go for it," said Audrey. "I can geek out on a little philosophy now and then."

"Take us down, Strider!" said Vincent.

"All right then," Strider said. "We are miles from the nearest city lights. On a moonless night like tonight, you'll see a shooting star every few minutes. The more your eyes get used to the darkness, the more stars you'll see. Take a look for yourself."

Strider extinguished the lantern he'd hung from the rigging and let a few minutes go by so the happiness delegates would have a chance to "ooh" and "aah" over the night sky. As he'd predicted, shooting stars made frequent appearances.

"Lenore, you're our space expert," said Strider. "Tell us how far away all those amazing lights in the sky are."

"The closest star is our sun, Sol. It's ninety-three million miles away. Light from the sun takes a little over eight minutes to get here. The next closest star is Alpha Centauri. It's 4.2 light years away—a light year being the *distance* light travels in an Earth year. Some people get confused by that because it's called a 'year,' but it's a measure of distance, not of time. One star in the constellation of Cassiopeia is thought to be about 16,000 light years away, though it's difficult to measure those kinds of distances accurately.

"See those four bright stars just to the right of the front mast?"

"That would be called the *foremast*," corrected Strider, "but I'm being pedantic as usual. Continue."

"About two thirds of the way between the 'Great Square' and the band of the Milky Way is a little smudge. That's actually a whole galaxy much like our own."

Strider reached for the ship's binoculars so his guests could hand them around while Lenore continued.

"You're seeing it as it looked two-and-a-half million years ago. When that light left Andromeda and began its journey to your eyeballs, the continents on Earth had separated but were still clustered together. The very first hominids had just begun to use tools. Mammoths and mastodons and saber-toothed tigers were alive and well."

"So as beautiful as all this is," asked Strider, "is it safe to say that all these stars are yesterday's news? If some Darth Vader type wiped out Andromeda last week, nobody here on Earth would know about it until a flash appeared in the sky two-and-a-half million years from now?"

Lenore chuckled. "I'm not laughing at the idea of some nut-job blowing up a galaxy. I'm just amused at Strider's observation. He's absolutely right."

"Now let's back up a bit," suggested Strider. "What about the light from the marina over there? Or the reflection off the tip of my nose? Aren't you still seeing these things as they were a tiny fraction of an instant ago—in the past?"

"Hmm. Yes."

"So nothing you perceive with your eyes can be said to represent absolute truth—things as they *are?*"

"I guess not."

"And since sound moves a *lot* slower than light—a little over 750 miles-per-hour—it's safe to say that our ears also bring us echoes from the past?"

"What about touch, taste, and smell?" asked Micky Tomm. "Aren't those senses immediate?"

"All the senses are immediate for practical purposes. Nearby sounds and light sources are perceived quickly enough so we can react to them in the moment, but even when we touch or taste something, our nerve cells have to convert those sensations into electrical impulses that travel through chemical pathways. Our brains have to perceive those impulses, decode them, decide whether or not they merit paying attention to, and then choose an appropriate reaction—which also takes time.

"Everything you perceive is past tense. We lack the ability to have any knowledge of the immediate now."

"In music, we call this the problem of latency," added Vincent. "If you add too many special effects processors between the sound source and the recording device, the delay not only becomes audible, it throws off the timing of the music. That's why videoconferencing works for speech, but musicians can't use it for virtual jamming. The timing in music is subtle enough that the latency kills the groove."

"Interesting, and I'm glad you mentioned time, Vincent. Who here thinks the future exists?"

"It probably doesn't," said Kaitlin. "It hasn't happened yet."

"Does the past exist?"

"I think only in our memories—in recorded form," offered Doug.

"So the only thing that truly exists is the moment—the tiny instant of now?"

The Essential Absurdities

"It's hard to imagine it," said Audrey, "but logic suggests it's true; truth is an instant—a point. The past is gone and the future hasn't happened yet."

"So if messages take time to get to you, everything you *think* you know technically no longer exists. You can only perceive past events—and they're gone."

"Back to Lenore, our physicist: What happens if you slow matter down to absolute zero degrees Kelvin—if you slow it down to where all molecular motion stops—which is essentially what happens when the Universe exists in a single moment?"

"It falls apart. It collapses into fundamental particles of matter and en..."

"So as promised, I have just destroyed the Universe."

"Where's the kaboom?" asked Doug in a cartoon voice. "There was supposed to be an earth-shattering kaboom!"

The happiness delegates laughed, grateful for a moment of relief from Strider's philosophical gyrations.

"But since we haven't all collapsed into a haze of quarks and neutrinos and electrons and protons and morons and such, perhaps one of our assumptions is wrong? Maybe the past and the future do exist?"

"What do you mean?" asked Micky Tomm.

"Maybe we can think of time as a river—as a continuum. If we put a clock on a spaceship that travels very fast, when the traveling clock returns, it will show an earlier time than clocks that remained on Earth—it ticks more slowly relative to the stationary clock—and I say 'relative,' because the so-called 'stationary' clock on earth is still rotating around the earth's axis and whizzing around the sun like we are. The same is true about the wristwatches of a standing person and a walking person, but the time difference is too tiny to measure."

"Einstein called this 'relativistic time,'" explained Lenore. "Events that occur at one time for one observer can occur at different times for another. He talked about space and time as being interwoven. According to Einstein's special relativity, any object that has mass causes a distortion in space-time—which is responsible for what we call 'gravity.' One quasar about 8 *billion* light-years from Earth sits behind a galaxy that is 400 million light-years away. *Four* different images of that same quasar appear around the galaxy because the intense gravity of the galaxy bends the light that comes from it. Astronomers call it 'Einstein's Cross.'"

Walter broke in. "This science lesson under the stars is interesting, but what does it have to do with happiness, connection, engagement, or your Essential Absurdities, Strider?"

"My point is that *everything you know* is a story," Strider raised his index finger. "And it's a story built from flimsy evidence; our senses are inadequate. The human eye can only see about 38,000 colors; the average computer monitor can display over sixteen

The Essential Absurdities

million. Only a tiny range of the spectrum of energy is visible to our eyes. Imagine what the world would look like if we could see X-rays and ultraviolet and infrared. Is that picture of the world truer than the one we perceive? Our senses only receive past tense information; we can't perceive what's happening now. Our clocks all tick at different speeds.

"These are the Essential Absurdities—things we can never see directly—things we draw conclusions about based on their effects on what we *can* see—magic forces we struggle to understand and explain with tools and instruments and brains that aren't up to the task.

"Take connection for example. How do you explain what that is? What does it mean to look into a lover's eyes? What does it mean when we call someone a friend? What does it mean when four hundred people sitting in church feel like they're part of a community? What does it mean when a woman in California calls her identical twin sister in Germany because she 'feels something is wrong' and finds out she's sick? Does connection even mean the same thing to you as it does to me?

"And then what is meaning? What does it mean to ask, 'what does it mean?'?

"The world is full of mysteries—things science or the senses will never adequately explain. We give them labels like 'God,' 'love', 'self,' 'connection,'—'truth'—and we throw these labels around as if they mean anything we can remotely comprehend. All these things are *stories* — and if you happen to love those stories, I'm not saying they're not valid; I'm just saying that stories are the building blocks we use to construct our world. Stories bring us closer to the Mystery. Stories help us deal with the enormity of the Universe. *Everything you know or think you know is a story.*"

"That's fine and dandy," said Walter. "But I'm not sure I want stories on my pancakes instead of the happiness I ordered. How do I use this? I mean ... philosophy is fun, but the reason I signed up for the Happiness Congress is so I could gain insights into new ways to make my audiences happy. I know you weren't the one who offered the happiness workshop — or at least I don't *think* you were — but since you offered to take up Mr. King's baton, I'm feeling lost in space here. Why are we learning about stories?"

Looks and murmurs circulated among the happiness delegates. Several of the happiness delegates shared Walter's concerns.

Strider took a moment to choose his words. "I think happiness is a by-product of other thoughts and actions — and non-thoughts and non-actions. Happiness, itself, qualifies as one of the Essential Absurdities. If you embrace your stories as absolute truth that lives in a world free of logical contradiction, you're going to end up feeling crushed under the weight of The Mystery — and you're probably going to blame that on the differences between your story and someone else's.

The Essential Absurdities

"Walter, you're the one who speaks about the mind-body connection—about the relationship between a healthy body and a healthy mind. You have *evidence* of that connection—the fact that you survived cancer while others didn't being one of your compelling arguments. But you can't *prove* you didn't just get lucky. You can't *prove* that the next person with a healthy body and a positive outlook won't get the bad news and keel over a week later. With your limited senses and past-tense data pulled from a world full of contradictions, you can't prove much of anything. The best you can do is use the story that makes the most sense to you. And by *sharing* that story, by *connecting* with others who share the same conflicts and goals as you, you can hope to catalyze the same transformation in them that you *believe* your story gave you. And that's fine and noble and beautiful as long as you don't get so invested in your story that you're unwilling to accept someone else's healthy living story or modify yours to accommodate theirs. If you eat four bowls of oatmeal for breakfast every day, and some researcher finds a link between oatmeal and cancer remission, you need to be willing to adjust your belief system to accommodate a new theory that explains your survival—even if that invalidates everything you've been telling the world.

"Let's go back to this idea that stories are instruments of inference and not of direct observation. One more space example—In the desert in New Mexico lies a mile-wide crater caused by a

300,000-ton asteroid that struck the earth about 50,000 years ago. That's a lot of iron and nickel, so over the years, a lot of people wrangled over the mining rights. But though scientists calculated the mass of the meteorite by estimating the force required to move that much earth, and though they've found fragments of iron that confirm the crater *was* caused by a meteorite, the actual rock vaporized when it hit the ground.

"That massive force could have destroyed a small city, but we only know about it from its *impact*. We gather evidence, we do a little math, we write a story, and we walk away satisfied that we 'understand' what happened—even though the actual giant meteorite is gone."

"What is it with you and meteorites?" asked Doug.

Strider chuckled at himself. "I was a bit of a space nerd when I was a kid. I didn't always live on a schooner, you know.

"But if you gather your evidence and write your stories and file them under absolute truth, you miss out on the wonders of the Essential Absurdities. The role of stories in our lives is not to put life's wonders in intellectual specimen jars so we can stop thinking and worrying about them. It's to bring us closer to the incomprehensible and the unknowable—to the Essential Absurdities.

"When you connect with someone, you may not know what that means or how it works, but it makes you taste some flavor of happy. Mint chocolate chip, anyone? When you ponder the magnificence of the vast physical Universe and develop some vague notion of how some part of it behaves, you feel a different flavor of happy—maybe peanut butter vanilla swirl?"

"Definitely chocolate!" Audrey laughed out loud.

"And when the Universe serves up a cone full of chicken mint or artichoke fudge ripple—which it inevitably does—you can either question all your stories and your place in the world, or you can accept that these are just more stories that can co-exist with all the stories that contradict them.

"Your conscious mind may reject this, but to the subconscious, contradictory stories are just more colors for the palette. Story conflict doesn't *have* to be an impediment to happiness. If we rewrite the story of ourselves and the world and accept our limitations, we grow closer to the Mystery, less anxious about life's absurd contradictions—and therefore *happier.*

"And you can be happy and experience other emotions at the same time. People cry tears of joy. People get so angry they laugh. I'm happy as can be here in my little wooden castle in Paradise, but that doesn't stop me from feeling lonely at times. The story that you can get past all your other emotions and arrive at a pure, happy 'happily ever after,' sounds appealing, but it isn't authentic. This is where embracing the Essential Absurdities becomes meaningful. This is where people find hope while in prison or lost in the desert or stuck in a refugee camp. Even when they're painfully aware that their life stinks in the physical world, the ones who embrace the Essential Absurdities keep writing stories; they don't abandon their search for meaning."

"Where does God fit into this?" asked Audrey. "Do you think God created the Universe or do you think God is a story?"

"I think you — *we all* — create the Universe — when the pictures we take of it come back from the PhotoMat in our brains. But that's another of life's Essential Absurdities. When you look at our beautiful, perfectly ordered planet with a gorgeous moon circling it that causes the tides, with the sun just the right distance away to support life — life that seems to have generated itself by accident — and you become aware of yourself and say, 'It's me … thinking and feeling and trying to figure out who I am and why I'm here,' you can only conclude that you're the result of some benevolent, intelligent force that consciously intended to produce that result.

"And then you look out into the night sky and see all those lights, and you realize that some of them are whole galaxies that contain billions of stars with planets of their own — and we can only see a microscopic sliver of the big, big, *big* picture. It makes just as much sense that even if the odds are one in a trillion-trillion-trillion, what happened here on earth is bound to happen without any intelligent force playing with the Legos of the Universe. Maybe we're the lucky winners of the celestial lottery? It's statistically probable."

"So which is it, Strider?" Audrey tilted her head and opened her upturned hand toward the captain. "Which story do you think is true?"

"And here we have the absurdity," chuckled Strider. "You're asking me — *me* — an expatriate boat bum on an antiquated schooner in the wilderness — to kill or rescue God. If you have to decide on a story, by all means choose the one that makes you feel best. Believe or don't believe in anything you want. Both of the stories are magnificent, wonderful, mysterious, sensible, and beyond comprehension. Belief is like space-time; everything is relative. Einstein's quasar shows up four times — and each image is the 'real one.' Shoot at any one of them and you'll hit nothing — eight billion years later. Why not believe *both* stories — if you buy into the story that you're *required* to make such a decision? As absurd and illogical as that sounds, you can carry two stories in your head at the same time.

"Kaitlin…"

"No sir, I'm taking a night off. Your Universe is not so easy to gift wrap."

"C'mon. Give it a try."

"Hmm… okay… but don't hold me accountable if I don't make any sense.

"You can't hold an infinite Universe in a finite mind or see it with a limited set of senses. This means most of what's *out there* is mysterious and unknowable. The distances are too far to comprehend, and everything we perceive potentially no longer exists or is inaccurate because, by nature, it's past tense.

"As conscious beings who want control over our lives and destinies, we fabricate stories out of whatever information we can gather. Because of the limitations of our perception, we often end up running into paradoxes and contradictions—the Essential Absurdities.

"For example, the future doesn't exist because it hasn't happened yet, and the past doesn't exist because it's over and done with. At the same time, nothing can exist in a single instant because it would fall apart. And time will pass at different rates for any two people—or clocks—moving at different speeds. I think I'm starting to understand that paradox of quantum physics I keep reading about where, depending on the observer, sometimes energy looks like a particle and sometimes it looks like a wave."

Strider smiled but let Kaitlin continue without interruption.

"We encounter a variety of magical forces in the Universe—Strider's Essential Absurdities—that we can only *infer* the existence of because of their impacts on what we *can* feel and see. We refer to these magical forces or concepts or whatever-they-ares with words like "love," "God," "art," "meaning," "truth," and "connection"—which are nothing more than spoken placeholders that allow us to discuss them—to create stories about them—even though it's impossible to define what they actually are.

"And in spite of the fact that it makes a mess out of our nice, tidy picture of how the universe works, nature plays by some counterintuitive rules. If light, space, and time are malleable, things can be in several places at once—or they can be different things to different people. If we become frightened of these paradoxes, we choose the most comforting story and stop being curious. If, instead, we allow our minds to be in multiple places at once, we can accept conflicting perspectives and emotions as part of our natural order. If we settle on one story because we're afraid of the Essential Absurdities, the danger is that we might think of someone else's story as wrong or untruthful or less valid than our own. That's probably the root of all the world's conflict."

"Oh, Kaitlin," crowed Strider. "You so totally rock! That's another absurdity—that the way we handle the Essential Absurdities themselves is responsible for a great deal of the happiness *and* the misery in the world. Since all we have to know the Universe by is the stories we create about it, stories become the vehicle through which we get closer to the Mystery. But if we become *invested* in a story—or we lack the communication skills to work out the incongruities in a shared story—we end up with conflict. We all want connection—but when we find it, we have to find ways for our stories to mingle harmoniously. And as essential as that particular absurdity is, you won't find a word about it in any of the popular *homo sapiens* operating manuals — which is why we're all sitting here collectively pondering the unponderable and trying to figure out how to be happy."

"One question, Strider," said Kaitlin. "It's one thing to look at a quasar eight-billion light years away and then twist the focus knob on the telescope until we can see the tip of your nose. Your story of how we perceive the Universe told on the deck of a boat in this remote place makes a great twist on 'outward bound.' But what about who *we* are? What about 'inward bound?' What's *our* story?"

"Ah my dear," sighed Strider. "I am tired from a day of sailing, destroying the Universe, and putting it all back together. If nobody objects, I won't be killing anyone until tomorrow."

How the Story Goes

After breakfast, Strider fired up the diesel, and motored *The Metaphor* a mile-and-a-half over to Settlement Creek at the southeast side of the island. There, he tied off to a mooring off the town of New Plymouth. Doug and Vincent helped him launch the second dinghy.

"Anyone know how to row?" asked Strider.

"I'll give it a go," offered Vincent. "How hard can it be?"

"Not that hard ... but why don't you take the *Yin* out for a test run before we entrust your friends' lives to your seamanship?"

Vincent eased himself over the side into the dinghy. After some rocking and a near tip-over, he got himself balanced on the low center seat, placed the oarlocks noisily in their holes, and began to splash about in circles.

"Think each stroke through," called Strider. "Hands low, together, and forward—oars even. Drop the blades just below the water's surface. Pull back. Lift the oars. Repeat. Draw a box with the oar handles that extends out from your heart in front of you with your hands."

The calm harbour waters offered an ideal place to learn. After a few minutes of practice and a minor collision with the *Yang*—*The Metaphor's* other dinghy—Vincent was able to guide his craft elegantly between the moored boats.

"Try letting the oars do the work," called Strider. "Makes no sense, but imagine all you need to do is drop them in the water. Let them 'pull themselves,' and then lift and drop. You can row all day without expending much effort. It's magic."

Vincent took a few more exploratory runs around the neighboring boats and then returned to the side of *The Metaphor* to face his colleagues with a grin on his face. "Your chariot awaits!"

The two dinghies soon landed at the town dock with all hands still aboard and in good spirits. "The rules are simple here," explained Strider. "Have fun. Explore. Talk to people—especially locals. You'll find a lot of churchgoing folk in these islands who will be more accommodating if you keep your language rated PG or under. Swim off the beach if you want—all these islands have beautiful beaches—but don't wear your suitless bathing string in town—no 'Spring Break at Daytona Beach' stuff.

"Vincent, let me show you how to tie off the dinghy. That line attached to the bow is called the 'painter.' If anyone's interested in learning about bowlines and clove hitches, I can—literally—'show you the ropes.'"

"Aren't you going to lock up the boats?" asked Kaitlin.

"Steal a boat in these islands and you'd better pray it's the police who catch you and not the locals. People here make their livings on boats. If a car represents self-identity in the American subconscious, boats are the Bahamian equivalent. Cruising sailors—whether rich or poor—are the same way. Our dinghies are our lifelines. And you may have noticed I didn't lock up *The Metaphor*, either. Stealing a man's boat is like stealing his soul—and island churchgoers spend a lot of time making plans for theirs. I wouldn't leave a dinghy unlocked in a busy industrial harbour like Nassau, but here in the out-islands, you can leave your bags on the seats and nobody will dare touch them. If you buy stuff in town and get tired of hauling it around, drop it in the dinghy. It'll be here when you get back."

"I like that," said Walter.

"I'm impressed," added Lenore.

"It all has to do with connection," explained Strider.

"Better find a shady spot," laughed Micky Tomm. "He's off and running!"

"I'll keep this one quick," chuckled Strider, "because I want us all to get time to enjoy New Plymouth, and I have evil plans for you after dinner." Strider raised his eyebrows and glanced comically over each shoulder.

"Sailors are much more dependent on one another than the average city-dweller. Our homes hang on a few pieces of rope affixed to the sea bottom. If something comes untied, our houses end up on the beach. We deal with storms and tides and other natural forces that sometimes demand we pull together.

"And contrary to popular belief, most of us are not out here living on trust funds. The number of people who sail out to the islands to live a simple life on a social security check would surprise you. It's often the ones who sell the company and retire on a multi-million-dollar yacht who are the first to get bored and move on. For all the money they spend, they're the least invested in their cruising stories.

"The same is true for the people of these islands. They know who their neighbors are. They understand the value of fresh water. They understand what a hassle it is to get supplies from the mainland to here. They know how isolated they can be if there's a hurricane or a local epidemic.

"All it takes is one yahoo who thinks he can exchange somebody's outboard motor for a few rocks of crack cocaine, and suddenly the whole society is under threat. But if that happens here, people don't start locking up; they *all* start watching over *everybody's* stuff; they become *vigilant;* they stand watches if they need to—because they're not protecting their *property*; they're protecting their community, their way of life, and even the symbolic source of their psychic identities.

"So...lecture's over. Feel free to leave your stuff in the dinghies. The taboo protecting your gear is more powerful than any lock.

"And I have a tip for you: As you stroll around town and look at the sculpture garden and all the pretty colonial-style houses with pastel shutters, pop into a tourist shop and buy a half-dozen postcards. Sometimes cruisers make their own and sell them to local merchants—you'll find some arty stuff—but the traditional tacky ones with the sunset or the bikini girl with a lobster in each hand will do. My friend Caroline taught me about the magic of postcards and I'm going to pass her wisdom on to you."

The Happiness Congress proceeded into town. Walter and Lenore lingered in a local art gallery while Doug, Micky Tomm, and Vincent detoured into the sculpture garden. Strider briefed them on the story of the sculptor, Randolph Johnston, and the bronze foundry he'd set up at Little Harbour during the 1950s. Then he and Kaitlin proceeded to the local grocery store to stock up on supplies.

"I'm not used to shopping for eight people," Strider explained. "I could use your help."

"No problem, Strider." Kaitlin brushed a hand against his shoulder.

"We'll hit the big grocery store in Marsh Harbour the day after tomorrow, so we only need enough supplies to get us through until then."

"Some of the groceries here are interesting. They're quite different from…"

"Remember that these islands were an English colony until the crown cut them loose in 1973. Those ties are still strong; you'll find all sorts of junky European imports instead of junky American ones.

"The sad thing is that apart from fresh fish, the people in these islands live on a lot of prepackaged white flour, sugar, and salt. They've forgotten that shrink-wrap is not found in nature. Many of them suffer from the same obesity and malnutrition problems that Americans do."

"I wasn't going to say anything," said Kaitlin, "but I have seen some people around here who could stand to lose a few pounds."

Kaitlin paused, opened her arms, and turned a full circle. "It's funny, but even though this is all new to me, I feel *connected* to this. This makes me want to grow my own vegetables and bake my own bread. I can eat out of a can at home, but—and I wanted to tell you this—I *loved* that seafood rice you made last night. I love that you went into the ocean and came back with fresh, healthy food. That and a few carrots and onions and potatoes gave us something you can't buy in any grocery store. And here are people who live in the heart of this magic place who are eating white bread and frozen chickens and TV dinners and…"

"Be careful, Kaitlin," warned Strider. "You're beginning to *get* it—and you're beginning to sound like me. You're writing your own story about who these people are and how you think they could live better lives—and believe me—I create similar stories for how other people could be happier.

"But that's a slippery slope. If you want to make lifestyle evolution in the Abaco Out-islands your personal priority, nobody's stopping you from buying a straw hat and a pink-shuttered house here. Grow vegetables and raise chickens. Buy a small fishing boat and put solar panels on your roof. Live the good life, stay thin and beautiful and happy, and see if the locals want your story to become their story. You wouldn't be the first American to land in a foreign country on a mission to reform everyone. You wouldn't be the last to leave wondering why they didn't value your gifts. People are heavily invested in their stories, and they're not going to dump theirs for yours—even if you put hearts and a bow and chocolate kisses on it. Do what makes *you* happy and let the rest of the world figure out its own way to accomplish that."

Kaitlin laughed. "I guess it's easy to look at other people's hypocrisy when you've just stepped out of your own world and don't have to look at your own contradictions every day. I can see how people get caught up…"

"Caught up in their stories?" interrupted Strider. "Yes. The more invested we get in our stories, the harder it becomes to let go of them. Take the divorce rate as an example. So many people get together, but they don't stay together. Each partner finds they've written a different story about how their shared life is supposed to go—and often that's because the story of how their *own* life is supposed to go is poorly crafted or incomplete or incompatible with their psychic makeup; I'm certainly guilty of that. And then you get people who stay together despite their story conflicts. They never resolve the incompatibilities, but they buy into some story about marriage being sacred and forever, and they spend six decades pounding one another slowly into the grave.

"But lest you think me more of a cynic than I am, there's another story we can tell about revising our original story, and compromise, and forgiveness—about flexibility and the ability to imagine multiple endings."

Strider selected a bag of potatoes and a bag of onions. He looked over the carrots, but didn't find any fresh enough to pass inspection.

"Supply boat's comin' this aft'noon, Strider," the woman behind the counter reassured him. "Should hev s'm fresh ones here by 'roun' three a'clock."

"Thank you, Miss Hattie." Strider placed his groceries on the counter. "I think this'll take care of what we need. Look,

Kaitlin—you inspired me. I got some yeast and flour for bread. We'll make our own this afternoon."

He turned back to the grocer. "Got any fresh fish?"

"Go down t'd' docks and ask for Mike. Tell 'im I sent ya. I 'ear 'e got some fresh hogfish and plen'y o' crawfish this mawnin'. He'll fix you up."

Strider smiled and turned to Kaitlin. "Grab a few packs of postcards off that rack there—I need to mail some, myself."

"Sure, Strider." Kaitlin selected a few postcards featuring prints of watercolors by a local artist. "But why do we need to buy fish when we can jump in the water and...?"

"The fishing's much better out on the reefs than it is in the harbours. Instead of organizing an expedition, it makes more sense to put tonight's meal on the expense account and stay focused on The Happiness Congress."

He thanked the store clerk and they walked back out into the Bahamian air. A light breeze had come up with the sun. It wafted around the wooden houses and drifted down the streets of New Plymouth, past the big breadfruit tree and the coconut palms and a tall papaya tree bearing a cluster of dark green fruit. "Kaitlin, tell me about that sense of connection you said you feel here while we haul these cardboard boxes back down to the dinghies."

"It's difficult to describe ... but perhaps that's what I like about it. As we discussed last night, there's *something* here. I can't tell you what it is. I can't tell you why I feel it here, but I don't feel it back home in Seattle—and I *like* living in Seattle. It may very well be my sub-conscious responding to the vivid colors and the cool air—and the unusual company is kind of fun." Kaitlin directed a smile at Strider. "But I'm in a completely alien environment where I kind of just have to surrender; I don't have to change lanes or pay my electric bill or bang on the air-conditioner to get it to stop rattling. Aside from washing a few dishes, I don't have to worry about all the tiny, daily responsibilities of urban life. I feel free.

"And as a writer, I see a challenge here. If my job is to take experiences and ideas and convert them into text on paper that other people can reassemble into potent, powerful, meaningful stories, I'm going to have to become one hell of an alchemist. It's easy enough to write about 'blue skies' and 'white beaches' and 'quaint towns' and 'turquoise water,' but how do you write about the 'Bahamian positive energy vortex' without inspiring readers to refer you to Audrey? Before I came here, I dealt with plot, characters, and settings. Now I have to deal with plot, characters, and settings—and *this!*"

Strider took a deep breath and thought for a moment. "I think, Kaitlin, that you don't have much to worry about. Real writers—real artists—know that plot, characters, and settings—and color and brush selection and melody and tempo and key—are just ways to get at whatever version of this they're trying to convey the enormity of. The ones who have no connection to the Mystery are out there just tossing words onto pages and blabbing about the endless circle of human gossip and politics. They're the ones who show up with 'crafts' at the 'arts and crafts' show. They're the rebels without a cause. They're trying to figure out what to write about because they've retreated inside a fortress of stories that has no windows."

They walked together down the narrow Bahamian streets. "Here's something for you," said Strider. He reached over to a bush, plucked a few leaves, rolled them in his hand, and extended his palm under Kaitlin's nose. "Allspice—one of nature's perfumes."

"You're pretty cool, Captain Strider. Can I buy you an ice cream?"

"That would certainly forestall hauling these boxes the rest of the way down to the dock, wouldn't it?"

"It'll be my pleasure," Kaitlin said. "Peanut butter vanilla swirl for you or the dreaded chicken mint?"

"This be the islands, sweetheart. Aim for chocolate, vanilla, or strawberry!"

Kaitlin put a finger on the back of the captain's callused, sunbronzed hand. She withdrew it immediately and blushed, turned quickly to mask her embarrassment, and walked into the ice-cream shop.

Strider put his hands behind his head and leaned back in the chair he'd adopted at the small table outside the shop. He closed his eyes and took a long, slow breath.

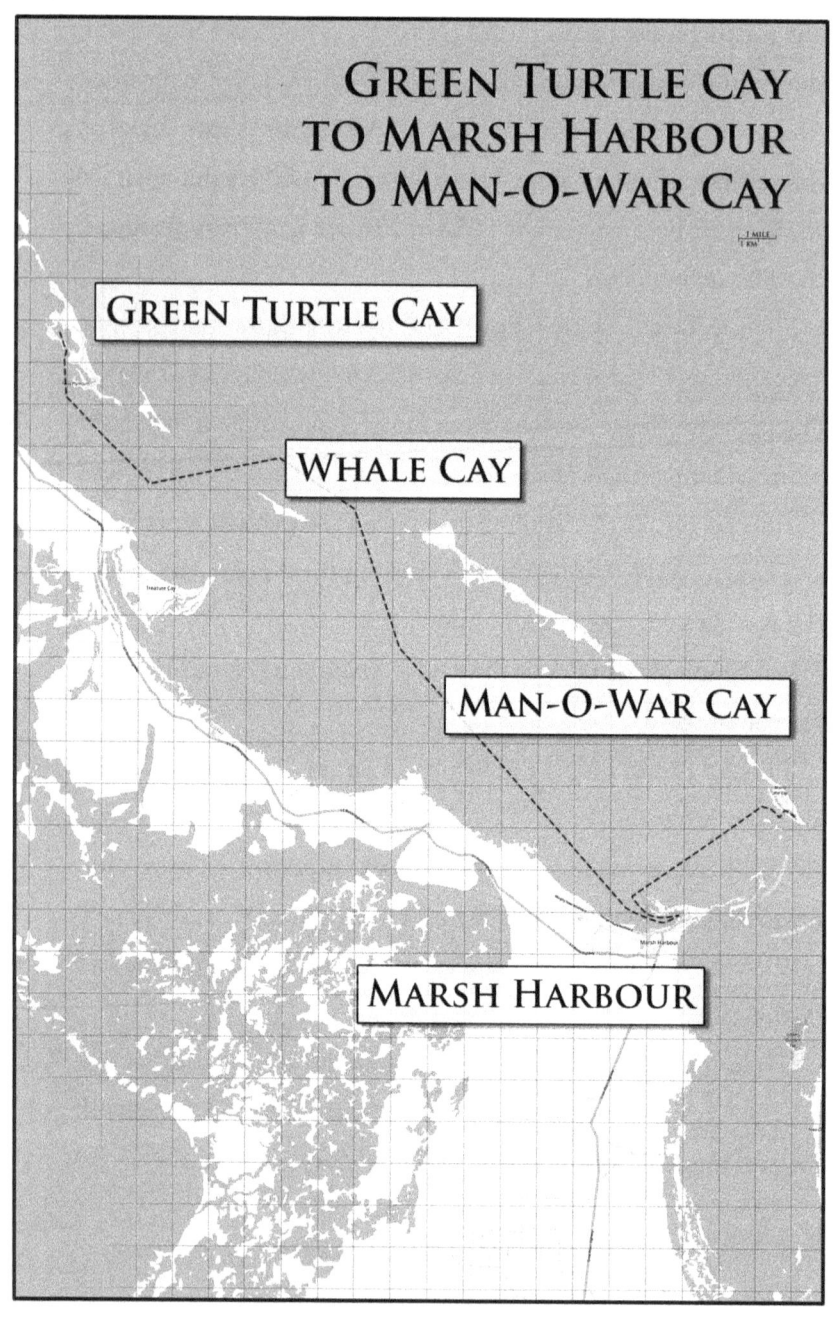

Physical Evidence

The two dinghies ferried happiness delegates and groceries and beach towels and souvenirs back and forth between the dock and the ship throughout the day. By 3:00, all were reassembled on *The Metaphor* where they took to their bunks to enjoy a nap with the light, cool Abaco breeze streaming gently through the hatches.

Strider had set aside bread dough, enough for two loaves, to rise before lying down in his cabin. By 5:30, the seductive aroma of bread baking had summoned everyone from their bunks to the main cabin to eagerly await its emergence from the ship's small oven.

"Here's a piece of connection to the Mystery we'll never figure out," said Strider. "It's pretty clear this bread isn't going to last two minutes after it clears the oven door, given the Pavlovian response it produced. If I'd brought it straight from the local bakery, you'd all have stayed in bed. Instead, I made it right here on board; that seems to give it a special mojo. But though bread is easy to make, there's something magic about kneading your own dough. I'll show anyone interested how to do it while we're under weigh tomorrow. If you've never done it — and even if you never do it again — I suggest you take me up on the offer. If you're single and want attention, fresh baked bread is better bait than red roses or a playful kitten any day. The ingredients are simple and cheap, and the recipe is easy to modify in endless creative ways.

"In the meantime, did everyone get postcards when you were ashore?"

All hands nodded groggily. They'd slept deeply after their walk in town.

"Well, go get 'em — Captain's orders!" barked Strider.

After a series of complaints about the indignities of "Why is he making me get up? I was *so* comfortable there on the settee," the guests returned with their cards.

Strider handed out pens from a heavy mug that sat on the corner of the galley. "Grab yourselves a book from the shelf on the bulkhead to use as a writing surface — and despite how you might choose to describe how you feel after a deep Bahamian nap, a 'bulkhead' is a wall that runs across a boat … and those horizontal boards that line the curved sides of the cabin along the inside of the hull are called 'the ceiling' and the bit above you is called the 'overhead.' To confuse matters more … well … perhaps I'll resist digressing into too much nautical nomenclature … back to postcards.

"What I love about postcards — especially as someone who tends toward verbosity…"

"Not you!" quipped Audrey.

"No! It can't be true!" Micky Tomm said, laughing.

Strider bowed his head gently and allowed the laughter to subside before continuing. "As I was saying … *ahem* … what I love about postcards is that they don't give you any room to go all Tolstoy on your loved ones. A postcard takes three minutes to write, it costs pennies to send, and it brings a smile to the face of anyone who receives it. Nobody writes letters any more — except me. It's too easy for people to send emails or make a phone call. You can jot down a few words about the sculpture garden or learning to row or sailing *The Metaphor* or the bizarre company you're keeping these days, but the one important message a postcard conveys is 'I'm thinking about you.' Draw a smiley face on the goddamned thing if you want, but make sure your kids, friends, and loved ones know they're in your thoughts.

"Why more business and salespeople don't spend an hour a week writing postcards is beyond me. At one point, I had a thousand of them printed up with a photo of *The Metaphor* on them. I used them all up. I can't believe I wrote and mailed a thousand postcards, but I'll have another batch printed and do it again.

"If you want to connect and engage with people, send them a piece of *physical evidence* that you're thinking about them. Emails and phone calls aren't physical evidence; you can't hold them in your hands. Writing someone a letter is big-time voodoo magic these days, but it takes time that nobody has any more because the world is supposedly so much more efficient. But a postcard! 'Wish you were here, Bill.' 'Just thinking about you, Denise.' 'Can't wait to tell you about my adventures in the Bahamas, Jim.' 'Hope your gout hasn't been acting up again, Margaret.' Write something short — *anything* — and see what kind of response you generate."

"I feel like I'm in summer camp," said Vincent. "The counselors used to force us to write letters home."

"I remember that," said Doug. "I sent my parents the most boring drivel about archery and go-karts; there's nothing quite so inspiring as being *forced* to write a letter to your parents — especially when you're at that age when you think everything they say is bullshit."

"Well as soon as you've got your postcards done, I'll carve up this bread. I have good olive oil or — and this is one of those things you can't get in the States — fresh, unpasteurized butter in a can from New Zealand. That with some honey or maple syrup will put a big exclamation mark on the end of our New Plymouth expedition. And if you want to try one more absurdity, olive oil and real maple syrup are sublime together.

Physical Evidence

"Then after you've got all the crumbs off your bums, we'll clean up this boat—it looks like *The Titanic* down here—and bang back over to White Sound to see if last night's mooring is still available. It's darker and quieter there—less noise from drinking tourists and boats motoring in and out of the harbour.

"Kaitlin, my dear; any thoughts?"

"Only that there seems to be a relationship between connection and what you call 'physical evidence.' I could buy a loaf of bread from the grocer in town, or even get one fresh from a local bakery—I think we passed one in New Plymouth—but making it yourself makes it special. I watched you mix the ingredients and knead the dough, and even got to help a bit. I can tell you with certainty that I have *never* smelled anything so delicious in my life.

"And then there's the postcards. Putting a little bit of handwork in makes the connection happen. Sending a tiny piece of physical evidence is much more powerful than an email or a call."

Doug grew animated. "I've never thought about this before, but I've taken students to Art Basel—the big art show they have on Miami Beach every year. I've seen original works—sometimes even mediocre ones—by famous artists fetch *enormous* prices. You can get a serigraph—a signed, numbered print of the same piece for a lot less, but you'll still pay four or five figures—or you can buy a $10 print in a poster shop. From six feet away, they all look identical, but the value to collectors appears to correspond to the amount of 'physical evidence' that the artist personally worked on the piece. An original Picasso sells for massive amounts of money, I suppose because people are buying the *story* of the Master sweating over the canvas; it's evidence of the magic transference of pure inspiration into physical form—*evidence* of the Essential Absurdities, I suppose...."

"Good," said Strider. "I hadn't thought about that one."

"The serigraph has value because it's a limited edition and it still has Picasso's signature on it," continued Doug. "I guess it's more like a prayer and the original is more like a miracle. And though the poster version carries the same image, it bears no physical evidence that the artist ever touched it or cared about it."

Strider removed two brown, steaming loaves from the oven. "So get to it, ye students of happiness. Get physical. Start connecting. Produce something original. Finish those postcards so I can slice up this bread!"

The Metaphor's cabin grew quiet but for the scratching of pens on paper.

Chop Wood; Carry Water

Strider collected his guest's dirty dishes in a five-gallon bucket of seawater. Micky Tomm scrubbed the plates and cutlery and handed them to Strider who rinsed them lightly with fresh water. "Fresh water is not something that flows out of the tap like magic, here," explained Strider. In the U.S., you flip a switch or turn on a tap or flush a toilet; lights glow, hands get clean, and waste disappears—hocus-pocus. In the islands, we collect rainwater or buy it when we have to. Here you'd never throw away a *gallon* of fresh water every time you pee. And soon enough, Americans are going to find out that their story of the magic faucet doesn't hold water. A lot of folks are *not* going to be happy about that. The average American uses 80–100 gallons of water per day. That's almost the full capacity of *The Metaphor*'s tanks. The story that magic flows out of our pipes and walls is a seductive one, but it's dangerous, and because water and energy—especially energy—are *big business,* industries are capitalizing on that phony story to collect money while they destroy the planet."

"So how do we rewrite that story?" asked Doug. "We teach about fresh water in junior high school, but I'm not sure we're changing minds."

"There's a famous Zen saying: 'Before enlightenment: chop wood; carry water. After enlightenment: chop wood; carry water.' It refers to the idea that life is full of mundane tasks, and that pursuit of a spiritual existence doesn't excuse you from getting your laundry done and washing between your toes. You don't get to sit around chanting with a robe on while the angels follow you around and wipe your bottom for you. But the problem, as I see it, is that nobody's chopping wood or carrying water *after or before* enlightenment because enlightenment flows out of their tap. Chop the wood yourself and you won't burn so many logs. Carry the water yourself and you won't use a gallon of it to rinse away a cup of pee.

"What you can do about it is exactly what you *are* doing about it. Live out in the world for a few days and sleep under the stars. Find out what so many people are insulated from. Take your newfound appreciation back to the land of clocks and calendars and encourage others to have the experience you're having.

"Another aphorism—it might be contemporary; it's attributed to a few sources, but it has the ring of 'an old Zen saying,' and it might even be one: 'If you wear shoes, the whole earth is covered with leather.' How can we teach children to love the earth when we don't teach them what it feels like to walk barefoot in the grass?"

Strider wiped the last of the plates and rose from the galley. He ascended the first step of the companionway ladder and poked his head out into the fading Abaco dusk before returning below to address the happiness delegates. "We have a south wind," he explained, "which means we probably have a cold front coming. That in itself is probably not a big deal, but assuming we haven't missed our weather window, we want to hightail it out of here at first light, get around Whale Cay—which we can't do once the wind clocks around to the north and starts hissing and spitting—and get anchored up over at Marsh Harbour. If the weather gods find us worthy, maybe they'll bless us with enough time to get supplies at the big store there and then move on to Man-O-War Cay before the rain comes."

The captain surveyed the cabin. "Before we transition oh-so-appropriately from Zen sayings into tonight's assault on reality, let's get the gear stowed and the sail covers stripped off. If we do see any rough weather tomorrow, I don't want stuff crashing all over the boat."

The happiness delegates busied themselves tidying up for a few minutes and then reconvened on deck.

"How do you know there's a cold front coming," asked Kaitlin, "and at the risk of sounding ignorant, what *is* a cold front?"

Strider smiled and fingered the brim of his hat. "I'll give you the short version: The wind in this part if the world blows slightly south of east most of the time. But an approaching weather system—in this case, a bubble of cold air moving down from the Arctic—a 'cold front'—can affect the local wind direction before it actually gets here. Think of it as a 'weather shadow.' When the wind moves past southeast, it will most likely clock all the way around to the north and then back around to the southeast once the front has blown through.

"I'm sure Lenore could tell us all about the Coriolis effect and other interesting physical properties that affect the weather..."

Lenore nodded.

"...but let's skip the science lesson and plug that back into the world of 'things the average homeowner doesn't pay much attention to.' If you take off those leather shoes, the earth will talk to you in all sorts of wonderful ways. When you tune into it and listen, you gain a different appreciation for it."

Walter raised a wine glass. "I'm going to play the skeptic again."

"Please do," encouraged Strider. "If no one questions, it usually means no one is listening—which usually means I'm ranting about something."

"I'm all good with your 'tune into the earth' message; I get that—but what's the relationship between that and connection and engagement and happiness? I'm not challenging what you're saying, but I'm challenging you to keep it on-message."

Chop Wood; Carry Water

"Good," said Strider. "Knowing me, that's always a wise idea."

"If there's *one* thing we *should* all be able to connect over, it's the idea that we have a common interest in caring for the planet that sustains us. When we live in a way that puts us in touch with what the wind says, when we engage with the seasons in a way that runs deeper than choosing between the heater and the air-conditioner, when we learn to time the tides so we can cross the shallows when the water is high, when we watch the stars instead of the ceiling tiles, the earth becomes a *character* in our shared story. Technology is wonderful—and how many of us would even be here if it weren't for antibiotics?—but when I see people walking down a beautiful beach and they're staring at their stupid-phones, I want to shake them and wake them up.

"Ten thousand years ago, humans were still living in caves and hunting mammoths. In geological or evolutionary terms, that's a blink of an eye. Now we're flying around in airplanes and sending people to the moon and navigating with satellites and curing cancer and making microchips and talking to friends on the other side of the world. That's all wonderful, but we've grown too fast; our stories—including some important ones—have been left behind. Our psychic story writers can't keep up.

"Walter, you've been connecting to and engaging with the earth on a different level since you arrived in these islands three days ago. You've had to conserve fresh water and use kerosene lanterns to read by and travel to and from shore with a rowing dinghy, but you've seen the reef and the stars and used the wind to push you from one island to another. What do you think?"

Walter closed his eyes. "It's all magnificent. It's beyond words. It's..."

"So when you get back to your home and work—to your so-called 'real life,' how will you use this experience to enhance the way you connect and engage with audiences at your speeches? Hasn't this journey been one big exercise in connection and engagement?"

"I'm not sure. That's why I asked…"

"And that's the answer; I wish I had a better one for you. Too many people don't speak 'earth.' Their stories are missing a vitally important character. Try starting a story with, 'I stuck my head out the hatch the other day and noticed the wind had gone south.'" It'll be crickets and tumbleweeds for sure—no applause for you.

"Our culture is losing stories. Its smile looks like mine." Strider showed off his missing front tooth. "You can't use the wind and the tide and the ways the birds are behaving to connect with people—but you *should* be able to.

"Audrey, you're a psychologist. You deal with the effects of missing stories all day."

"What do you mean?"

"Men and women see the world differently. How many times have you taught couples how to listen and respond in each other's gender language? A woman marries a man thinking he'll change; a man marries a woman thinking she won't. Why do couples get together and struggle to harmonize their stories? Why isn't conflict resolution a required class for fourth, seventh, and eleventh graders? Why is Sex Education all about body parts?"

Audrey shrugged.

"For all our technology and the millions of books we've published, you still have to spend thousands of dollars to attend a workshop if you want to discover the 'secrets to happiness.' That's because the tapestry of stories that makes up our society is full of holes. That drafty blanket isn't keeping us warm any more."

Walter pushed harder. "All good stuff, Strider, but I don't think you answered my question. You've given me ways I *should* be able to connect and engage but can't. How do I turn this around and use it?"

Strider raised an index finger and looked at his guests. "Write the missing stories," he said. "Find the gaps and fill them in. Steal some people's shoes. Turn off their main breakers and shut off their water. Kidnap them and take them out to sea or deep into the woods. Write the missing chapters in the *homo sapiens* instruction manual."

"That's a tall order," said Micky Tomm.

"Of course it is," replied Strider, "but that's what leaders and happy people do. Chop wood; carry water."

I Am Not That

"Moving on," said Strider. "I want to get into a different take on the Essential Absurdities. This is another deep dive, but I don't want to blab all night; I want to rack out early so I can get this ship under weigh at first light. You all can sleep in as late as you want, but my plan is to keep us ahead of the weather.

"I'll start with a little joke: Buddy was born without arms or legs or a body. He's a medical miracle, but aside from the fact that he's got nothing going on below the neck, he's an affable and intelligent young man. His friends carry him around in a cereal bowl, and because it's his 21st birthday, they take him to a bar to enjoy his first beer. He takes his first sip and all of a sudden, a foot pops out of the bottom of his neck. *Pop!* His friends stand him up on it and he takes a minute to find his balance. 'I want more of that,' he says. He takes another sip and a moment later, the foot becomes a leg. You can imagine what happens. Buddy keeps drinking and body parts keep sprouting. Pretty soon, his friends have to run and find a towel to wrap around his waist because he's turned into a perfectly normal, full-bodied man.

"Buddy's quite happy with the results of his first drink, and his friends congratulate him. They find some clothes for him and he dances for the first time in his life with a girl he meets at the bar.

"And then he decides to have another drink. After all, his friends have had a few. He takes a sip and begins to look uncomfortable. The next thing you know, there's a horrible stretching and tearing sound and poor Buddy explodes all over the bar. It's a nasty mess.

"One of his friends looks at the others. 'Poor Buddy,' he says. 'He should have quit while he was a head.'"

"Oh, Strider," moaned Audrey. "Drop the oxygen masks."

"That was horrible," complained Doug.

"And Strider has the audacity to do this to a captive audience," noted Micky Tomm. "That's just cruel."

"I call for a mutiny," said Kaitlin.

"You just try that," Strider retorted, "and I'll show you the *pun* is mightier than the sword."

"I can't take it any more," cried Doug. "Someone kill me now!"

"I did tell you I had evil plans for you," laughed Strider, "but as painful as that was, I told that joke to make a point. If we are to be characters in our own story, and if *we* — whoever and whatever that is — are to connect and engage with others, we need to understand that we are made up of stories as much as our Universe is;

I Am Not That

we need to understand who and what is creating all those stories. Who is *I*?

"I could have started with the moon and asked you, 'Are you the moon?' and you would have given me a funny look and thought, 'Oh, Strider's off down one of his crazy rabbit holes again.' Then I could have asked you if you were the mainsail, and you'd have said 'no' again. And then I'd get closer and closer and you'd keep saying, 'No; I am not that.' What's interesting about that very bad joke is that nobody has any trouble accepting the premise that Buddy is a 'person' in spite of the fact that he's AWOL below the neck.

"Vincent, if someone chopped your legs off—and let's hope they don't; I hate when that happens—would you still be *you?*"

"I suppose so," replied Vincent. "I don't see why not?"

"And if I kept removing body parts, you'd still be you?"

"As long as I could think and be aware, I suppose."

"But what happens when you go to sleep? Are you still you? You're thinking, but you're certainly not aware in the same way you are when you're awake."

Audrey chimed in. "I think you're still *you* because you're still engaging with the same symbols and meanings you deal with when you're *not* sleeping. You might process that information differently, but you're still dealing with the undersides of your own unique stories."

Strider placed his hat in its resting spot on top of the compass. "So *you* has to do with thoughts and awareness. If you got sick and I put your brain in a robot body—or if I could take all of your conscious and subconscious thought processes and put them in a computer, would you still be you?"

"I don't know," said Micky Tomm. "I'd have to think on that one."

"That's fine," said Strider. "I don't have answers; only questions. All I can do is feel around in the darkness and try to assemble stories that make sense. In this wilderness of thought, you can disagree with me and I won't have—sorry—a *leg* to stand on as far as persuading you you're wrong."

Doug slapped his forehead and shook his head.

"But we've established that *you* are not your body. As far as anything you can point to and identify goes, all you can say is, 'I am not that.'

"Let's take this to a deeper level. Are *you* your thoughts? Your feelings? Your ideas? Your dreams?"

"How are we supposed to answer *that?*" protested Kaitlin.

"I ask because it's easy to say, '*I* have a feeling' or '*I* had a dream' or '*I* have an idea.' Who is this *I* that is doing the having? When I speak about '*my* subconscious,' to whom do I ascribe that ownership? When you say '*I* was asleep,' who or what is that witness that's beyond sleeping and waking—the one who *knows* you were asleep or tripping on drugs or unconscious on an operating table?

"The way we think and speak about our own thought processes and mental states suggests that *we are not them;* deep down, there's a witness — an observer. All our senses and cognitive processes are designed to look *outward.* We can watch the movies we create, but we have no tools for viewing the projectionist. All your thoughts and feelings and memories and inferences are like so much asteroid crater in the desert. It's as if we're the meteorite and all we can do is spin around and look at the wall of earth we've thrown up around us. We can see the results of the impact, but we can never see what caused it.

"Do you realize that as long as you live, you'll never see yourself. You can stare in a mirror, but you'll only see a reverse image — a reflection. Other people can see you — at least within the limitations of what space-time allows — but you will never see yourself with your outward-facing eyes."

Walter waved his hand. "Official ship's curmudgeon weighing in, here. What does this have to do with happiness, connection, or engagement? I really want to love this stuff, but is there a 'nuts and bolts' aspect to this psycho-spiritual identity crisis you've confronted us with?"

Strider nodded. "As far as wrapping your head around the idea that *you* are nothing you can point to and say you are not, we're caught in a conceptual quagmire because the only tool we have to examine it with is negation. At some point we run out of things to say we are not, but we still can't turn the metaphorical camera inward.

"A theory: I like to think people are like power tools or kitchen appliances. The microwave oven and the blender and the electric carving knife all have different functions. Think of them as having different stories or personalities as well as different physical attributes. Those properties make them into unique 'individuals' even though they're all plugged into the same AC current. At some point, the mechanical parts of those machines will no longer be able to convert that electricity into the work they were designed to do. At that point, we can consider them 'dead' in much the same way we pronounce a person 'dead' when their body can no longer support life."

"I'd like to be a blender," said Vincent.

"No way, dude," said Doug, "I'll be a refrigerator."

"Ice cream machine!" shouted Audrey.

"You guys take all the fizz out of metaphysics," said Strider. "But let me get back to Walter who is doing such a good job keeping me on the rails. Maybe those machines—or to bring the metaphor home, we conscious people—are biological appliances that are capable of taking in some sort of life energy and putting it to some purpose. Maybe our physical bodies and brains and that wall of stories we create around us define the kind of impact we have on the world around us. Maybe what we *truly* are is what we're plugged into. That would explain part of the mystery of connection, but who can know? Whether that life force is one big power source for all of us or whether each of us has some sort of 'battery' at the center of their consciousness is anyone's guess. This is 100% theoretical stuff, but the logic of 'I am not that' is pretty compelling."

Walter crossed his arms. "Still waiting."

"My main point is a macro view of the one I made last night when we looked eight billion light years into space—everything you know or think you know is a story. Everything we know of it is a product of our own imagination.

"But it also suggests that we create imaginary connections between ourselves and our stories. We think a car or a sexy life partner or a new degree will make us happy. We attach ourselves to values like wealth and status. The only things that actually do seem to bring us happiness are those that help us fulfill our purpose as a metaphorical refrigerator or blender or ice-cream maker—or sailor or writer or psychologist or big pharma exec. When you take the light of pure consciousness and filter it through an individual's unique 'story lens,' you find whatever that person was *meant to be*—their *destiny*.

"If you want to connect to others in an authentic and honest way, you have to figure out how to connect to your self first. If you're called by your nature to be a watercolor artist and some 'practical' person convinces you to be an accountant, you might reap the material benefits of that advice, but you'll always be at odds with your own story.

"Walter, given your interest in the mind-body connection, do you think there might be any link between disease and internal story conflict? How can you maintain a positive attitude if you're working against your own nature? We both know it takes a lot more than a gym membership and a brightly colored wardrobe and a potted plant next to the bed. We know it takes more than telling people to 'stay positive.' When you eliminate the concept of 'I am that' from your list of possibilities and shift to 'I am *not* that,' you eliminate *attachment* — and any Buddhist will tell you that attachment is the root of all suffering.

"Strider, are you suggesting I caused my own cancer. Victim-blaming is…"

"Yes and no." Strider smiled and took a breath. "To some degree, I think *you're* suggesting that. Nobody knows whether their cancer was triggered by a single molecule from the exhaust of a passing truck or the burnt edges of the toast they had for breakfast a year earlier. Maybe it was just their turn to draw a genetic Joker from the card deck of life. But your message is about mind-body connection. You theorize that stress has a lot to do with a person's risk of getting sick and happiness has a lot to do with their odds of getting well or staying well. And that has a ring of truth about it; it makes sense.

"What I'm doing—if I understand your position—is reframing it in terms of story. If you have a toxic work environment or a stressful marriage, probably, your risk of illness increases. But the flip side of that is your implied daily decision to stay in the unrewarding job or abusive relationship. There's a level where you get up in the morning and think, *I really need to get myself out of this,* and then there's a 'completely submerged in the tar pit level' where you don't even question anymore. That's story conflict. I can't prove that living in a prison of your own making is unhealthy, but it sounds plausible."

"I'll buy it," said Walter, "but isn't that a shift toward 'I *am* that?' The problem is no longer the job or the nasty spouse; it's you and your willingness to stay in a bad situation."

Strider thought for moment. "Perhaps, but if the problem is seen as internal instead of external—if the trouble is not the job or the spouse but your own story conflict—you end up with a situation that's within your power to change. Jump from '*That* is my problem' to '*I* am my problem' to '*I* am not that.'"

Strider turned to Vincent. You said you love to play jazz. Go grab your guitar and play something for us."

Vincent ducked below and handed his guitar case up through the companionway. After taking a moment to tune, he closed his eyes, nodded a few times to lock in his tempo, and began to improvise. After playing for a few minutes, he brought his impromptu composition to a crescendo and ended on a lush, sustained chord.

"Marvelous," said Strider over the happiness delegates' applause. "How would you describe the *work* of producing that music. It looked technically difficult…"

"But it feels easy," Vincent assured him. "I just close my eyes and let the music flow out of me. And I enjoy the sound of an acoustic guitar; there's something pure and natural about it."

Strider directed his gaze at Kaitlin. "How about you? What do you like to write about?"

"I write a lot of things. I do some copywriting for a few local ad agencies—but I *love* to write poetry, novels, and short stories."

"A natural storyteller. I should have guessed," chuckled Strider. "And when you're in your writing groove, what's the work like?"

"It isn't work at all. It's kind of like I just hold the pen for God. That certainly doesn't happen all the time; sometimes I stare at my keyboard and the faucet doesn't even drip. But If I keep showing up—if I sit at my desk and open myself to *whatever it is*—sooner or later, inspiration comes. It certainly doesn't feel like work."

"And Vincent, you seem like the type who appreciates the spiritual qualities of your music. What if I asked you to compose a digital theme for a kids' video game?"

"Now, that would be work. I don't think it would be easy to do at all. It's just not me."

"Kaitlin, I need a patient information sheet for a new pharmaceutical product. Give me all the dosage information, side-effects, disclosures, and…"

"I'd hate that job. That would definitely feel like work."

"So like Vincent said, 'not you'?"

Kaitlin smiled. "I am not that."

"Exactly," said Strider. "The human being is the only animal on earth not in captivity that doesn't do whatever the hell it wants to do. When we become attached to stories that don't fit us, we imprison ourselves. When we do what we want to do, the work doesn't feel like work; it becomes an effortless, joyful expression of who we are. When we buy into other people's stories of who we're *supposed* to be, we become miserable. When our happiness cake collapses, we blame ourselves for being bad cooks. If we follow the recipe exactly and things don't work out, we conclude there must be something wrong with *us*. But plenty of bad recipes are supported by compelling stories. Plenty of those bad recipes work great for people who are not you.

"If you don't connect with your *self* and figure out what your purpose is, all you'll do is run around trying to figure out why it feels so wrong to be doing everything 'right.' All your connections with others will come from a place of neediness and falsehood.

"Kaitlin, I'm done. If there are no comments from the peanut gallery, I'll give you the honor of putting tonight's topic to bed. The foremast is all yours."

Kaitlin rose and looked over her notes.

"Strider's jokes are total *ship*. He should be banned from telling them—the *schooner* the better."

The Story Story

Kaitlin's comment provoked a chorus of booing. She bowed and proceeded. "If last night was 'outward bound,' tonight was 'inward bound.' Instead of moving out into the stars, we moved in closer and closer. Anything we could identify was logically not that which identified it—'I am not that.' At some point, we found ourselves at the center of a circular wall of stories—names of things, expectations, dreams, feelings, our bodies, our mental states—which supports last night's thesis that 'everything we know or think we know is a story.'

"Just as our eyes can only look outward at the stories we use to describe the Universe, our true selves can only look outward at the stories we create. I like the analogy Strider used about us being able to watch the movies but unable to see the projectionist.

"The way this relates to happiness, connection, and engagement is simple: If the core of our being is just an energy source or life force, the way each of us filters that light with the lens of our unique physical, intellectual, emotional, and spiritual characteristics is where we derive our sense of meaning and find our destiny—our purpose. But if we believe stories that encourage us to be something we weren't 'built' to be, we end up at odds with ourselves.

"So the *actions* we find joy in are the ones that express our true purpose. The *things* we find joy in are tools that help us accomplish that purpose. The *people* we find joy in are those who help us express ourselves fully.

"And that takes us to connection. Connection is all about finding ways we can help one another realize our potential. I'm going to go out on a limb here, Strider, but I think on a practical, business level, this circles back to stories being part of everyone's search for meaning. If I'm selling you a product, I need to understand what your *purpose* is so I can find a way to provide you with a tool that helps you realize that purpose — or a way to remove obstacles that *prevent* you from fulfilling it.

"In order for that to happen, I have to be clear about my own purpose. Otherwise the connection can never be authentic. The first step in connecting with others is to connect with your self. The first step in connecting with your self is to say, 'I am not that.'"

Strider walked over to Kaitlin, took her hands in his, and looked into her eyes. "You have a very special gift," he said softly.

"I hate to interrupt your moment," said Lenore.

Kaitlin turned bright red.

Strider composed himself and smiled.

"I'm just wondering how deep we're going to dive into this pool of what you call 'The Essential Absurdities.' It's all quite fascinating, but my brain hurts…"

"My dear Lenore." Strider smiled and raised an understanding eyebrow. "Though it may not be obvious, I get tired of all this deep exploration, too. If it makes you feel better, having taken you from the farthest reaches of space to the center of your soul, I am plumb out of new territory … and we all probably have enough to ponder for years. Consider the foundation built. From here on, we can all start writing truthful, meaningful, authentic stories that promote connection, engagement and—since I'd hate to see you come all this way for nothing—happiness."

Strider folded his hands together, touched his fingertips to his chin, bowed deeply to his guests, mouthed a silent 'thank you' to all, and retreated to his cabin.

Trust the Compass

Hmm. A light west-northwest wind. Strider took a sip of coffee, raised the big mainsail as quietly as he could, then followed it with the foresail. He let the mooring pendant fall into the water, pulled up the jib, and as *The Metaphor* began to fall downwind, he cranked the wheel to starboard. He released the main and adjusted the jib. Soon his ship was gliding gently through the boats in White Sound toward the channel that led from the protected lagoon into the sea of Abaco.

"Mornin,' Strider," whispered Kaitlin as she joined him in the cockpit. A tiny streak of red cracked a purple-gray sky above Green Turtle Cay.

"Take the wheel, love. I'll go get you some coffee. Cream and sugar?"

Kaitlin hadn't expected to find herself in control of a 50,000-pound boat, but she suppressed her momentary panic and embraced the moment. In less than a minute, Strider returned with a steaming mug, which he placed in a holder mounted next to the wheel.

"Watch the compass. Keep her slightly west of due south for about two miles until we pass New Plymouth and the southern tip of Green Turtle bears about sixty degrees."

Kaitlin experimented with the wheel, feeling how the ship and the compass needle responded.

"You're rounding up a bit, dear. Watch the compass. Feel the boat. When you get to the course the sails are set for, you'll feel 'the groove'; she'll move forward a bit more boldly. Come this way a bit." Strider nudged the wheel. The compass drifted back around to due south, and Kaitlin felt the wind embrace the ship.

"Beautiful."

"You're a natural, Kaitlin. For some reason, women often pick this up faster than men do. There's an intuitive side to sailing and there's an engineering side; it's a blend of science and folklore. You can study hydrodynamics and aerodynamics for years, and you can make fancy high-tech sails that work like an airplane wing; you can use science to coax tremendous speed out of a sailboat. At the end of the day, all those engineers and sponsor dollars only shine when there's someone at the helm who can *feel the boat.*"

The two sailed in silence for twenty minutes. Strider kept an eye on the compass, but mostly enjoyed watching Kaitlin learn to tune into the boat.

"These binoculars have a compass in them. Point them at the tip of Green Turtle Cay over there and tell me what that compass reads."

Kaitlin fumbled with the binoculars for a moment. "Right about 60 degrees now, Strider."

"Perfect. There's a shoal—a big patch of shallow water—we need to go around. To do that, we need to pass around the ocean side of Whale Cay. It's the only deep water we'll hit on this trip. If the wind blows hard from the north, it's a dangerous place; the seas get big and they break when they hit the shallow banks; I'm told a lot of wrecks lie on the bottom there. I wanted to weigh anchor early today so we can get through Whale Cay Passage before the cold front gets here. I expect we'll just see glassy swells out there; our timing looks good.

"Let's fall off about 20 degrees downwind so we're paralleling the islands." Kaitlin turned the wheel to port while Strider eased the sails out.

"See that island?" Strider pointed. "That's Whale Cay. Hold this course until it bears about 256 degrees; then we'll turn and pass a bit to the north of it."

A big powerboat appeared behind them. Its approach brought with it the thrum of surging diesel engines. It passed a hundred yards to starboard and continued toward Whale Cay, leaving a smudge of exhaust smoke hovering in its wake.

"Hang on tight," said Strider as the wake passed beneath *The Metaphor*. The ship rolled awkwardly and then resumed her steady course.

"I didn't see anyone in the cockpit!" said Kaitlin. "Was anyone actually steering that thing?"

"Usually, someone's at least keeping an eye out, but these days, you can hook a GPS up to an autopilot, plot a perfect course, and let the computer steer you within inches of where you want to be. Sadly, it's not uncommon to see boats with nobody at the helm."

"Wanna see *my* GPS?" Strider grinned.

"Really? *You?* I didn't think you were the type."

Strider went below and returned with a plastic box. He opened it and revealed its contents. "This is my GPS—my Gray Plastic Sextant. I use it to navigate with the stars."

Kaitlin smiled and shook her head. "I should have guessed."

Strider returned the box to its hiding place in the navigation station below and then returned to the cockpit. "Here's a fresh mug; I brought you a refill."

"So how come you *don't* use a GPS? I can see why you wouldn't want a computer to steer the boat everywhere; you'd miss out on the sailing. But it sure makes sense to do whatever you can to avoid the rocks and reefs and shallows and other hazards."

"I suppose it does, but haven't you had some fun using the compass and the wind and the wheel to get this ship where she's going? It's more work, but these powerboaters might as well send the boat over from the States on its own and then fly in to meet it. Those boats have engines and bow thrusters. With a computer coordinating them, they could pull in and stay stationary over a piece of bottom at Marsh Harbour until the owners got there. How *un*adventurous is that?"

Kaitlin placed a hand on her hip. "I hope you don't think less of me, but Seattle's a big city. When I have to get to a new place, I turn on the GPS and the robot lady tells me exactly how to get there. I find a lot of comfort in it."

"There's nothing wrong with GPS," reassured Strider. "It's an amazing tool, but it has a tendency to prevent you from finding new stories. You see, nobody ever had a true adventure where everything went right. Things break. The weather doesn't cooperate. Somebody flakes out.

"If you're on your way to a job interview or the church where you're about to be married, avoiding adventure is just plain prudent. Getting that job or marrying that partner will bring you more adventures than getting lost on the way there—it's a trade-off.

"But if your GPS is on all the time, you'll never learn to trust your internal compass. Intuition is another one of the Essential Absurdities. Sometimes that little voice in your head says, "turn back" or "don't trust this guy" or "go left here even though there's no sign." You might argue with yourself about whether or not that makes any sense, but if the voice of intuition is emphatic enough, it's usually a wise idea to pay attention to it. If you add an electronic voice to the mix—and that voice is tied to detailed street maps of the world—it's too easy to let a microchip compromise your compass. How will you learn to trust that compass if you place more faith in a computer than you do in yourself?

"You're equipped with your own, real, non-metaphorical, wayfinding compass. We usually refer to that as a 'sense of direction.' Betty and I visited Washington, D.C. once. The first thing I did was look at a map. The Capitol Building, the Washington Monument, and the Lincoln Memorial are all arranged in a straight line from due east to due west; that city might as well have a giant compass needle painted on it. Betty marveled at how I always knew where I was, but all I did was take bearings on the buildings and pay attention when we'd make a turn."

"So, for example, Seattle has the Space Needle as a visible bearing point, and one main highway—I-5—that runs north and south. If I use landmarks like the two stadiums and Harbor Island..."

"You probably do that without thinking about it. Where's the airport? Where's your favorite coffee shop? You probably don't need the GPS to find Pike Place Market."

"No. I've been up and down I-5 so many times to get to so many places that …"

"Get lost," said Strider sternly.

"What?" Kaitlin looked hurt.

"Get lost!" His frown turned to a smile. "God forbid you end up some place you didn't expect to. You might see something new. You might see a beautiful Victorian house to take a picture of or get to take a chance on a new Asian restaurant—or even a new Asian friend. All the while, if you know you're somewhere west of the highway, all you need to do to get un-lost is head east. You can always turn on the GPS if you get completely disoriented.

"Nobody goes exploring any more. When Columbus sailed down the coast of Africa and across to the Caribbean and up the island chain to North America, he had no idea where he was going. All he had was three square-rigged boats that wouldn't sail to windward. He was lost the moment the Spanish trees dropped below the horizon—and he was even *more* lost when the new trees showed up. He put his faith in his compass, and in what was only a theory at the time—that the winds and currents circled the Atlantic. He repeated that trick four times and was applauded as a hero every time he found his way home."

Micky Tomm made his way to the cockpit and surveyed his changed surroundings. "Good morning, Kaitlin. Good morning, Strider."

"Good morning, Micky. Your timing is excellent. Would you like a cup of hot coffee?" Strider ducked below without waiting for an answer and returned a moment later with a mug.

"We were talking this morning…" Strider began.

"Of course you were," joked Micky Tomm.

Kaitlin smiled and returned her gaze to the compass.

"We were talking about navigating—about trusting your compass. When you're up in the wheelhouse of a big corporation, how does that come into play?"

Micky Tomm took a sip of his coffee. "A lot of data comes across my desk," he explained. "I get profit and loss reports, analyses of competitors, market surveys, safety and efficacy studies…. You'd be amazed at the volume of material I'm expected to look at every day; it's *thousands* of pages. Then add meetings and conference calls—and unlike many managers, I try to spend time down in the trenches with my troops. My reps usually have a very different take on battle conditions than the folks up on the 23rd floor in the marketing department. I have some talented and patient staff members who act like my 'professional sub-conscious'; they help read through the stacks of information, and they discard stuff I don't need and circle the important stuff with a red pen.

"And then I get a 'feeling' about what decisions need to be made. Sometimes that goes against what the finance department thinks should happen. Sometimes the marketing people want to tar and feather me. Sometimes the reps end up with new business cards. Sometimes the product development folks need to switch gears ... Switch gears? Hell ... Sometimes they get a whole new transmission!" Micky Tomm chuckled. "Sometimes my decisions are very difficult to justify in a purely rational way, but there's a 'sweet spot'—a 'groove' where I know I'm taking the best road."

Strider raised a finger. "Sorry to interrupt, Micky. The wind's gone a tiny bit more north—and I think it's come up. Give me a moment." Strider hauled in each sail, glancing up at the canvas until he was satisfied the boat was humming along efficiently. *The Metaphor* heeled over slightly and picked up speed. Kaitlin looked vibrant at the helm.

"Do continue," he said to Micky Tomm.

"I've been at that job for fourteen years, and the reason I'm still there—as far as the board is concerned—is that the profitability graph keeps going up. The reason I'm still there as far as *I'm* concerned is that we keep producing products that cure diseases and make people feel better. I make decisions with my *moral* compass—and I try to make those jibe with my *business* compass. So far, I've either been extremely lucky or God has been on my side; I've seen a lot of executives come and go during my tenure. But whatever professional success I can lay claim to has nothing to do with what I studied in business school. I go with my gut—even when all the data are against me."

"So as metaphors go...." Strider gestured at the bronze compass that sat above the ship's wheel.

"Absolutely," affirmed Micky Tomm. "Part of being successful—I suppose at most anything—is to learn to trust your compass."

Strider inhaled a breath of steam from his coffee cup and took another sip. The sky, by now, was a conflagration of red and orange. "Red sky at night; sailor's delight," he chanted. "Red sky at morning; sailor take warning."

"Do we have to worry?" asked Kaitlin.

"Could be nothing; could be a gale," replied Strider, "but we'll get around Whale Cay before the weather turns. An hour from now, we'll be on a course for Marsh Harbour. There's shelter there and good holding ground for anchoring—the long and short of it being that there's stuff to pay attention to, but not much to worry about.

"Kaitlin, my dear, can you round up just a hair? Aim a hundred yards or so off the east end of Whale Cay."

A few minutes later, *The Metaphor* passed over the bar without incident. She soon found herself rolling in tall swells as she changed course to round the island.

"How come we slowed down?" asked Kaitlin.

"Wind's behind us and we're moving pretty much the same speed and direction as the waves. Look in through the cut and watch Great Abaco in the background move past Whale Cay. You'll see we're still skimming along. Just a few minutes of this and we'll be back inside in shallow water."

Strider stepped aft to where four fishing rods waited in holders on the rail. He deployed four lures and reeled in three painted mackerel. "Beautiful, aren't they?" The backs of the sleek fish glowed blue and green beneath a pattern of black stripes. Their bellies were silver. "From the top, they look like the sea bottom. From underneath them, they're the undersides of sparkling waves—perfect camouflage. Too bad for them, they're also a perfect breakfast. Sorry, my darlings. Some things were put on this earth to be eaten.

"Head back in about halfway between Whale Cay and Great Guana Cay. Pass to this side of Shell Island, which is that clump of casuarina pines over there, and then change course to 145 degrees. That'll take us right into Marsh Harbour—another thirteen miles or so. We'll be anchored up by lunch."

Lenore and Walter emerged from the cabin and stationed themselves in the cockpit.

"Howdja sleep?" asked Strider.

"Deeply and peacefully," said Lenore.

"Yup. Me, too," said Walter. "What was all that rolling around?"

"Just running downwind in some waves," explained Strider. "We're past the worst of it." As he spoke, the cobalt blue water lightened. As the water depth decreased, the familiar pastels of the shallow Bahama Banks returned.

"Kaitlin, since Walter and Lenore slept through our wonderful conversation, why don't you give them the short version? Doug and Audrey and Vincent will have to get your notes."

"Before you start stuffing our heads, I want coffee," complained Lenore.

"I second that!" added Walter.

Strider bowed and went below.

"Earlier this morning," Kaitlin began, "a big powerboat blasted by with nobody in the cockpit. I asked Strider why *he* didn't navigate with a GPS and things took the usual, philosophical turn.

"We talked about how we naturally take bearings on familiar landmarks, and how you can't really get lost if you know where you are relative to a familiar place. But if we add a computer guidance system, we add a 'third voice' to the internal conversation about where we are and how to get there. It's easy to assume that voice knows better because it's armed with all this *data*....

"Then Micky Tomm joined us in the cockpit. He talked about how leadership involves taking all that data and figuring out what it *means*. To do that, you have to trust your gut. And according to

Strider, if you never test your compass—the one you use to find your way around the planet *and* the one you use to make decisions—you'll never learn to trust yourself."

Walter smiled. "You know what I'm going to ask next."

Kaitlin looked at Strider who crossed his arms and smiled. "As stated during my initial introduction, I am the *agent provocateur*, not the oracle. I think you've got this, Kaitlin."

Kaitlin pursed her lips for a moment, looked at Walter, and then continued. "Walter, you're probably the ideal person to be pressure-testing this material. If you speak in front of audiences, you have to build direct relationships with multiple people at the same time. And since we've all been forced to sit through terrible presenters—like those morons administrators bring in to talk to employees about sexual harassment or 'humor in the workplace,' I imagine you have to gain the trust of skeptical audiences."

Walter nodded.

"I have to wonder if a lot of the people your speeches appeal to wouldn't describe themselves as feeling 'lost.' Is that a fair assumption?"

"Definitely," said Walter.

"So if someone feels lost, what do you sell them? How do you connect with them in the most useful and powerful and effective way? A lot of people would sell them a GPS. 'Here you go; now you never have to be lost again.' But maybe that isn't what they need. Maybe the lack of a GPS isn't what's making them feel lost. Everyone's got a GPS in their phone these days, but people are more lost than ever. Maybe we should sell them a way to start relying on their *own* compass and encourage them to have some faith in their intuition. Getting lost isn't such a terrible thing. Maybe we should turn the problem around and tell them about the joys and opportunities that come with getting lost. Maybe the people who never venture into unfamiliar territory are the ones who are really lost."

"You know what I think?" asked Walter as he turned to face Strider. "I think you're the missing Mr. King, and Kaitlin here is your assistant."

"Write any story you want," said Strider.

"But Walter…" Kaitlin began to object, but Strider held up a palm.

"Are you getting your money's worth?" asked Strider.

Walter laughed. "I certainly am. I'm asking the tough questions and you guys keep the answers coming. I'm impressed… and I'm certainly having fun."

"Then I suppose it doesn't matter whether I am who you think I am or not?"

"I suppose not," smiled Walter knowingly.

Strider adjusted his hat. "More coffee anyone? And who's interested in fresh mackerel and eggs for breakfast?

Live to Tell the Tale

The Metaphor continued sailing. "She's a bit rolly," Strider apologized. "When the wind's behind you, you don't have the same stabilizing forces at work."

Lenore belched loudly. "Greetings from the interior!" she chuckled, embarrassed. "I wasn't expecting that … but I am feeling a little …"

"Seasick?" Strider asked.

"I don't know. I was fine a minute ago, but I'm feeling a bit 'third person,' like I'm not really here—like this is all a strange movie."

"That's the first stage," said Strider. "Let's head this off at the pass before things get messy. Lie down on that cockpit seat for me, love. I'll be right back."

Strider returned a moment later with a roll of duck tape.[7]

Lenore looked at Strider weakly, "You're not going to…"

"No, I'm not going to tape your mouth shut. I have a bucket for you if we get to the point where those mackerel want to swim free

---

7. Often mis-corrected as 'duct tape,' the original was actually Duck-brand tape.

again." He opened his hand and revealed two dried pinto beans. "I'm going to cure your seasickness with magic beans."

Lenore rolled her eyes. "I think I'll be okay lying down. I'm a scientist. I don't do magic beans."

"So let's do an empirical experiment. Give me your hand." Strider tore off a six-inch strip of tape, placed a bean on her wrist, and taped it tightly-but-not-too-tightly in place.

"Come on, Strider. I appreciate…"

"Other hand, please; captain's orders."

Lenore extended her other hand. Strider felt the inside of her wrist with his thumb, and placed the second bean between the two flexor tendons. Another strip of tape completed the remedy. "Just lie still for a bit," ordered Strider. "Close your eyes. You don't have to believe in this for it to work. When you do feel better, you won't even have to believe you didn't get better on your own. I just want you to feel all right."

By and by, the rest of the Happiness Congress rose from their bunks and ascended to the deck. Strider cooked breakfast for the new arrivals and made a fresh pot of coffee. Doug brought a drawing pad to the cockpit, Audrey wedged herself into a cushion propped against the mainmast where she lost herself in a tattered novel, and Vincent perched himself on the cabin top next to the companionway hatch with his guitar.

"Oh, you power-loungers," Strider called out. "I am so impressed. You came here to study happiness and look what's happened. They say 'nothing is impossible,' but after a few days in the islands, I believe you all can do it all day.

"Who's got a camera?"

Walter handed Strider his phone. The captain ascended into the rigging where he snapped several pictures of his satisfied guests. "Look up from that compass for a second, Kaitlin. You've been staring at that thing for hours."

Kaitlin smiled a sincere smile for the camera. Strider returned to the deck and handed the device back to Walter. "How ya feelin', Lenore?"

"I'm doing okay. I think lying down really helped."

"Whatever works," replied Strider. "Kaitlin, do you want me to take the helm? You don't have to steer all day if…"

"No way. I'm tuned into the wind and the boat and the compass. When I turn this wheel, I don't turn the ship; I turn the whole Universe around the compass needle. I know where the wind is coming from—which is something I never paid attention to before. It's like writing—when you're in the moment and words just flow out of you. Here we have the wind and the sea—two immensely powerful forces—and this mighty ship—and somehow I get to direct this ballet of the gods with this tiny wheel. No, Strider, I don't think you'll be doing much steering today."

"In that case, I'm going to leave you all to your sloth and grab an hour nap. Holler if you need anything or think you might need something but aren't sure if you should wake me. There's no one here I trust," Strider joked, "so nobody's in charge. You'll find a bag of cutlasses in the lazarette if you need to sort things out."

Strider retired to his warm wooden cabin where the sound of waves lapping against the hull and the gentle rolling of the boat soon had him dreaming of whatever it is people who live on a sailboat in Paradise dream of when they dream happy dreams.

A few hours later, he rejoined his crew on deck, refreshed. He looked around and took some bearings. To the east, the sun shone white and hazy. "See those spotty clouds and those streaky, wispy ones way up high?"

Everyone looked up.

"Mackerel skies and mare's tales make tall ships wear short sails.

"Wind still northwest?"

"Aye cap'n," said Kaitlin. "She's been steady since you went down for your nap."

"Good, and how about you, Lenore? How's the gut?"

"I owe you one," Lenore confessed. "I was feeling better and the tape was a bit uncomfortable so I took it off. Fifteen minutes later, I started feeling pukey again, and I lost one of the beans down the cockpit drain. Poor Walter had to rummage in the galley for a replacement bean and figure out where you kept the tape. So I'm feeling better for the second time, and I'm now a scientist who believes in magic. Thanks, I guess."

After an uneventful two-and-a-half-hour sail across the Sea of Abaco to Marsh Harbour, Strider had Kaitlin round *The Metaphor* up into the wind. He dropped the jib and foresail quickly and paid out anchor chain as the ship drifted backward. Once satisfied that sufficient scope had been let out to keep the ship in place, he cleated off the line and let the momentum of the boat dig the anchor flukes into the grassy bottom.

"Okay, folks," Strider announced. "This weather is not going to hold much longer. It's not the end of the world if we get stuck here — there's decent protection and good bottom for anchoring — but I'd like to get over to Man-O-War Cay before nature gets *dramatic*.

"There are two big grocery stores in Marsh Harbour. Maxwell's is about a half-mile up into town. Hike on up there and get some eggs, fresh vegetables, and anything you want to turn into dinner. I need potatoes, onions, and a few cabbages. I could use some more flour and sugar for baking bread. Eight people can make short work of a case of wine. Expect to pay a lot more money than you do in the States. Almost all this food comes in by ship from other places. I'll do what I can to keep us in seafood, but no promises. If you want animal protein, grab it here, but remember that the icebox is small — and that reminds me, if you can grab about four bags of ice — two blocks and two bags of cubes — I can keep things cold and fresh. And if you don't mind, I have four blue plastic water jugs lashed up behind the foredeck. Can you take those and fill them up? Try to find a spigot over at the marina. Tell 'em it's for me if anyone gives you trouble.

"And don't forget to mail your postcards!"

"Grab a cracked conch sandwich on your way up to the grocery store—and pronounce it 'konk,' not 'konch' if you don't want to pay tourist prices. Then get yourselves back here quick so we can beat this cold front. If we have a gale, we'll be happier in Man-O-War Cay."

Kaitlin looked at the captain. "What about you, Strider. Aren't you going?"

"No, love. I'm going to straighten things up and grab a few minutes of quiet and solitude. Not that you all aren't wonderful company, but…"

"We get it," assured Doug. "No problem; I think I'd be the same way if I had seven guests in my apartment."

Doug turned to the task at hand. "I'm happy to row. Who's riding in my dinghy?" The happiness delegates clambered over the rail into the dinghies with backpacks and shopping bags.

Strider walked around the deck and inspected the lines for wear or chafe. Then he washed the breakfast dishes, stowed everything securely, and straightened out the main cabin.

Before long, the boats returned. A parade of bags and boxes passed over the rail and marched down into *The Metaphor*'s cabin. Doug and Vincent lashed full water jugs onto the foredeck while Strider stowed supplies in lockers in the galley.

"This isn't going to happen to us—especially here in these shallow, protected waters—but when you stow stuff on a boat, imagine what would happen if she were to roll 360 degrees. Would your gear stay put or would it go flying around the ship? I've seen one big, unexpected wave turn a tidy boat into an instant mess—though if it makes you feel safer, I've never seen an actual rollover."

Satisfied that everything was stowed properly, Strider ascended to the deck, untied the mainsail, and tugged on the two halyards that raised it. He jumped out of the way as a coil of line and pieces of a heavy wooden block crashed to the deck at his feet.

"Are you okay?" Kaitlin called.

"I'm fine. Fortunately that missed my head. But we have a bit of a conundrum. This block—this big pulley that the peak halyard goes through—looks like it has a failed weld or a stress fracture. I'm amazed it didn't fall apart when we were sailing over here, but falling to the deck didn't help it any."

"Do you have a spare?" Kaitlin asked.

"I did have a spare—two actually—but a buddy of mine had some problems on his boat and I gave him mine."

"Does this mean we're stuck in Marsh Harbour?"

"We could motor over, but engines are a lot more dependable when you have a backup plan. There are rocky shores here I'd hate to blow down on, and I worry about that a lot less when

I have sails to rely on. It might make more sense to just put down another anchor and…"

"I might have a solution," suggested Lenore. "I'll be right back."

A moment later, she emerged from the companionway with a shopping bag under her arm. "I was walking from the dinghy dock up into town and I found these old boat pulleys lying in the grass with some old rotten line. I picked them up because I thought they looked kind of 'nautical.' I figured I could polish them and keep them as a souvenir."

Strider began to laugh. "I love how things work in these islands. I wasn't going to say anything because you'd all have thought I was nuts, but if you stay here long enough, you see more coincidences than you'd expect. These blocks are exactly what I need. They're a little weathered, but they're perfectly useful. Lenore, if you don't mind, I'll oil them up, climb up and shackle one up on the mast, and we'll be off and running in ten minutes."

"Magic beans and magic blocks," mused Lenore. "Consider them yours. This story is a much better souvenir than a couple of wood pulleys I won't actually use for anything."

"And that's an important observation. I thank you for that as much as I do for the blocks … but we'll get to that later the next time Congress is in session."

A few minutes later, the sails had been hauled aloft and sheeted in tight. The wind had freshened and clocked a few points more to the north. Once past the harbour entrance, *The Metaphor* charged to windward into a smoky, hazy sky.

"Try the wheel now," Strider suggested to Kaitlin. "We ran downwind all morning to get to Marsh Harbour, but now it's blowing from about ten o'clock. If you fall off the wind, the ship will slow down. If you sail too high into the wind, you'll see the sails 'luff' or flap around. Find that 'sweet spot' and keep her there."

"What about the compass course?"

"It'll be around 45 degrees, but we have less than five miles to cover—about an hour's sail. Just aim for that island up ahead and keep the boat pointed where she sails best." Strider put his hat over the compass. "Sail the boat, not the course."

Kaitlin experimented with steering the ship on and off the wind until she found the 'groove.'

As the ship approached Man-O-War Cay, Vincent pointed ahead. "I've never seen anything like that before. It looks like a waterfall in the sky!" A sheet of gray clouds extended down from the north. Where it met the blue Bahamian sky, the gray clouds dived downward like an imposing wall.

"Those gray clouds are where the cool air is condensing all the moisture out of the warm tropical air—like a cold bottle of wine 'sweats' when you take it out of the freezer. That 'wall' is where the cold air is diving under the warm air—and that's why it's called a cold 'front.' You rarely see such a dramatic example."

"What does that mean, Strider?" asked Lenore.

"It means we're going to have a North Atlantic gale. It's going to blow hard and rain like hell. We'll probably get some lightning and thunder. "But we're also a few minutes away from one of the world's finest hurricane holes. And that means our timing is a little tight, but we're going to watch nature's freak show from a calm, peaceful anchorage." A rumble of distant thunder added an ominous note of punctuation to Strider's pronouncement.

"Doug." Strider tossed his hat onto a settee in the main cabin. "Opposite the head[8] is a locker with foul weather gear in it. Can you bring up a set for me, a set for yourself, and a set for Kaitlin?"

"How can the rest of us be useful?" asked Micky Tomm.

"Go down below and get comfortable. Be ready to close and dog the hatches when the rain starts. And once we're inside the harbour, can someone start a pot of coffee?"

"Got ya covered," said Micky Tomm.

Strider looked at Kaitlin and pointed to starboard. "See those two islands there? They're Grassy Cay and Garden Cay, and they're just off the entrance to Man-O-War harbour."

"I don't see the entrance," said Kaitlin.

"It's magic," said Strider. "It won't appear unless you're worthy—and until you're really close to it. But you proved your mettle today. I'm optimistic."

Strider held the wheel while Kaitlin donned her foul weather suit.

---

8. A "head" is a marine toilet. The room that encloses it is likewise referred to as the "head."

"Kaitlin, let's round up into the wind for a moment in the lee of the island. Doug, help me wrestle this foresail down. It'll be one less piece of canvas to deal with once we're inside the anchorage. It can get crowded in there."

Kaitlin executed the maneuver and stalled the schooner into the wind. As soon as the foresail was down and lashed to its boom, she resumed her course along the coast of Man-O-War Cay.

A few fat raindrops plopped onto the deck.

"Here she comes," called Strider.

He went back to the cockpit and started the engine. "Never hurts to have backup when mooring in a tight anchorage in a storm—no place for sailing purist's pride here."

A blast of cool air swooshed across the deck and grabbed the sails, then subsided as quickly as it had arrived.

Kaitlin looked concerned. "I still don't see the entrance, Strider."

"Keep going, Kaitlin; I know you're worthy." He smiled back at her confidently.

A distant flash preceded another rumble of thunder by several seconds.

"Still no entrance."

"Keep going...."

Sheltered in the lee of the island, *The Metaphor* glided forward. The waves made an oddly musical sound under the shelf they'd undercut in the island's coral shore over the centuries.

"Got it!" cried Kaitlin. "A tiny gap in the coral!"

"Once you're inside, head straight. You'll see a channel marker. Make sure you pass it or you'll end up on a sand shoal. Then turn to starboard—right—and when you pass through the anchored boats, try to pass *behind* them so you don't foul any anchor lines. We'll find a mooring down-harbour."

Strider showed her how to work the throttle lever and engage the transmission in forward, neutral, and reverse. "Watch for my hand signals up on the bow."

"This is gorgeous," cooed Kaitlin. It's like a lake inside a beautiful island!"

"And those hills to windward of us are sixty to ninety feet high. The weather's got to get pretty nasty before anyone feels it in here."

Darkness fell upon the anchorage. The blue sky disappeared.

"Doug, once we find an open mooring ball, I'm going to help Kaitlin get the boat in position and then I'm going to grab the line with the boathook. On my signal, drop this jib and tie it down. Try to be ready to take the line from me so we can get her tied off. We'll drop the mainsail last."

Doug nodded.

Kaitlin eased *The Metaphor* through the pack of anchored boats toward the end of the harbour. At last Strider spied an available mooring. He pointed at it and motioned for Kaitlin to approach from downwind.

Doug pointed at the north end of the harbour. An advancing curtain of rain obscured the entrance.

Strider raised a palm. Kaitlin shifted into neutral and let *The Metaphor* drift forward. The mainsail danced and shook. Kaitlin hauled it in tight.

The captain signaled Doug who dropped the jib and lashed it securely. By the time he'd finished, Strider had secured the line to the foredeck.

The rain arrived. The air turned cold as the mainsail glided down, suspended from the magic block Lenore had found in Marsh Harbour. Strider and Kaitlin held the struggling sail down while Doug got the sail ties secured.

"Kaitlin, thank you. Go get dry and warm. Doug will help me with the anchor."

"Why do we need the anchor if we're on a mooring, Strider?"

"Whose mooring is that?"

"I don't know."

"I don't know, either. I'm sure the owner will come by looking for rent money as soon as the weather clears, but probably, all there is down there is a block of cement. I call that the 'weight and sea' method, but without knowing what's actually down there or what shape it's in, I'll put my faith in my anchors. It'd *probably* be okay to trust it, but then again, we've already written some great stories today. Let's not push our luck."

In the pouring rain, Doug lowered a big anchor and its length of chain to where Strider waited in the dinghy at the bow. He rowed out to windward, paying out chain as he went, and then flipped the anchor off the stern close to one of the wooden docks that lined the harbour.

A bright flash of lightning accompanied an enormous boom.

Strider shrugged, flashed a gap-toothed smile, and returned to his ship.

"I sure hope someone made up that coffee."

The Elements of Story

"Ah, a rainy day," sighed Strider as he slipped two loaves of bread dough into the oven. "Is everyone warm and dry?"

"I thought being stuck down below decks was going to be a drag," said Walter, "but I enjoyed the sail here and the hike through Marsh Harbour. This place looks stunning; I can't wait to explore it, but for now, I'm relaxed and content to listen to the rain on the deck."

All agreed *The Metaphor* was no prison. Her cabin was warm and dry and on this, their fourth night aboard, full of friends.

Audrey pulled out a big can of mixed nuts and passed them around.

Strider pulled the corks on two bottles of pinot noir and began to pass out glasses. "I have a suggestion," he said. "I'm a human barometer; when the atmospheric pressure falls, I get sleepy and lazy. I have a hard time imagining myself staying up this evening once the sun goes down—but the adventures we've had between Green Turtle Cay and here are perfect on-ramps for a nuts-and-bolts discussion about stories. No metaphysics — no multidimensional philosophical quagmires — just what stories are and how they work. Who's game?"

Kaitlin smiled and raised two fingers.

"I'm amazed you have the energy after steering the boat all day — that's a lot of concentration — but I'm glad you're in. Any objectors?"

Everyone raised their glasses. The smell of fresh bread was beginning to fill the cabin and that, combined with the memories of an adventurous day, had the Happiness Congress in good spirits.

Strider rapped a wooden spoon on the galley top, signifying that the Congress was in session. "Remember we spoke about 'selling the benefits, not the features' back in Green Turtle Cay when we were making our introductions?

"Let's start with a variation on that. Every story has two horizontal elements — conflict and transformation. I call them 'horizontal' because they can be visualized as moving from left to right. Cinderella escapes from her stepmother; she's the conflict — or at least one of them. And Cinderella lives happily ever after with the prince — that's the transformation. The conflict in a story often gets too much attention while the transformation gets downplayed. We call these 'bad sales pitches.' Great stories and great storytellers focus on the transformation — on the benefits.

The Elements of Story

"Did anyone see Kaitlin's transformation today?"

Walter looked at Kaitlin. "I watched you change from someone who wondered why we weren't sailing with a GPS into a real sailor. You didn't take your hands off the wheel all day. Something happened. You *got* something. Something *got* you. I'm no hardcore sailor, but I've had enough daysailing experience to understand that running downwind is difficult. Any other beginner would have jibed[9] the boat a half-dozen times. When we headed upwind from Marsh Harbour to Man-O-War, you did it again; you stayed just off the wind without losing focus and accidentally tacking across it. As well as I'm able to judge, Kaitlin, that was some fine sailing today."

"Absolutely," agreed Strider. "So Kaitlin discovering her natural sailing ability is the transformation. We could extrapolate backward and propose that up until today, Kaitlin didn't understand that sailing—or tuning into the elements—was missing from her life. One could argue that we're all missing out on things we don't know we're missing out on—things that would make our lives richer and bring out our full potential if only someone would connect us to them. The notion that we might never get connected to what or whom will bring out our gifts is definitely a conflict."

---

9. *Jibe* — When sailing downwind, it's easy to unintentionally change course enough to cause the wind to shift behind the boat from one side to the other. When this happens, the sails can shift quickly and unexpectedly — sometimes with great force.

"And at the same time," added Audrey, "I think it's pretty darned special that Kaitlin just happened to be there to get stuck with us on Moraine Cay so she could end up sailing your boat and having that day of self-discovery."

"You're right," said Strider, "But that's magic—the fourth element of story—one of the vertical elements. We'll get there soon enough. In Kaitlin's story, we see a pure and simple example of the search for meaning—a passive search perhaps; nobody set out on a quest—but one that resulted in meaningful transformation.

"I'd like to read you a short piece written by someone who sailed these waters almost thirty years ago as a young man on a small boat. Walter, will you grab that blue book off the shelf behind you?"

Walter handed the volume to Strider.

"This is a vignette called 'Cathy's Island' from a book called *The Blue Monk*—which was the name of the author's boat. Strider cleared his voice and began to recite.

> I anchor at Powell Cay, a less-traveled island northwest of Green Turtle Cay. Uninhabited, it's serenely quiet, with beaches devoid of human footprints and a grove of tall, wild coconut palms. On the lee side, dramatic coral cliffs shelter tropicbirds nesting in their season. Affixed to the rocks near the anchorage is a small, bronze plaque— "Cathy Swedenborg Loved This Island"— a shrine to a young woman who died here with her boyfriend in 1979 when their boat burned.

Her epitaph is unconcerned with what was lost. Instead, it connects her forever to this special place she found and appreciated, and to her enduring suggestion that I might love it, too.

Late at night, I awaken and step into the cockpit. Unadulterated by urban incandescence, untinted by the azure hue of day, the nocturnal world projects its magic for those fortunate to bear witness.

The moon is high and bright; the white sand bottom illuminated like a stadium; the lunar light brilliant enough to read by.

I step astern, grabbing the backstay for support.

A diamond shape moves in the water below me.

And another.

Giant Atlantic stingrays glide over the bottom—dozens of them. Their dark forms undulate, slow and graceful against brilliant, sub-aquatic sand; an Escher woodcut brought to life; a moving tapestry of figure and ground; a dream landscape.

Such sights may be common. Stingrays may congregate here regularly on moonlit nights—or perhaps—maybe only once, tonight. It doesn't matter; I am blessed to witness a secret world of shadows and light.

Cathy Swedenborg loved this island.

I understand.

"Maybe the conflict is that there's this sign placed on the rocks without any context that might explain its meaning; it's a riddle that can't be solved. But it's a story because it's loaded with transformation. Not only does it transform the reader by sharing a beautiful experience; it tells of the author's transformation. And by the way, I've anchored at Powell Cay on many a moonlit night and though it's as beautiful as he says it is, I've never seen the stingrays. He finds this plaque on the island and stores its memory in his psychic 'junk drawer.' Then he gets up to pee—which is the only reason he'd be standing on the stern holding the backstay in the middle of the night—and he has this epiphany—this revelation. He experiences this moment of connection with this woman who died years before he got there. In an unexpected way, he solves the riddle."

"I love it," said Kaitlin. "Thanks for sharing that."

"One of today's best stories was Lenore's seasickness." Strider looked at his guest. "Sorry, dear, I know feeling queasy wasn't any fun for you, but your story had an easy-to-define conflict—you wanted to avoid blowing your oats all over the cockpit sole. And it had an easy-to-define transformation—you felt better after I taped the beans to your wrists.

"That in itself is more of an anecdote than a story—a factual recounting of events is an anecdote; it doesn't necessarily speak to anything *meaningful*—but there was a larger transformation. Lenore is an empirical scientist—and as such, things like "magic beans" and eastern medicine—acupressure—are stories that don't always harmonize with her meticulous study of how the gears of the Universe mesh. Because Lenore got seasick, the skepticism—the very thing that makes her an effective researcher—lost a wrestling match to a pair of beans. Now I'm sure Lenore thinks there's a scientific explanation—even *I* think there is—but nevertheless, because of that event, Lenore now lives in a world of expanded possibilities. Living in a Universe full of unexplained science is no different than living in a world full of magic, is it?"

Lenore twisted her hair. "What's funny, Strider, is that I've been thinking about how much fun it will be to tell that story when I get back to work. I endured a lot of skeptical sarcasm when my co-workers found out that I—the astrophysicist—was going to spend my vacation time at a happiness conference. One reason I've enjoyed our discussions so much is that I'm always uncovering overwhelming evidence for things that make absolutely no sense; we've talked about plenty of examples of that. But some of my most brilliant colleagues have been driven since childhood to put the Universe in order. I've never called them 'Essential Absurdities' before, but these things—these stories of the inexplicable—are great fun to drop on the anthill of scientific inquiry."

Vincent extended his empty wine glass to Strider. "I slept in through the whole seasick story—though I'm not regretting that. The one that blew *me* away is that Lenore came back to the ship with the exact part you needed to fix the boat. What are the odds?"

"They say truth is stranger than fiction," added Kaitlin. "If I wrote that in a novel or short story, my readers would never accept it as plausible."

Strider uncorked another bottle, refilled Vincent's glass, and passed it around. "So what are the conflicts in that story?"

Micky Tomm volunteered an answer. "We needed to beat the weather to Man-O-War Cay and, at the last minute, we had a mechanical breakdown that got in the way."

"Exactly," said Strider. "Pretty simple. And the transformation?"

Doug raised a finger. "We got here—at least *almost* got here—before the weather got nasty?"

"Yes, but that's not the *remarkable* transformation. That's not what gives an anecdote the gravitas to call itself a story. What's the *deeper* transformation?"

Walter refilled his glass and passed the bottle back to Strider. "The transformation is that whether we're accepting or skeptical, we're all mulling over the idea that either something *magic* happened or we witnessed an *epic* coincidence. You used the word 'remarkable'—which means 'worthy of making a remark about.' Whether it was an act of God or a work of Shakespeare accidentally written by the zillionth random monkey on the zillionth random typewriter, it's remarkable."

"That sounds more like a conflict," said Doug. "We don't know whether we've witnessed magic or coincidence."

"Perhaps," replied Strider, "but when a coincidence strikes us as so highly improbable that we begin to acknowledge expanded possibilities, that's transformation.

"So to come back to you, Walter," Strider continued. "The story is a story because it brings us closer to the Essential Absurdities—to the Mystery. You don't have to explain *how* acupressure cures seasickness to marvel at it. You don't need to explain *why* Lenore found an old boat part lying in the grass that's been obsolete since the 1950s and stuffed it in her bag an hour before mine broke to marvel at it. The biggest story transformations are transformations of perspective. You don't have to come away with anything resolved; every time I see this kind of stuff happen, I'm more confused than ever."

"So we have the 'horizontal' story forces of conflict and transformation," added Micky Tomm. "What are the 'vertical' forces? You mentioned magic."

Strider sliced his hand slowly through the air in front of him. "Imagine a story moving through conflict to transformation. A football team is twenty points behind in the last quarter. Can they throw some long passes and win the game? An undervalued female employee summons the courage to ask for a pay raise that will align her income with the salaries of her male colleagues. A group of professionals is stranded on a remote island without shelter or leadership. Will they spend a cold night on the beach? Will they find the insights they came there searching for? Those are conflicts.

"The transformation may be predictable. The football team may win the game and get icy Gatorade poured on their heads. Or they may lose the game but use it as an opportunity to let that nerdy kid who's been sitting on the bench all season play quarterback. Maybe the transformation is that they all realize there are more meaningful stories in life than pushing a ball down a field. They finish the season 0–14 but everyone's a winner.

"Maybe Gladys gets a raise — or maybe she gets turned down and goes home rejected. And then while she's home getting ready to move out of the apartment she can't afford, all her officemates get together and organize a big employee flapdoodle that challenges and embarrasses the management into paying everyone what they're worth."

"What about those idiots stuck on that island?" laughed Micky Tomm.

"We'll see," replied Strider. "I think that story is still being written … but stories move from conflict toward transformation. In sailing terms, that horizontal motion is like the course of the story—the path it takes. The 'vertical' forces are like the wind that fills the sails and the sea that keeps the ship off the bottom.

"The force that stabilizes and supports the story is *authenticity*. That doesn't mean the story has to be true or even plausible. It means that the story is representative in some way of our human search for meaning. Take the football story for example. We're sometimes so engrossed in the game of human competition that we fail to find value in people who can't contribute directly to the team. How many of us were ever rejected because we stunk at sports? Or had to endure the pressure of performing well on the ballfield because our social status was riding on scoring those points? How many young girls don't feel pretty enough or worry about looking too smart? For lots of kids, sports teams represent winning through conformity and competition. Non-conformists and non-competitive kids get benched. In our story, when little Joey gets out onto the field and he's carried on the shoulders of Billy the bully because he's got fiberglass legs, he gets to be a hero for everyone who never got the chance to play ball or was never any good at it. We all feel his pain.

"When Gladys shows up at work ready to suck up to the boss because she can't buy Wheaties unless she does, and she finds her colleagues standing outside the office with protest signs, that story is authentic because we've all been treated unfairly at one time or another. We all have a sense of justice built into our moral compass. We've all had to bite our lips for a paycheck or deal with some sort of inequity. When those conflicts get challenged, we celebrate because we can relate to the story. That's authenticity.

"If I tried to sell you a story about how Dudley Dashley Junior is chaperoned to the Porsche dealer in a white limousine by his father's chauffeur on his sixteenth birthday and forced to choose between a red convertible and a black one—even though he really wants yellow—there's simply not enough authenticity there to keep that ship from going aground. Dudley is a privileged and ungrateful little snot. The challenges he faces at the car dealership are not meaningful to us—they're shallow. He may be ripe for transformation, but unless the story takes us there, it's not authentic. We don't care."

"I knew a kid like that back in high school," said Doug. "He was loaded, but he was miserable—lots of drugs and low-life friends. I think he had everything but love and approval. Wonder what happened to him…"

"The 'poor little rich kid' is an authentic and oft-written story," said Strider, "but let's move on to magic. Even *fantastic* magic has an important place in effective storytelling. Let's circle back to Cinderella. She's left behind; she can't get to the ball. The fairy godmother shows up and waves her wand. The pumpkin turns into a coach and the mice turn into horsemen. Her shabby dress turns into an elegant dancing gown and a pair of sexy glass stilettos. Off she goes to meet the prince. The story is *utterly implausible*, but nobody wants to hear how Cinderella tied bedsheets together into a rope and shimmied out the window, how she broke into the house next door and 'borrowed' a gown, and how she summoned a cab and made it to the castle. Why not?"

Everyone thought for a moment. Audrey spoke. "I think the Cinderella story is not about what it appears to be on the surface. As children—especially as teenagers—we all want to take control of our own destinies. We all want to meet our special prince or princess and live 'happily ever after.' Those slippers we leave behind aren't red or sparkly; they're glass—they're subtle and transparent. Symbolically, they're 'our walk,' and you have to look through the glass to see what they represent. Not everyone will notice or appreciate them, but they fit only us; they represent our unique qualities. The great love of our life is someone who will seek out and appreciate what only *we* have to offer. The Cinderella story is about love and connection. It's about realizing our human potential. It's about growing up and controlling our destiny."

Strider put a thumb up. "I think you nailed the authenticity part, Audrey. What about the magic?"

Audrey closed her eyes and then clapped her hands together. "It's simple! The mechanism through which Cinderella escapes to the castle is not a series of clever strategies; it's a moment of realization, a burst of insight. It's real, symbolic magic. Maybe a voice in her head says, 'I know I'm just a cleaning maid and I only have talking mice for friends and my stepmother is a bitch. I have a million excuses for not going out into the world to connect and engage— *but tonight I'm going to go for it!*'"

"Bravo," said Strider. "I told you I wasn't going to play the professor here. I'm outgunned on several fronts. Magic is like the wind that moves a story along—an invisible, powerful force, a catalyst for transformation."

Strider grinned, reached inside the oven door, and placed two steaming brown loaves on the counter. "I give you *transformation!*

"Kaitlin, why don't you wrap up the elements of story while this bread cools?"

"I always start these summaries off wondering what I'll say, but then I end up feeling like I've got it. It's one thing to think about this stuff—to *talk* about stories—but today we navigated around Whale Cay, we went ashore in Marsh Harbour, we broke the boat and fixed her back up with the help of a minor miracle, and we sailed here to Man-O-War just ahead of a storm. Once I start verbalizing these ideas, I understand them in a more concrete way. Once we go out and actually navigate and sail and row and fix things and race against the weather, we're *engaging*—we're *doing*. That suggests that if you want to be an effective storyteller, if you want to understand how this works, you have to get out there and make the search for meaning an active, conscious part of your life. That's how the Blue Monk—whatever his name was—managed to squeeze a story out of waking up to pee off the back of his boat. You have to *live* to tell the tale.

"And I think this was why Strider had us do all that theoretical deep space and conscious-and-subconscious and 'Zen of the soul' stuff in the first days of this trip. We talked a lot about what meaning is all about and what it *isn't* about. We loosened up the stranglehold we have on so many of the stories we take comfort in and opened ourselves up to expanded possibilities."

Strider handed out plates of fresh, hot slices of bread and followed them with a small tray of butter, honey, maple syrup, and olive oil. "Don't let me interrupt you, Kaitlin. Take a bite and continue."

"Today, we got a formula of sorts — a way to visualize what makes stories work or not. On a linear, horizontal plane, stories sail across a sea of conflict toward the safe port of transformation. That transformation can be anything that's meaningful to the main character in the story — and the transformation is the most important part of the story. Too many advertisers and salespeople focus on conflicts; they talk about data and ingredients and the mechanics of avoiding obstacles. But then they fail to talk about the transformation in a meaningful way. They sell the features instead of the benefits. A product or service takes a customer on a voyage through conflict to transformation.

"As a story travels across the sea of conflict, it needs metaphorical water to hold it up — *authenticity*. The reader or listener will stay on board only if the transformation being sought is meaningful to *them*. It has to be 'deep enough' to keep the ship afloat. Connection and engagement succeed when we demonstrate that we understand the people we're telling stories to. You have to speak their language and understand their challenges. We have to find the deeper, more meaningful goals hiding behind the shallow ones.

"Finally—and this bread is a remarkable story unto itself, Strider—we have the wind that pushes the story-boat—magic. If we approach the conflict and transformation in an innovative and authentic way, we can create stories that open people's eyes—stories that change the way people see the problems and challenges in their lives. Readers, customers, audiences, art lovers, music lovers, employees—even stranded happiness seekers—are all looking for a magic shortcut, for a fairy godmother to show them the shortcut to grandmother's house. Being a storyteller—and I'll take a chance on this and add 'being happy'—is a process of connecting with others authentically so you understand their needs and goals and win their trust. It's a process of discovering your own magic and learning how to use it—which is probably why the story of Harry Potter and his friends at Hogwarts School of Wizardry and Witchcraft is so popular.

"Conflict and transformation. Authenticity and magic. A story is a ship on a sea with a course and a destination—and a fair wind to push it."

Kaitlin paused, closed her eyes, and raised a finger to signal her listeners that she had more to say. "I think there's one more story element we haven't talked about yet—and that's the boat that sails from conflict to transformation. The boat contains people—a captain and maybe a crew; they're who the story is about. A boat has a compass, a rudder, and a sail. How many stories are about people who don't trust their compass? How many people end up on the rocks of conflict because they won't take the wheel and steer? How many people are stuck because even with the winds of magic blowing all around them, they won't put up the sails? How many of us have taken on passengers who interfere with the safe navigation of the boat? How many people carry too much gear with them or not enough? A poorly maintained ship can sink in deep water on a calm day.

Conflict, transformation, authenticity, and magic represent the *environment* in which the story takes place—the forces that confront the characters, the degree to which their story is meaningful to the listener, and the insights and experiences they gain that allow them to advance. The boat represents the resources available to the characters in the story, the choices they make, their power, and their potential. A story is a sailing lesson.

"Welcome to *The Metaphor*. Is there any more bread?"

MAGIC
the invisible force that moves your story forward
(wind) (perspective) (awareness)

storms   *resolution*

CONFLICT  **TRANSFORMATION**

rocks   *safe harbor*

is the story (or the water) deep enough to keep the ship afloat?
is the story a metaphor for the listener's story?
AUTHENTICITY

One Mosquito

*B*y morning, the rain had passed, and though the wind was still gusting to 50 m.p.h., the sky was clear and *The Metaphor* rode gently at anchor. The sound of the surf booming against the rocks reverberated from the far side of the island. As was his custom, Strider summoned his guests to the main cabin with the smell of hot coffee and pancakes.

"I didn't sleep too well last night," Strider complained. "It's odd for February, but I had a *relentless* mosquito in my cabin last night." He sighed and began to mix a second bowl of pancake batter.

"We'll sit here for a day or two and let this wind die down a bit. When I saw that red sky yesterday, I was worried we might get socked in somewhere. Marsh Harbour would have been safe, but Man-O-War is much more fun for exploring. You can row down to the public dock in town, or tie up at that dock over there; friends of mine own it. Hike about fifty feet up the hill and then take the Queen's Highway down the spine of the island. The first half-mile is just a coral rock path through the jungle; it turns into a regular paved road when you hit town. The island's less than three miles long from tip to tip. Between the old colonial town and the harbour and the beach on the ocean side, you'll find plenty to explore and lots of history to uncover. If you can find the 'baseball field at the end of the world,' it has the most exquisite view of any ballpark on earth. Look out and watch the reef; it'll be in a 'rage' today."

"What's that?" asked Walter.

"We're sitting right at the eastern tip of the Little Bahama Bank. Some of the waves that arrive here have traveled thousands of miles across deep ocean water — and with this wind blowing, they're big and moving fast. Imagine swimming pool-sized hills of water rolling across the surface of the ocean. All of a sudden, they hit a shallow coral wall. Kaboom! The only place they can go is up; they explode. A friend and I got crazy once and rowed out there to see it. One of nature's freak shows; it's spectacular — but please watch it from the shore."

"What's the town like?" asked Vincent.

"This is another quiet Bahamian church-going town. There's a boatyard and a traditional wooden boat-building industry here that account for some of the island's income. They ferry tourists in and sell them tote bags and ice cream, and then they send them back to Marsh Harbour. You'll find lots of white colonial houses with pastel-colored shutters. And Man-O-War is a dry island; they don't sell any alcohol here."

"That's too bad," said Walter. "I've been enjoying our wine."

"And you'll continue to—just not on shore in Man-O-War."

"Why do you think that is?" asked Doug.

"It's rather enlightened of them," said Strider. "They haven't made alcohol illegal—just the sale of it. That means their sleepy, quiet little town gets to stay sleepy and quiet. It means the spring break party tourists will thumb their noses at Man-O-War and go rent a cottage in Hopetown or New Plymouth. It means nobody's trying to remember all the verses to 'American Pie' while they stagger through the streets after the bars close at 3:00 a.m. It means the town stays neat and tidy because nobody's making it their mission to go out and paint it."

Walter poured syrup on his pancake. "I suppose, but it does penalize people who want a glass of wine when they go out to dinner."

"Compare it to the way tobacco laws work in the States," suggested Strider. "You can buy cigarettes anywhere, but you can't smoke them in a restaurant or public place. As soothing as they might be to a nicotine addict, they smell horrible, have unhealthy side effects, and invade people's space."

"Back when I was first starting to play music professionally," added Vincent, "I used to come home with my amp and my guitar and my clothes absolutely reeking of smoke. My eyes would burn and my throat would itch. I would have had to change careers a long time ago if the smoking legislation hadn't passed."

"What about narcotics?" asked Doug. "Where do you draw the line? Drugs are illegal but you can buy them on any street in America."

Strider refilled his coffee cup. "Now there's a chain of dominoes where a wrong story has sent a ripple of painful and expensive consequences across Western society."

"Why do you object to drugs being illegal, Strider? The health effects…"

"Yes. Drugs are unhealthy, but look at how the story goes—and understand that out here, where I live, a lot of these things are non-issues for me; my interest is in stories. Most people *follow* stories; they accept them at face value and read their part in the script. Leaders *write* the stories; they create the framework for laws and culture and social mores. When bad leaders write bad stories, we end up with tragic and expensive problems.

"But while it's a shame to waste a beautiful morning in the Bahamas debating whether narcotics should be decriminalized, we might be able to use that topic as a tool for learning a few things about connection and engagement.

"Good morning, Kaitlin. Did you catch the tail end of that?"

"Mm-hmm. Coffee, please."

Strider handed her a mug. "Let's look at the drug addiction story using the tools we discussed yesterday. What's the desired outcome—the hoped-for transformation?"

"A drug-free society," offered Doug.

"That only works as long as we exclude alcohol from the 'drug' category. Given that alcohol inhibits motor skills, inhibits judgment, and arouses passions, is there any rational reason it shouldn't be considered a drug?"

"What about people like us who want a glass of wine with dinner?"

Strider raised his coffee cup. "What about people who want a kick of caffeine in the morning? What about people who want to take a few puffs of marijuana to wind the day down? Look, I haven't smoked pot since I was in college, but nobody ever got high on dope and beat up his girlfriend. It's easy to argue that alcohol is a far more dangerous drug than marijuana—but instead of going down the rabbit hole of deciding which drugs are worse than others, which is part of the problem with the whole story of drug interdiction, let's get back to desired outcomes, to transformation. I reject your premise that a 'drug-free society' is a valid goal, and if it were, it would be a means to a larger end. What are the actual societal ends we aim to accomplish with the new, enlightened drug policy story we're about to develop—despite the fact that no one will ever implement it? If nothing else, it's a great exercise in story leadership."

"A safer, healthier society?" suggested Vincent.

"People connecting instead of disconnecting?" offered Audrey.

Kaitlin extended her empty cup to Strider. "Supporting the freedom to walk in public without having to deal with inebriated people?"

"What about opioids and solving the problem of addiction?" asked Strider. "What about stopping organized crime and the Colombian cartels? What about reducing gangs and violence in American cities? How about recovering the costs of law enforcement and imprisonment? These are real costs and negative impacts of drugs on society."

"All those are important goals," agreed Walter. "But how do you see this as a story problem?"

"Somewhere along the line, some well-meaning imbeciles decided that if drugs were a problem, that problem could be solved by making them illegal. The logic is undeniable, but that story is simple and one-dimensional. The law identified a conflict and attempted to eliminate it without any concrete notion of what the desired transformation was and whether the action taken would produce that outcome. Since Richard Nixon declared his "war on drugs" in 1971, a trillion dollars has been spent on drug interdiction — *a trillion dollars* — and yet that appears to have had negligible impact on supply or use or crime. The U.S. now has the largest prison population in the world — about two-and-a-half-million people. Almost half of them are incarcerated for drug-related crimes. That's a lot of mostly poor, mostly black people who have lost their freedom and their right to vote. And it's given rise to a five-billion-dollar private prison industry.

"Meanwhile—and maybe you'll have something to say about this from an insider's perspective, Micky Tomm?—the pharma industry cranks out opioid drugs. Got a toothache? Here's a prescription for Oxy or Percoset or Vicodin. Most people pop a few and move on, but Helen Handbasket swallows her first one and sees Nirvana. When she dies from an overdose ten years later, the coroner can't tell if it's from heroin or pills because they're chemically identical—and if she can't get a prescription for more pills, she ends up on the street stuff."

Micky Tomm nodded silently.

"Let's start with a more realistic premise for this story: No matter what the legal system does, people are going to use drugs for pain and pleasure; always have—always will. That's part of what makes a smart drug strategy story authentic: it's statistically proven that the legal system has no ability to reduce drug use—especially given that some of the most harmful drugs are legal. It's absurd."

"So how do you solve the problem?" asked Micky Tomm.

Strider shrugged. "What's the problem?"

"Drug abuse."

"If the drug interdiction program has been ineffective and drug use is happening all around us, maybe the law is a larger problem than the drugs. This is a perfect example of using decapitation to treat a headache. If you decriminalize narcotics, you put the cartels out of business. You empty the overcrowded prisons. You reduce crime. Problems of drug-related crime are far more severe than problems of drug use."

"But do you really think crack cocaine and heroin should be legal?"

"For all intents and purposes they already are; the people who want those drugs are getting them and using them. Whether you make them officially illegal or not has no effect on what you cite as the problem—drug abuse. And by some people's standards, the fact that we share a few bottles of wine after dinner makes us drug abusers. That word—abuse—is a subjective and devious bit of story manipulation. Who's to decide where use turns into abuse? Who's to decide whether marijuana is a 'gateway drug' or a 'harmless pleasure' or a 'stress reducer'?

"Can I propose a more realistic story of conflict and transformation?"

"We're all ears," said Audrey.

"The world will always be full of ways to engage and disengage the senses. Some of those have physical and mental health consequences, and some are good for the body and the soul—and all of them are open for debate depending on who's writing the story. Let me propose a story to tell our children: 'Here's the ocean. It has beautiful corals and colorful fish, and it also has sharks and jellyfish in it. Sooner or later you'll get stung. Go swim and play. Learn and observe. Find your way and write your story. Pay attention. If you get your foot stuck in the rocks and the tide is rising, don't be afraid to call for help....

"And since we stopped trying to make swimming illegal, you won't be treated like a criminal when you're ready to be rescued. If you legalize chemical recreation, people will continue to drive under the influence and fight in bars—just like they do now—and people will continue to become addicted to drugs they knew better than to try in the first place—just like they do now—but they'll have better options when they need a fix and better options when they're ready to *be* fixed."

"I still don't know how comfortable I am with drugs being legal," said Doug.

"That's because the 'drugs are evil' story is a myth that 'respectable people' are deeply invested in. And yes, drugs *are* evil—but so are fire and television and pole dancing and shopping. Look at the diamond industry. Look how cattle and corn are raised. Ninety percent of the big fish in the world's oceans have been harvested by factory fishing boats. Capitalism is evil. Communism is evil. Those people who live in that neighborhood are evil. You're not going to solve any of those problems by making stupidity illegal; people will always want it and they'll always find a way to get it."

Vincent laughed. "Frank Zappa said, 'There is more stupidity than hydrogen in the Universe—and it has a longer shelf life.'"

Audrey clasped her hands together. "So what's the solution? How do we reduce crime and addiction and poverty and all the other problems in the world?"

"First, stop trying to write everyone else's story. Each of us has to define his or her own relationship with the Universe. Everyone will ultimately succeed or fail at that on their own—even if you try to intervene. But if the conflict in Helen Handbasket's story is opioid addiction, you're not going to move her story any closer to transformation if you lock her up or force her underground. Help her find her way through the colorful corals and the stinging jellyfish. And if you disapprove of your cab driver or your teacher or your pilot or your President having a beer or a toke after their work is done, anything you do to stop that will probably do more damage than good.

"You have a full plate trying to swim on your own. Accept the ocean—the Universe—as it is—beautiful and dangerous—and figure out how to thrive in it. And when you do figure that out, live that story; be an example. I haven't asked any of you to buy a boat and move to the Bahamas, but it works for me. Maybe it will open up options and ideas for you. My goal is not to change you, unless you think what I have to offer is better than what you have—in which case, you'll still have to change yourself. I think commuting fifty miles to work is stupid, but what good would I accomplish if I passed a law against it?

"Start off by being happy and successful. Then connect and engage with others. Be a leader who writes stories worth following—stories that help others write their own healthy stories. Every accomplished author starts off by writing a lot of junk."

Kaitlin nodded.

"But if we outlaw bad writing or bad thinking or stupidity, we make the path to excellence and intelligence illegal. How's that for an essential absurdity?"

"But Strider," replied Walter. "Even if we buy your notion that laws that prohibit certain behaviors are ineffective compared to laws that guarantee rights and freedoms…"

"I didn't say that exactly, but I like it," interrupted Strider.

"Even if we stop trying to legislate our problems out of existence, don't you think you're being idealistic? I'm glad you're happy here on *The Metaphor*, but most of the time, you're out here alone in the wilderness. It's not like you're touring schools with a slide show or publishing books about utopian lifestyles. How do you expect one person to make a difference under the best of circumstances?"

Strider thought for a moment. "As for me being alone in the wilderness, all I can say is when the time was right, we were there to meet each other in the most unlikely of places. The timing and appropriateness of that is so outrageous that you're still wondering if the whole thing wasn't a setup and I'm your missing teacher.

"But putting that question aside, we're all here sharing ideas. I put myself in the teacher's chair and maybe my ideas about storytelling will change your life—or maybe they'll amount to nothing more than an interesting vacation—or maybe you'll fly out of here and roll your eyes and say, 'I'm sure glad *that's* over with.' That's between you and me and the Essential Absurdities. But I'm here making a difference for anyone who's ready for my kind of different—one guy in the middle of somewhere telling stories and exploring the Universe, connecting and engaging for whatever good can come of it.

"Mohandas Gandhi made a difference. He pioneered non-violent resistance on a scale that had never been seen before. Instead of arguing against the British story, instead of fighting, he wrote a sensible story of connection and engagement for his people. When the Indian people did not participate in the British story, when they refused to dignify it by engaging with it, it collapsed under the weight of its own stupidity."

Strider yawned. "Perhaps the Dalai Lama said it best: 'If you think you are too small to make a difference, try sleeping with a mosquito.'"

That Connection

With breakfast dispensed with and one of society's great ills dealt with, Strider ordered his crew ashore. "Get ye all to the boats," he ordered. "Go find stories."

"You're not going?" asked Kaitlin.

"I'll go later," replied Strider. "I'm used to a lot more alone time than I'm getting—and I'd like to do a little 'curriculum' planning for the Story Congress … er … the Happiness Congress."

Kaitlin shot him her best lonely puppy look. "Do you mind if I stay aboard and share some of your alone time—if such a thing is possible?"

"I'd be delighted," said Strider. "You can help me make some bread."

The other members of the Happiness Congress exchanged knowing glances and then arranged themselves three per boat. Audrey and Lenore headed for the nearby dock with Micky Tomm flailing at the oars. Walter and Doug reclined luxuriantly in the bow and stern of the other dinghy while Vincent's graceful strokes carried them swiftly down Man-O-War harbour.

Strider and Kaitlin stood on deck watching the crew leave. Once they were out of sight, Kaitlin turned, wrapped her arms softly around Strider, and buried her face in his shoulder. Centuries passed while she breathed in his scent and he felt the soft tickle of her hair against his cheek.

Kaitlin collected her thoughts. "I've been wanting to do that for days. I know you felt that electricity when I touched your hand at the ice cream shop back in New Plymouth. And I see how you look at me."

Strider offered a self-conscious smile.

"This is the part of our story where I get scared and vulnerable, but Strider, you're the most remarkable man I've ever met. You have this way of looking at the world … this beautiful, infinite tapestry of stories you weave … and everyone else's story is just a thread in that tapestry … and your story is just a thread in everyone else's—in the story of the Universe … and…" The words caught in Kaitlin's throat. "Here I am, the writer; I'm supposed to be articulate and I'm blubbering.

"I … well … Strider, would you say something, goddamit? I don't have words for this, but I'm damned sure you know how it goes … and I just want to know if you … I mean … do you …?"

Strider took Kaitlin's hands in his. "Of course I do, Kate. Of course I do. I felt a special connection with you the moment I saw you look down at me from the dock back at Moraine Cay with your eyes all full of 'who is this odd guy with the zebra pants?' and 'is he here to rob and kill us?' It startled me."

Kaitlin sniffled and laughed. "So here we are—two oddballs from two different planets. What do we do? How do we…"

"Get together?"

Kaitlin nodded.

"You might not like the answers—a big part of *me* doesn't like the answers—but those answers are 'slowly, maybe, not on this trip, and we already are.'"

"Too complicated, jungle man." She stepped closer and looked into his eyes.

"You're not going to make this easy for me, are you, Kaitlin?"

"Jesus, Strider! I've never been this aggressive with a man in my life. Short of crawling into your bunk naked, I can't think of a way to make this any *easier.*" Kaitlin sniffled. "I'm the woman; *I'm* the one who's supposed to be telling *you* to cool things down. Strider, I…"

Strider sighed, embraced Kaitlin again and led her down below to the main cabin. "Sit," he ordered gently.

"I guess this means we're not…"

"Please … sit."

Kaitlin sat stiffly on the settee. Strider handed her a pillow and sat facing her.

"Kaitlin, the first thing I want to say is 'thank you.' Yes, I have feelings for you, too. Yes, I feel the same way you do. Yes, I want to take you to my cabin and start making tsunamis in the harbour. You are brilliant and articulate — and quite a beautiful woman — and thank God you had the courage to say what I was afraid to.

"But though the best inspiration shines like a sunbeam into the window of the soul, it was you who suggested that it is *we* who have to 'hold the pen for God.' Let's not pretend that you won't be getting back on an airplane in a few days and flying 3,000 miles away. You have a job and a cat and…"

"I know, but that all feels like another world. It's all so far away and surreal and…"

"This is probably one of those really stupid things men do at the most inappropriate times, but I'm going to tell you an ex-girlfriend story. Will you humor me?"

Kaitlin nodded.

"I used to make a little money chartering this boat. I never had an official captain's license or a Bahamian work permit — and I got tired of sneaking around the islands trying to make it look like this week's fresh group of 'old friends' weren't part of an illegal business so I don't do it any more — but one day, Katya came aboard. Katya: Kaitlin. Perfect, huh?"

Kaitlin smiled weakly.

"Katya was a professional contortionist. Not only could she turn herself into a human pretzel, she could climb around the rigging like a gibbon and perform aerial stunts with a gigantic red ribbon. Katya had an IQ of about 600. She got on board, wrapped her brain around the aero- and hydrodynamics of sailing and did things with this boat that made me look like an amateur.

"To make a long story short…"

Kaitlin smiled. "Strider, I didn't think you had it in you!"

"I have to keep you on your toes or you'll lose interest, my dear … but by the end of the cruise, we were…"

"Now *that* must have been interesting!"

"I wasn't going to mention it, but yes, Katya's unusual elasticity afforded some opportunities for intimate connection that … well … let's just say that added to my certain knowledge that I was never going to find another Katya Kuznetsov."

"So what happened?"

"By the end of the cruise, all the other guests were pretty uncomfortable. Boats aren't very private places, and though I'm used to having couples aboard who want a romantic holiday, it's different when two giant magnets clank together and start pretending they're eighteen years old again."

Kaitlin giggled.

"And then we made *plans*. It was all so *perfect*. She called Cirque du Soleil and told them she was going to drop out of the tour. She flew home to settle some affairs and came back a week later, and we started looking at navigation charts. We bounced around the Abacos and then we headed south through the Exumas and down to the Turks and Caicos. We jumped off to the Dominican Republic and the Virgin Islands, made love on deserted moonlit beaches, gazed at the stars, talked about life and stories and..." Strider paused.

"One day, the fantasy got old — at least for Katya. She woke up one morning on a boat in the middle of the British Virgin Islands and realized she'd seen a lot of islands and a lot of beaches and a lot of *me*. Whatever it was that we'd set out to achieve together had been achieved. I was content with 'happily ever after,' but few people are. I think it was starting to feel like a beautiful prison sentence to her. We'd had all our deep, philosophical conversations and explored the outermost limits of sexual intimacy. We'd sailed together in calms and storms and each of us had learned to sleep soundly when the other was at the helm. It was perfect — *for me*.

"You see, I was happily ensconced in the metaphor I'd made for myself; this was my story. Katya hadn't grown up dreaming about pirates or adventure voyaging or sailboats — and she wasn't a writer or a painter. The sailing life didn't free her up to work on a novel or develop a theory or write a business plan. Her full-time job ended up being having me as a loving pet. She needed me to distract her, to divert her from her supposedly glamorous life swinging from the top of a circus tent. She left that to share my supposedly glamorous life sailing through the tropics. What she got was the *tabula rasa* — the blank slate she needed to write her destiny on — and that wasn't a destiny she was ultimately meant to share with me."

Kaitlin closed her eyes and visualized beautiful Katya with a painted face and a feathered headdress atop her long flowing hair, balanced on the tip of *The Metaphor*'s bowsprit[10] clad only in a shimmering silk ribbon.

Strider inhaled and let out a long breath. "I poured her into an airplane. We were both sobbing like babies. But she wasn't happy. She needed to write her story, but she couldn't do that as long as she was riding on the back of mine. We had a beautiful connection, but she had this bright, beautiful mind and this talented, flexible body. She had all the tools she needed to change the world — but hanging from a silk ribbon in front of an audience hadn't helped her do that, and sailing in Paradise hadn't, either."

"So what happened to her?"

"She went home to Siberia and started the 'Red Ribbon' women's organization. When young girls in Eastern European orphanages turn 18 without getting adopted, they get turned out into the street because the government won't support them any more.

10. *Bowsprit* — a wooden spar extending forward from the bow of a traditional boat,

You can imagine where too many of them end up. She teaches them to use their minds and their bodies in whatever unique ways best help them pursue their destinies."

"She sounds perfect—and perfect *for you*. How am I supposed to compete with that?"

"Stay with me, Kate; don't go into the light."

Kaitlin laughed.

"Katya and I needed to write a piece of our story together—and we did. But Katya's a lot like me—probably *too much* like me. She likes her own story to be barebones and uncomplicated—like I do—but she loves helping other people with their conflicts and transformations. I think we came together and she wrapped her head around the storytelling bit and then needed to go somewhere where she could apply her talents. We loved sharing life, but our time together—and the fact that a hot romance in Paradise wasn't keeping her glass full—helped her find her true path."

"Are you still in touch?"

"We send postcards here and there, and an odd letter shows up at the little Man-O-War post office once in a while. She married a sweet, pudgy little guy who's got a generous heart and a successful export business. He puts the girls to work in his warehouse, and she puts that massive brain of hers to work helping them write life stories of happiness, success, and fulfillment. She's got

That Connection

a couple of little rug rats to chase around, and stories of circus life and sailing life to share — or to reflect on quietly and smile over depending on which stories she's thinking of."

"So where does that leave us?" Kaitlin twisted one of her braids.

"Where it leaves us is that we have an obvious connection, but I'm not going to get hot and heavy with you on a boat with six other people aboard. I'm not going to split our group into the Happiness couple and the Disgusted Congress.

"Where it also leaves us is that the connection is there and the interest is there, but if you'll allow me to be brutally unselfish about it — for both of our sakes — I think you need to go home and put your story in order. You don't have enough data about either me or sailing to drop everything you're doing in Seattle and move in here — and that's not a recipe for a lasting relationship, anyway. Living on a boat can be romantic as hell, but there's a lot of 'chop wood; carry water' stuff that catches up with people."

"But Strider, how are we going to find out…?"

"Kate, I think we already know. We have a connection. We feel it and we acknowledge it. We're sitting here talking about it. If you want to write a story where we spend time together and see what that connection grows into, I'd be thrilled and honored to write it with you, but I'm not going to let you abandon whatever story you've spent your whole life developing so you can hitch a ride on mine. If you want to explore our connection, if you want to share a story with me, you have to write a complete, self-standing story of your own that intersects with mine."

"What about you, Strider? What about *your* story intersecting with *mine?*"

"We're not two people sitting in the dark writing independent secrets—at least not since we started this conversation—but if we are to be whatever it is we are to be, it will come from both of us writing good stories and getting those good stories together. Come back and spend a week sailing. Go home again and let the experience settle."

"Would you visit me in Seattle?"

"I'm not good with crowds and tall buildings and traffic, but with a very understanding tour guide, it might be fun."

"And then…"

"And then we'll become acquaintances or lovers or life partners or friends or spouses—spice?—or whatever silly labels we need to apply to make sure our connection rolls into the appropriate tube once we drop it into the sorting machine. We'll get together and we'll bounce off each other or we'll stick together or … Do you really want to screw this up by writing the whole damned script after spending half a week together? We're here—now—together. Let's hold the pen for God, but let's acknowledge that's all we have to do. Let's not 'work on the relationship' or put ourselves in a position where it's more important to write a mediocre ending than a cliffhanger. In a month, we'll feel how we feel. In a year, we'll feel how we feel."

"But how will we know…?"

"Kaitlin, look at the stars. How will you know? You can't. Look deep inside your soul at everything you are not. How will you know? You can't. We're adrift on an endless sea of stories. Stop analyzing the water. The important story is that you and I are sitting here holding hands, confronting the Mystery together. Everything else is just politics. Take a minute and burn this moment into your memory—the having, the wanting, the fear, the joy, the certainty, the confusion, the complexity, the simplicity—the big ocean of conflict and the promised land of transformation that lies beyond imagination. What happens to us after we 'get together'—whatever that means? What happens to us after we die? It's the same abstract question and the same 'hazy white light with harp glissandos' answer.

"A lot of vacationing women came on and off this ship when I was in the charter business. For a while, I thought I must be pretty special; I got propositioned left and right—and I'd never thought of myself as unusually attractive. But whenever someone would stay on, the relationship would last a week or a month or two or three.

"After a while, I realized I was that 'grass that's always greener.' Plenty of women want to leave all the drudgery of urban life behind and go swinging through the jungle on a vine with Tarzan.

'Me Tarzan. Me climb tree. Get coconut. Protect Jane from lion. Ride with Jane on elephant.' But eventually, the jungle gets old if you like air-conditioning and Chinese takeout. My story is attractive to a lot of people, but it's attractive like Disney World is attractive. Nobody rents a permanent room at the Polynesian Village; it's a fantasy.

"Meanwhile, as much as it would be *fun* to change scenery for a week, I'm not fantasizing about going to Jane's world. I'd enjoy myself some, and then remind myself why I don't fit in with 'normal' company. I'm sure I'd be a great curiosity—the intelligent ape—the noble savage. And then I'd fly back to the Bahamas and curl up in a fetal position in the chain locker for a week."

Kaitlin closed her eyes and breathed slowly.

"But Kate, a connection is a connection. It isn't *necessarily* a crazy fantasy, and it isn't something I'd toss away. I'm just like you. I am hardwired to find my princess and live happily ever after—even if I already *am* living happily ever after.

"You're a writer and a thinker. You *get* all the crazy stuff that floats out of my mouth. You hear it and spit it back to me—and it makes sense. You have your own dreams and goals and writing projects to stay engaged with—and I could support those. Most women your age have a biological clock that's chiming like Big Ben, but maybe you don't. I don't know. I just think we need time — and I know we won't get that if we go fog up the mirrors in my cabin.

"Keep your hand on the wheel of your ship and your eye on your compass and your horizon. Hold the pen and start writing. Good books take time. How often have you found yourself writing a story or a book where you watched the story unfold without having much to do with the process? Have you ever surprised yourself with the ending of your own book?"

Kaitlin sniffled. "I stressed out about that for months while I wrote my first novel. My characters did what they wanted and went to places I knew nothing about. I had to do all sorts of research to keep the story authentic. I had all these loose ends; I got all the way through the story, but didn't know how to tie those ends together. And then I woke up at 3:00 one morning and knew *exactly* how the book would end. I jumped out of bed and finished it. I claim no conscious responsibility for it. The book wrote itself."

Strider kissed the backs of Kaitlin's hands. "Do you think *our* story is any different? Do you think *any* good story is any different?"

Kaitlin shook her head gently.

"I know a different story of how our morning together might go had magically written itself in your mind. I hope I'm not a massive disappointment."

"Not *massive*, but ..."

Strider chuckled. "Believe me, I've been rewriting and rereading that same story for days. I just sense that you and I run a little deeper than a quick island frolic. I'm a story snob, Kaitlin. As much as I'm a guy who lives alone in the wilderness who would desperately love to fall madly in bed with a pretty girl once in a while, I prefer a sophisticated story over a knock-knock joke any day."

"One kiss?" asked Kaitlin.

"You drive a hard bargain, my dear. One kiss ... and I'll throw in all the hugs you can handle."

Stories, Stories Everywhere

By late afternoon, several dinghy-loads of explorers had gone ashore on Man-O-War Cay and returned. Strider and Kaitlin visited the ice cream shop and the baseball field at the end of the world. Man-O-War was, as expected, a delight for all. Strider's fresh bread dough had risen to perfection as it always did, and he slipped it in the oven to bake.

"All right, folks," he called once the full complement of happiness delegates had been accounted for. "Hopetown is five miles away—about an hour's sail. It'll be just a bit bumpy but the wind's down to twenty-five knots and it'll be on our beam the whole way. We're in for a short, exhilarating sail. Let's get our gear stowed, blast on over, get anchored up, and spend tonight and tomorrow night over there."

Strider raised the big mainsail and sheeted it in tight. As soon as he dropped the mooring ball, he raised the jib and walked to the stern to back the rudder. *The Metaphor* drifted backward, grabbed the wind, and moved gently forward down the harbour.

"No engine today?" asked Micky Tomm.

"Nah. I have a clear shot down the harbour and the wind'll be behind us when we go out the cut. Plus it's sheltered in here; we won't catch the *real* wind until we're past the tip of the island."

"Heads down!" Strider called as he headed out the cut. The heavy mainsail boom jibed across the cockpit as *The Metaphor* turned with the wind behind her.

"I see you left the foresail down," observed Micky Tomm. "Why is that?"

"A sailboat has a certain maximum speed—a 'hull speed.' Physicists say it has something to do with the length of the wake equaling the length of the waterline, but if you carry more sail than you need to get to top speed, all you do is overpower the boat. She'll heel over more and you end up dragging the rudder sideways through the water to keep her from rounding up into the wind. Watch the charter boats. They usually carry too much sail on windy days because most of their captains don't have the experience they should have, and they're unfamiliar with the boats." Strider pointed to a white fiberglass boat crashing through the chop a quarter-mile away. "Those guys could reduce sail by 30% and go just as fast—and they wouldn't have to fight the wheel to steer a straight course."

Micky Tomm studied the overcanvased sailboat. "I assume there's a story in there?"

Stories, Stories Everywhere

"I hadn't thought about it, but there's a story in everything. What do you think it is?"

"Something along the lines of 'less is more.' Seems like if the speed limit is 55, a Ferrari isn't going to offer you much advantage."

"There you go," smiled Strider. "How would you use that in your pharmaceutical business?"

"Hmm. Maybe there are places where we're trying harder than we need to. Maybe if we have an expensive marketing campaign going, but our competitor is far behind us with an inferior product, it makes more sense to shorten sail and go just as fast. And maybe less fighting the wheel means less stress on the people who are crafting messages and crunching numbers to keep the lines on the graphs climbing upward. Maybe that energy could be put to other use—or saved for the storm that eventually comes.

"I like this," said Micky Tomm. "I haven't ever thought about mining stories."

"Stories are everywhere, but there's a problem with this one: if you tell it at the staff meeting, you have to explain about hull speed and talk about the boat you saw carrying too much sail. Your corporate listeners won't have a clue what you're babbling about."

Strider adjusted the chinstrap on his hat as *The Metaphor* slipped past the southeastern tip of Man-O-War Cay and grabbed the wind. "Can you find another metaphor you can use to tell the same story?"

"I'm not sure. How do I translate something like this?"

"I think you already have. What about the Ferrari?"

"Of course. Everyone pushes the speed limit just a bit—just enough to keep from attracting police attention. As long as we're performing just ahead of the 'speed limit,' we don't need a big engine or a lot of high-test fuel. In fact, what we need isn't a Ferrari at all; it's four-wheel drive for the steep climbs and rough roads. There are places where we need a lot of 'horsepower,' but we need torque not speed—and only in strategic places."

"See how your story writes itself? You took the daily commute—the most boring and mundane and despised part of your employee's day—and you turned it into a story that connects and engages. What's the conflict and the transformation?"

"The conflict is that we get into 'warrior mode' and we deploy a lot of unnecessary horsepower where it doesn't give us any advantage. It's an ego thing. We get off on all the potential energy—the car's top speed—and forget that we can't use it. Then we get into a rut—an FDA compliance issue or a product recall—and we don't have the muscle to get ourselves out of the mud and over the obstacles."

"Good. Good," said Strider. "I like how you're framing your conflict in terms of your metaphor. See how natural that is?"

"And the transformation is that we hit our numbers with less effort—with fewer dollars and hours spent—and we're ready to get where we need to go if the road washes out.

"Only problem is that if we don't burn our budget, we won't get the same allocation next year."

Strider adjusted the mainsheet. "Sounds like a high-class problem to me. I can't help you there. What about authenticity?"

"Easy. All my employees deal with traffic and speed limits. I'm sure a lot of them would love to be driving a Ferrari. Funny thing is the CEO *does* drive a Ferrari. I think the employees might have some fun with that."

"And the last story element is magic." Strider fingered the brim of his hat. "I see it clearly in your story."

"I'm not sure. It all sounds like a pretty straightforward story to me. Nobody waves a wand or casts a spell. We just buy cars that match our goals."

"You underestimate yourself, Micky Tomm. *Leadership is magic.* If you can tell that story and make it part of your corporate culture, and get your people to start thinking in terms of horsepower and speed-versus-torque, you transform the conversation; you change the way everyone thinks about the resources they request and send out on the road. Everyone talks about corporate performance in terms of the terrain and the speed limit, and everyone thinks about choosing the most appropriate vehicle for the job. You eliminate the race driver mentality that probably sucks away big dollars from your bottom line. What's that story worth up there in the corporate stratosphere where you fly? Hundreds of thousands? Millions?"

The Story Story

The Metaphor bounded across the shallow Sea of Abaco. Micky Tomm shook his head but offered no reply. Strider left him to his thoughts.

By and by, the rest of the crew assembled in *The Metaphor*'s cockpit at the stern of the ship where there was less spray.

"Strider, it looks like we're still a little ways out," said Kaitlin. "Do we have time to circle back to your personal story? I've been thinking about your four story elements, and you mentioned you had some ideas about why your story works—why people like it. Did you table that discussion because we hadn't covered the four elements yet?"

"I'd be happy to come around to that. Micky Tomm and I just finished up a little story work along the same vein before everyone migrated back here. And yes, that's why I thought we should postpone talking about it.

"Kaitlin, I know you were taking notes. Do you want to summarize in case anyone got bored and fell asleep while I was introducing myself?"

Kaitlin grabbed her phone and flipped through her notes on the screen. "Give me a second to go over this."

Strider engaged the self-steering vane to allow the wind to keep the boat on course before letting go of the wheel and reclining against a sail bag.

Kaitlin smiled at Strider and began. "You grew up on a farm and were raised to be curious about the world. Your mother was a poet, and that exposed you to writing and the idea of transforming ideas into words. You loved sailing adventure books and movies.

"You graduated college but were underwhelmed by traditional education, then got married and found a job as a guidance counselor. That paid the bills and got you set up to live the American dream: the job, the kids, the car, and so on. But you weren't satisfied that you were actually giving kids the guidance you knew they needed. I guess the focus on job skills and placement was a lot like the focus on sentence structure and syntax in your English classes at college; you were intuitively much more engaged in the search for meaning."

"You're a better me than I am, Kaitlin." Strider raised an eyebrow. "Keep on goin'."

"So then your Aunt Freddie died and left you some money. You and your wife went to the funeral in Maine and there you spotted *The Metaphor*—up for sale and ready to drop in the water. That triggered an identity crisis, a divorce, and the purchase of the schooner—and the rest is geometry."

"That's pretty much it. Lenore, what's the conflict? I'm going to pick on you because you're the quiet one in our bunch."

"The conflict? Okay ... you were doing everything you'd been told would make you happy, but it wasn't working. I think a lot of people feel like that."

"I think everyone feels like that at least some of the time," replied Strider. "And you jumped right off of conflict into authenticity.

Part of the reason the story works is that everyone gets forced to pick a lane at various points in their life story. We get lots of advice about what lane to pick, and we act according to our own prejudices. How many accountants would love to have become artists or musicians or chefs, but they didn't see those as viable professions?"

"My mother was a lawyer and my father was a doctor," added Vincent, "… and I was a disappointment. It took me a lot of head-banging to find peace with my decision to do what I love."

"But…" added Micky Tomm. "I have some very right-angled people in my finance department who wouldn't tap their feet if a marching band paraded through the office. Some of those folks are very well suited to crunching numbers, and they're blissfully happy doing that job; let's not write every accountant and book-keeper off as a dissatisfied artist."

"Excellent point," agreed Lenore.

"So coming back to Strider's story," Kaitlin continued, "what's the magic?"

Walter spoke up. "I think it's fantastic that the money and the boat presented themselves at the same time. It's as if the Universe said, 'Here's your chance — *your one chance* — to make a quick turn and get on the path to your destiny.' Those chances don't come by often — and if this one hadn't, we all might still be sitting back on Moraine Cay fighting over the last potato chip crumbs and sucking on toothpaste tubes. The combination of the two opportunities—the fact that they happened at the same time—*that's magic.*

"And the transformation is easy: Strider broke free of the expectations he and others had placed on himself, and he's now qualified to preside over the Happiness Congress."

"Can you see how my model works?" asked Strider. "Conflict, transformation, authenticity, and magic make a great lens through which to look at stories. And if you're writing a story, you can work backward from the transformation—from the intended result—from the way you want your reader to think and feel. Figure out what obstacles you have to overcome to produce that transformation and you'll understand the conflict. Wrap your literal story in a metaphor and tell it in the language of your listener. That process—that alchemy—is often all the magic you need. If you can frame your lesson in a *relevant* way that helps readers and listeners find *meaning* in your ideas, you can consider yourself adept at the magic art of storytelling."

"I'm making progress!" shouted Walter. "I have all sorts of ideas about how to use this. I am officially happy."

"Glad to hear," said Strider. "Congratulations."

"I'm happy that Walter's happy," said Kaitlin, "but when I write a story, I usually have no idea what characters will appear, what conflicts they'll face, and where they'll end up. In some ways, writing a novel—or even a short story—isn't much different than reading it for the first time—or dreaming it. I certainly don't map out where my characters end up and work backward."

"You raise a good point," offered Strider, "but we may be caught in a semantic trap. If you're a creative writer producing a *literary* story, you probably won't get very far until you dump all the formulas and just let it flow. But if you're a presenter like Walter and you're writing a speech, it makes sense to focus on what the takeaway for the audience is. If you're marketing a pharmaceutical product, understanding the meaningful outcome for the patient will lead to campaigns that connect. If you're a scientist trying to get your research funded, the best way to accomplish that is to convert data into meaning so you can convince the man with the wallet that your work offers benefits and positive, profitable outcomes. A teacher plans a lecture to produce a specific learning result for students. There are stories and there are *stories*.

"And Kaitlin..."

"Yes."

"What do you do when a story just doesn't work? How do you evaluate someone else's creative writing? After all the mysterious creative channeling is done, sometimes you need a mechanism you can use to break things down. Once you know where the characters have ended up—what the transformation is—you can work backward through the conflicts to figure out what parts of the narrative road aren't leading the reader home. Storysailing is a formidable editing tool."

Kaitlin nodded.

"I have a few more story tools to share," Strider continued, "but after that, I want to switch gears. This whole trip is supposed to be about your happiness. Start thinking about your own life story—and your professional story—and how you might tell them in a way that clarifies what transformations your unique magic facilitates. Whether you're shopping for customers or a mate, your magic is your true product.

"And as we go on, pay attention to the experiences you've already had and to the ones you *will* have. How can you translate, 'we sailed to Hopetown'—an anecdote—into a *story* that connects and engages and transforms?"

Strider reached back and disengaged the steering vane. "Wind's perfect. I love when I can blow right into a harbour and not have to start the engine. How could anyone fail to find magic in that?"

The Magnificent Seven

The Metaphor skated through a mangrove-bordered entrance into a harbour embraced by traditional white colonial buildings and coconut palms and watched over by a tall, red and white candy-striped lighthouse.

After dinner, the Happiness Congress convened in its traditional configuration—scattered about the deck with cushions and blankets. "Who's got Man-O-War Cay stories?" asked Strider.

Doug looked at Vincent. "Go ahead; you tell it Vince."

"We found the baseball field while we were walking across town to the beach. You weren't kidding about the reef being in a rage. The exploding waves out there were spectacular. One of the locals told us about the *Adirondack,* a ship that wrecked out there in 1862. Apparently you can still see her cannons and boilers. We started talking about how totally nucking futs you were, Strider, to *row* out there in those conditions, when some wacko came blasting across the scene—*on a windsurfer!*

We watched him dancing and playing in the waves, having the time of his life. I mean—the guy obviously knew what he was doing, but…"

"So far, that's an anecdote," said Strider. "It's a potent one, but in this story—our story—the one where I dupe a bunch of castaways who came to study happiness into studying stories instead—the one where you all become master storytellers—you have not yet achieved transformation."

Vincent looked flummoxed. "I don't know where to start. I just found it impressive that that guy was out there sailing…"

Strider interrupted. "I think you found it *meaningful*. Otherwise, you wouldn't have remembered it or told us about it. Did everyone get a good look at the reef today? Can everyone picture the conditions this windsurfer was out facing today?"

The happiness delegates all nodded.

"Take a minute and let your imagination wander. Create a story. What's the reason for him to be out there doing that?"

Vincent crossed his arms. "But how are we supposed to know why he's out there, Strider? We don't know anything about him."

"Ah, but we are not his biographers. We are simply observers of the Universe. This guy inadvertently shot a flare over your mind's horizon. Let something about this man windsurfing over a hazardous reef pique your curiosity. Whatever that triggers beneath the surface of your own psychic water is not required to dovetail with Mr. Windsurfer's personal set of factoids. Don't let the truth stand in the way of a good story."

Lenore put up a finger. "Is there any possibility he went out there and got in over his head—maybe he wasn't expecting the conditions to be quite so hazardous—and then he managed to sail his way out of a bad situation?"

"No way," said Doug. "You should have seen this guy blasting back and forth across the reef with waves exploding all around him. He was definitely out there on purpose."

Audrey raised her wine glass. "Maybe he lost a loved one on that reef—and now, whenever the sea gods get angry, he goes out there to tease them—to challenge them?"

"That's it," encouraged Strider. "Find the stories."

"I say he's the world windsurfing champion," offered Micky Tomm. "He's won every contest and beaten every record. There's nothing else left to win so he's out there pushing his limits. He's no longer content to win trophies; he needs to find ways to impress himself and keep the adrenaline flowing—even though he knows it will kill him one day."

"A few days ago, he got really drunk," said Kaitlin. "He bet $100,000 that he could windsurf up and down raging Man-O-War reef ten times without wrecking. If he falls off, he'll lose his house and his fortune; his family will have nowhere to live—and he'll probably die. If he wins, he'll find his confidence, make amends to his family, and never drink again. This is his day of reckoning."

"Anyone else?" Strider looked around the circle.

"I think there was a hot girl on the beach who wouldn't pay attention to him," said Doug. "Some meat-head was bragging about his car and asking her to keep count of how many pushups he could do in the sand. Mr. Windsurfer's no bodybuilder, but he knows what he's good at. Next thing you know, he's rocketing through the coral heads and exploding waves out on the reef. Now *all* the ladies are cheering and paying zero attention to the hunky guy."

"He's got to be a motivational speaker," said Walter. "The NSA holds a big convention every year. This is the National Speakers Association—the NSA that talks, not the NSA that listens. Some of the best speakers in the world attend, and so do a lot of up-and-coming newbies—which is all well and good. This convention is an absolute freak show. It's full of brilliant and talented artists, scientists, thinkers, teachers, trainers, entrepreneurs, masters of inspirational hot air, narcissists, egomaniacs, and some of the most amazing and wonderful people you could ever meet. 'Finding your story' is a big theme within NSA, especially for new speakers who feel called to the platform but don't necessarily have any idea what to speak about. You can have an absolutely outrageous story and then find the person you're seated next to at dinner was born with no arms or legs, got burned in a fire, was wrongfully imprisoned for a crime he didn't commit, went blind, and then climbed Mt. Everest naked with his upper lip before spending seventy-two days in a life raft. He'll sell you his international bestselling book, too. *Someone* at NSA will have you beat by a mile. Like I said, it's a freak show. I have a good friend in the speaking business who's in a wheelchair because of a plane crash. The joke he hears over and over — and it's told as friendly sarcasm; people are not being insensitive — is that he's *lucky* to have had his story find him. Everyone else has to figure out their stories and speaking topics on their own.

"I think Mr. Windsurfer is out there on the reef trying to find his story. He's been cleaning up the park and changing out the trash bags, but he wants to inspire people. If he survives his trip across the reef, he'll have the requisite bragging rights to exchange stories with the rest of us wackos at the next NSA convention."

"You know," offered Vincent, "it could be that this guy is just a really good windsurfer who has been sailing these waters for years. Maybe what's extraordinary to us is just old hat to him. I have a friend who runs marathons all the time. I can't begin to imagine myself running two-*point*-six miles — never mind twenty-six — but that's just what he does. He'll pop off fifteen miles as a typical workout and think nothing of it.

"I know that's a boring story, but take Strider for instance. Everything he does is new to us — sailing, rowing, baking bread, navigating — and talking about all sorts of stuff that has no business floating around in the head of a guy who grew up in a small town in Oklahoma. We're all on an epic, mind-blowing journey through a world that's as common as air to him."

Strider crossed his arms behind his head and leaned back against his sailbag seat. "I'm so proud of you all. You're all telling stories. Let's explore a few ways to think about them.

"Traditionally, it's been taught that story plots all revolve around a conflict between an individual and one or more of seven forces: the individual himself, another individual, nature, the environment, technology, the supernatural, or a higher power."

"There's a lot of overlap there," observed Kaitlin. "Why have a separate category for nature and the environment?"

Strider tossed his hat over the compass. "Some stories take place in cities or schools or other non-natural settings. Out here, there's not much difference, but you could conceivably write a story about a confrontation that took place here in Hopetown. Your conflict might be with the townsfolk and not with the natural environment."

"What about the supernatural versus a higher power. What's the difference?"

Strider stroked his chin. "I think a 'higher power' is usually thought to be benevolent. If you write about witches or evil spirits, you're closer to supernatural. Though … the supernatural isn't necessarily evil. You might write about an earth spirit or an ocean goddess or a mermaid—and though that entity might be more powerful than you, it wouldn't be a 'higher power' unless its role is to guide you or teach you or let you use some of its power so you can achieve transformation."

Lenore held out her wine glass for refilling. "What were the conflicts on your list again?"

Strider counted them off on his fingers. "The individual, another individual, nature, technology, the supernatural. I left out 'a higher power' and 'the environment,' because I think 'nature' and 'the supernatural' have those covered for our story's purposes.

"Let's list the stories we have so we can see what the conflicts are:

"Lenore suggested he got stuck out there and had to make it home alive. I say that's man versus nature.

"Audrey said he lost a loved one on that reef, and now he goes out to challenge the sea gods."

"That would be man against the supernatural," suggested Doug.

"Or maybe it's man against himself," suggested Audrey. "He's out there trying to deal with his own anger and grief."

"I'll do you one better," said Strider. "What's the difference? Most supernatural forces in a story are just personifications of some aspect of human consciousness."

Audrey mulled that idea over for a minute and then nodded gently.

"Micky Tomm thinks Mr. Windsurfer is an adrenaline junky. He's reached the top but still needs to climb."

"Man against himself," said Kaitlin.

"Kaitlin says windsurfer dude's drunken ways have caught up with him. He has one last chance at salvation."

"It's the New Testament," said Doug.

"So it's man against himself," said Walter.

"Or," said Audrey, "it's man against a higher power—Biblical law personified as the individual's inner conflict."

"I guess we needed 'higher power' after all," said Strider. "Good."

"Doug thinks windsurfer dude wants to impress the ladies. What's the conflict?"

Kaitlin jumped in. "This one is Mr. Windsurfer against another individual … though if you want to get psychological, you could say it's man against nature. On a biological level, the women are attracted to a muscular man who can provide for them and their offspring. Windsurfer stud challenges the idea that brawn and braggadocio are ideal mate selection criteria."

"That's great," agreed Audrey. "This is all pretty simple but not quite as cut and dried as I expected."

"Walter, I love your story," exclaimed Strider. "I like it because it's a story about someone trying to find their own story—and I like it because most people have no idea that professional speakers have a community and an annual convention. You made it funny and colorful. You made me want to check it out."

Walter smiled. "It's man versus himself, I suppose—in the story, I mean."

"Or if the guy feels peer pressure to find his story," asked Audrey, "could it be man versus the environment?"

Strider gave his guests a moment to test-fit that idea into their expanding perspectives on stories.

"The right answer is the one that feels right to you," he reminded them. "It's not like scientists autopsied dead stories and created a taxonomy of seven precise story 'blood types.' All this stuff comes from people pondering the Universe and trying to write an engaging story about how their own stories work. Linguists analyze stories and graph the frequency with which specific words appear. They produce graphs of 'emotional arcs' and other interesting tomfoolery. It's a bit like trying to measure the interior volume of a football with a ruler, but you can't fault anyone for using whatever tools feel comfortable in their hands to try to sneak a peek at the Essential Absurdities."

"Where does my story fit in?" asked Vincent. "What if we're making much ado about nothing? What if the people of Man-O-War go play on the reef every day? What if it's our own perspective that's limited?"

Strider exhaled deeply. "I think your story is the best of all, Vincent. You didn't feel comfortable writing a story about Mr. Windsurfer's conflicts so you wrote one about your *own* conflicts. Your story suggests that we can find extraordinary magic in ourselves if we stop thinking everything that impresses us is beyond our reach. Your story is a very upbeat take on 'man versus himself.'"

"And that's a powerful story theme," added Kaitlin. "Harry Potter lives in a dingy room under the stairs at his abusive aunt and uncle's house. The next thing he knows, he's being whisked off to wizard school to study the magic arts. Readers ask themselves, *I wonder if I have any untapped magic potential?* and the books sell by the millions."

Walter raised his hand over his head. "I thought I was doing so well, but I'm back where I was before. I understand *how* to do this but I have no idea what to use it for. I'm not going to be teaching English any time soon."

"Walter, as a speaker, if you understand your audience's pain points, you understand their *conflicts*. These seven conflict categories we just discussed are universal themes. Use them to think about who and what your audience members are in conflict with. Tell stories that work with those conflicts. If you're talking about teambuilding and conflict resolution, tell stories about an individual versus other individuals. If you're talking about ethics, tell stories about man versus a higher power or the supernatural. If you want to motivate people, challenge them to think of extraordinary achievement as ordinary. If you want to teach them not to dump waste in the river, tell them a story about man versus the environment."

"Okay, I get it," said Walter, but how do I reconcile the seven types of conflict with the four elements of story?"

"First, you don't have to reconcile anything. Study the story—or the listener—through the telescope and then through the microscope. Use either or both perspectives—or follow your gut if it says to use neither."

"Okay, but…"

"Walter, when you're hired to speak to an audience, how long do you talk for?"

"Usually about forty-five minutes."

"Why does a company put you on a plane, rent you a car, put you up in a nice hotel, and cut you a check for forty-five minutes of *talking?* What do they expect you to accomplish in that short time that they can't accomplish with all the talent and expertise they already have on board? I'd bet your hourly rate is often higher than the CEO's."

"Okay … I think I get it," said Walter. "I'm the fairy godmother. They don't want a new planning process or a new technology initiative. They want someone to *inspire* them. They want fast transformation."

"Yes. Yes. Yes." Strider raised his hands heavenward. "If you understand what they really want to achieve, you understand the *transformation*—and that has to be *meaningful*. Beating last year's numbers is important, but not meaningful. You have to be a good enough storyteller to figure out where the real story of human struggle is—how showing up for work on Monday morning and punching a clock can somehow connect people to the Essential Absurdities. *That's* transformation. If you tell a story in a way that demonstrates your understanding of the real path from conflict to transformation—in a way that connects with the *types* of conflicts your listener is confronting—you'll be trusted and listened to because you'll be perceived as *authentic*. Show them how to navigate from conflict to transformation in forty-five minutes, and you will have delivered powerful, undeniable, real-life magic that changes lives and fortunes.

"Kaitlin, summary time."

Kaitlin stood up. "Strider, we've got eight different stories here about one anecdote. I'm going to keep this super simple. We didn't talk about it much; we just did it—but we took that windsurfer anecdote and each of us used it as the basis of a story. That took a lot of pressure off of me as a writer. I don't have to find fully formed stories in my surroundings and write them down; I just have to take whatever the Universe gives me and create a story around it. Given what we talked about back in Green Turtle—that there's no such thing as absolute truth—that we can't see anything but a tiny fraction of what reality contains—everything is fiction, anyway. If the purpose of a story is to connect a listener to its *meaning*, as long as that story isn't expected to be a journalistic recounting of facts—which suggests it isn't really a story, anyway—it makes no difference whether the narrative is true or not.

"Once we shared our stories, we got into conflicts. Story plots revolve around a conflict between a person and one or more of seven elements: the person who faces the conflict, someone else, nature, the environment, technology, the supernatural, or a higher power. You gain insights into stories by examining the types of conflicts they present.

"When it comes to connection and engagement, use the seven conflict types to shape your story so it resonates with the conflicts your listener is confronting. Feel free to mix and match. Invent new kinds of conflicts or cross a few off the list as needed."

As night fell, the light at the top of the Elbow Cay Lighthouse at the west side of Hopetown Harbour began to glow and rotate slowly.

Story Shift

"Think about this," suggested Strider as he distributed hot pancakes and poured coffee for his well-rested guests. "We'll head over to the lighthouse this morning and climb up the big spiral staircase inside to the top. From the balcony, you can see for miles in every direction. If you want to take a panorama photo, this is the place. The light mechanism is the original kerosene equipment. The rotating lens floats on a pool of mercury. It's as close to frictionless as you can get; you can move it with a finger.

"What's a lighthouse, Audrey?"

"A tall structure that warns ships away from reefs and rocks?"

"Smartass! Come on. You know what I mean; dream about a lighthouse and…"

"It's light from on high … illumination … perspective … awareness."

"Enlightenment," offered Vincent.

"Protective insight," suggested Kaitlin.

"A 'higher' power," said Lenore.

Strider flipped a pancake. "Ah ... I have screwed all of you up so royally. Listen to you! I am *diabolical!* Well, after breakfast, we're going to row over and survey God's kingdom from that marvelous tower. Then we'll go to town and buy postcards."

An hour later, the happiness delegates had tied their two dinghies to the dock and made their way up the path to the Elbow Cay lighthouse.

"This lighthouse was built in 1863," explained Strider as they ascended the 101 steps to the balcony at the top. "Many of the locals objected because they made their living salvaging ships that went aground on the reef just offshore."

"That's just evil," observed Lenore.

"Perhaps," replied Strider, "but the spider who builds a web near the porch light probably thinks he's reaping God's bounty. If the light goes on every night and that's where the moths go, any smart opportunist — even a churchgoing, island-dwelling opportunist — would probably have seen someone else's poor navigating as the Lord's will. These islanders salvaged a lot of cargo and ship's gear — and they saved a lot of lives. Wrecking was their livelihood. It wasn't their fault that ship captains were writing 'man against nature' stories in their backyard. As far as they were concerned, what happened out on the coral was 'man against a higher power,' and what the government was doing was thwarting God's will."

"It's still evil," said Lenore.

"Of course it is," laughed Strider. "It's despicable! But sometimes following your compass means steering into the rocks. That's the ugly side of stories. The Spanish chopped people's heads off during the Inquisition to *save their souls*. What about Nazis—regular people like you and me—who got caught in a story shift? They rounded up Jews and built concentration camps. Look at slavery and the American Civil Rights movement. Women's rights. Gay rights. All those people are trying to flip ancient, capsized stories and get them to sail upright. These islanders arrived after the American Revolution and what did they have? Fish, pine trees on the mainland, a sheltered harbour, and lots of sand and rock—*nothing* but a colorful landscape that screamed *potential*. Think of what it must have been like to set up shop here back in 1778. No electricity. Heck, they're *still* catching fresh water off the roofs and storing it in cisterns beneath the houses. No phones. No news or airplanes. This wasn't the tidy little postcard town it is today.

"And then someone would ring the bells and the men would gather in the boats. Some poor wretch was stuck on the reef. And in return for risking their own lives to save those aboard, they lay claim to the cargo. Insurance companies covered the losses back in the ship's home port, and as long as everyone made it home, there were no losers."

"What they didn't foresee back then is that the lighthouse would make them the epicenter of Abaco tourism," added Kaitlin. "I read up on it in Strider's *Cruising Guide*. Imagine how many postcards have been sold with pictures of the lighthouse on them over the years. That's got to add up."

Strider looked over the rail at Man-O-War Cay. "And the hotel rooms and restaurants and guest cottages and dive expeditions and boat rentals have more than made up for the ships that no longer go aground on the reef."

"Sounds like story shift can be a good thing or a bad thing," observed Walter.

"Absolutely," agreed Strider. "It's difficult to say where transformation ends and shift begins. If Cinderella moves from being a cleaning slave to being a princess—or from major self-esteem deficit to realizing her potential and finding love, that's a shift; that's a transformation.

"But societal stories are tapestries—thousands or even millions of stories woven together. Sometimes that produces ugly patterns. Take women's liberation as an example. Women got the right to vote in 1920. Then during World War II, all the men went off to fight. Women started welding and manufacturing—taking on professional roles that had traditionally gone to men—and some of them did those jobs better than the men ever had. Women started going to college. The pill came along in the 1960s and women decided they could have a little fun, just like the guys did. The story shifts associated with that are still in progress. Today, when little Lenore wants to become an astrophysicist, we don't buy her a toy oven and an apron and tell her 'Don't be foolish.' Women account for 47% of the U.S. labor force. They're still squabbling over pay equality—and they should—but the story has shifted."

Audrey gripped the rail. "I think that's a good thing, don't you?"

"Yes and no. Back in the 1950s, a working man with a high school education made enough money to buy a modest house, a car, a television set, and a vacation every year. The wife kept the house and the kids' butts clean. Now all those women are working along with their husbands to bring home collectively less money. A dollar in 1950 bought ten times more than it does today. Women made important social progress, but the economy swallowed it all and kept eating. Now it takes two struggling people and an underpaid illegal immigrant to keep the walls up and the diapers changed."

Audrey swallowed. "Are you saying we'd be better off if women were still housewives?"

"It all depends on how you measure 'better off.' If women are happier and writing life stories that align with bolder, brighter destinies, I'd say we're better off. If we pour 66 million more talented, educated, capable people into the workforce and the economy shrinks and negates that input, we're clearly *not* better off. If we focus on empowering women to work, but we don't find ways for that work—or anyone's work—to bring value home, we need another, larger story shift. The economy, gender roles, how we raise children in a professional culture, whose job it is to provide healthcare, our dependence on foreign energy sources, climate change—all these stories are elements of a much larger story. Story shifts can *divert* our attention from what's right or what's smart, or they can focus our attention on what's important and meaningful."

Walter smiled and wordlessly turned up his palms. "Who decides this?"

"All too often, it's the robber barons we elect to write our stories for us," Strider responded. "But beyond my natural cynicism, you'll find a challenge in this—a call to leadership. If you have an informed take on the conflicts and an inspired notion of what transformation looks like, you can shift a story by voting, running for office, hiring or firing someone, pushing an enlightened idea, refusing to take part in implementing a bad one, or just by acting courteous, responsible, encouraging, and honest. Leaders catalyze story shift.

"Let's look at a story shift that's been used throughout history. At the Nuremburg War Crimes Trials, Hermann Göring, one of Adolf Hitler's party leaders said, 'The common people don't want war; that is understood. But they can always be brought to the bidding of the leaders. All you have to do is tell them they are being attacked, and denounce the peacemakers for lack of patriotism and exposing the country to danger. It works the same in any country.' The Germans employed a classic recipe for tectonic story shift that destroyed Europe and killed over fifty million civilians.

"Some story shifters are still out there luring people onto the reef. They put in phony channel markers that trick ships into sailing up on the coral. They loot and plunder, and they don't care that coral reefs are endangered and vital to life on this planet. Ask any one of them and they'll tell you 'There's no other way' or 'It's God's will' or *'Someone's* going to do this; why not me?' or 'I'm just following orders.'"

"So what can we do about that?" asked Walter.

"Walter, you're a speaker. You get in front of thousands of people every year and inspire transformation. Audrey connects with patients. Micky Tomm connects with employees and they connect with doctors and patients. Doug connects with students. Lenore challenges her fellow scientists. None of us are alone in what we do. We all make observations and transmit stories to people around us.

"If we understand how stories work, and how they interconnect—if we pay attention to that man behind the curtain and expose his fraud, we storytellers assume a very important role in society. Most people blindly follow the bogus stories they're handed because they're afraid of the truth, or some salesman promises them a shortcut to happily ever after. Write 'big picture' stories that catalyze 'big picture' transformations. Examine the conflicts and separate the symptoms from the diseases. Look at the transformations people aspire to and encourage *meaningful* goals. Pressure-test the authenticity of the stories that take root round you and pull the weeds. Being magical—being a powerful witch or wizard—is simply a matter of knowing how stories work. When you understand how stories work—and how they get manipulated by advertisers and politicians—you can use your magic to write better ones."

"What about the idea that history is written by the winners?" challenged Walter. "Some of the ridiculous and divisive social narratives that invade our political discussions and contaminate the news media are story shifts that…"

"It all comes back to leadership," said Strider. "Be the winner. Write the good stories and unwrite the bad ones. Whether you're Anne Frank or a painter who protests through abstract art, if you're a passionate storyteller you'll find a way. Some horrific stories have risen and fallen throughout history. In the long run, a bad story will ultimately collapse under the weight of its own stupidity. It may crush some good people before it does, but a powerful storyteller—a Gandhi—can do a lot of good by rewriting the narrative."

Story Shift

Walter smiled. "So what you're saying is…"

"Be a lighthouse," said Kaitlin. "The world is full of beautiful, treacherous reefs and ships full of good people that have gone off course. Be a big candy-striped lighthouse that shines as a beacon for miles around. That might not make you popular at first, but once the tourists show up and start buying postcards, a good story shift can work out for everyone."

What's Magical?

"Y' know what's magical?" asked Strider as the happiness delegates gazed out from the top of the lighthouse over the islands and shoals of the Abacos. "Think about the places we've been: Moraine Cay has that arm of coral reef that shelters the anchoring area. Green Turtle has *two* inner harbours—White Sound where we anchored to get some sleep and Black Sound where we anchored to visit New Plymouth. Then we went to Marsh Harbour—a port town with another sheltered anchorage. That wasn't good enough for us so we went to Man-O-War Cay which has an inner lagoon so well protected from the wind and waves that we were able to ride out a North Atlantic gale there without feeling a ripple. Now we're here in Hopetown—again, *inside* the island in a sheltered harbour, and tomorrow we'll head to Little Harbour, which you might guess, has a sheltered anchorage. What are the odds that this could happen—that these islands could be so perfect for sheltering boats and sailing between? Is it stupendous luck or divine providence?"

"Geology is not my forte," offered Lenore, "but when I found out I was coming here, I did a little research. This place was once submerged. The water level here has come up and down with various ice ages. When the global temperature changed and the sea level dropped about four hundred feet *lower* than it is now, the Bahama Banks were high and dry. What looks and feels like magic is just a reflection of how the land reacts to the polar ice caps advancing and retreating over millions of years.

"Great Abaco is a geologist's playground; it's hollow. That island is full of cave systems and blue holes, lenses of fresh water that sit on top of salt water, high ground, and low ground. The high areas are ancient sand dunes that turned into solid rock. Low-lying areas collect water that flows underground. When the sea level rises again, Great Abaco will be mostly inundated. The high areas will become new islands, and when the underground cave systems under the lowlands eventually collapse, you might see the same 'protected harbour' phenomenon repeat itself. It only makes sense that the out-islands were once part of the same…"

"Thanks, Lenore." said Doug sarcastically. "Thanks for bursting our bubble. You scientists must sure…"

"Not at all," said Strider. "Look what happened to Galileo. He started looking out into space with his telescope. Even with his primitive equipment, he was able to prove that the sun did not revolve around the earth—that Copernicus was right. He was summoned to Rome and put on trial, and forced to recant his findings. He spent the last eight years of his life in house arrest. The Catholic Church didn't formally pardon him until three hundred fifty years later in 1992. That's conflict and transformation that came way too late—a tragedy...

"So here I am going on about my 'impossible coincidence versus divine providence' story, and Lenore steps in and says, 'there's a simple explanation for all this.' How many times do we choose the story we *like* instead of the story that makes sense? How often do we get stuck in our stories?"

Audrey joined in. "What's wonderful about *this* story is that we don't have to let go of our sense that this place is magic—even if we accept that there's a rational explanation behind it. The colors, the symbols, the shallow water, and their effects on our psyches are no different whether you're a scientist, the Pope, or a romantic. And the fact that the centers of the ancient islands turned into perfect sailboat anchorages—is that any less remarkable now that we understand how it happened? I'm just as blown away—not only by the appearance of these islands, but that they're so perfectly suited to human play. We're dancing on top of millions of years of geological happenstance. We're here to share it at a time when the sea level is just right."

"Well," said Walter, "given what we're doing to the planet, the top of this lighthouse might soon be the only thing above water here again."

"That's a sad story, and it's all too probable," said Strider, "but think about it; *this is the greatest time in human history to have ever lived.* We have airplanes and diesel-powered ships, you can pull out your phone right here on top of the Elbow Cay lighthouse and talk to a friend in Tahiti. We have electricity and fresh running water in our homes. We have a network of smooth, well-lit, paved roads that you can drive on from Key West to Kaitlin's place in Seattle. How many of us would even be here if we didn't have antibiotics to stop an infection? What about anesthesia? Who here has had surgery or a tooth pulled? Who gets polio or smallpox any more? I worry about kids who are born today, but even if the whole thing goes spiraling down the toilet tomorrow, I can look back with my last breath and know I threaded the needle of history. I wouldn't want to have been born anywhere else or at any other time. I wouldn't want to get stuck in any other story. Now *there's* some magic to think about. Grand coincidence or divine intervention? Hallelujah either way."

The Happiness Congress climbed slowly down the spiral stairs through the lighthouse's pink interior to the earth, boarded the dinghies, and rowed across the harbour to the town docks. From there, Vincent, Doug, Walter, and Micky Tomm all headed to the beach. Strider opted to accompany the women on a walk through town.

Lenore spoke first. "I didn't mean to bum Walter out with the geology lesson back there."

"I think he'll get over it," said Strider. "It's nothing a day at the beach won't cure."

"I've been thinking, Strider..." said Audrey.

"About ice cream?" Kaitlin interrupted.

"That, too." Audrey giggled. "But mostly about how *everything* I do is tied to stories. I'm a counselor—a therapist. Take a rocky marriage, for example. Picture two frowning faces with thought bubbles over their heads that say, 'That's not how our story was supposed to go.' My next patient is overcome with grief; she's lost her mother. Her story just lost a central character. She's in crisis because she doesn't know how to continue the story without her. She's reading and writing the book of her life and *boom*—one of the protagonists blows an aneurism and keels over. Kaitlin, what if you were halfway through writing a novel and then, for some strange reason we can't think of, you weren't allowed to include one of your favorite characters?"

"I think I'd have to dump the book and start over."

"Exactly," said Audrey. "A story crisis! She's also got a thought bubble that says, 'That's not how my story was supposed to go.'

"The next person who comes in is a twelve-year-old girl who won't talk or do homework or pay attention in class. Her uncle abuses her, and any time she's tried to get help, her parents tell her she's making things up. She's trapped in a nightmare story and her parents haul her in to my office to find out what's wrong—get this—with *her*. I've never looked at these issues from the standpoint of story conflict, but between the girl, the parents, and dear Uncle Jack, their stories are a tangled mess."

"Everything you know or think you know is a story," repeated Strider. "Understand the problem by mapping out the story elements and categorizing the conflicts."

Audrey adjusted her sunglasses. "That doesn't necessarily solve the problem, does it?"

"No, but try to solve a problem you don't understand and see what happens. Have you ever suffered the indignity of wrecking an unscrambled Rubik's cube?"

"I had one on my shelf," laughed Audrey. "I was so happy when my dog finally destroyed it."

"And yet, I have a friend whose eleven-year-old will take your scrambled Rubik's cube—assuming Max hasn't chewed it up—stare at it for three seconds and then twist it around behind his back for thirty more. You don't want to see the haughty look on his face when he hands it back to you all put together."

"I gave mine away," confessed Kaitlin. "How about you, Lenore? You're a mathematician. Any luck with the Rubik's Cube?"

"Let's just say it brought me 'closer to the mystery' and leave it at that."

"Okay," said Strider. "Let's assume we're not going to write a Rubik's Cube-solving story today. Audrey, how can you use storytelling in your psych practice? Start with the unhappy marriage. Think about what a marriage is in storytelling terms."

"A marriage is two people wrapping their stories together. They're still separate stories, but the authors have agreed to share settings, directions, et cetera. They have also, to some extent, bought into the social narrative of what a marriage 'should be,' what a husband is, what a wife is, what a marriage is for."

"Good. So how will you resolve the story conflict?"

Audrey thought for a moment. "I think it makes sense to teach the two partners about the elements of story. I might have to let them blow off steam first, but if I can teach them about conflict and transformation, I can get them to meet with me individually to talk about what problems they face and what goals they want to reach. I can get each of them to focus on authentic, meaningful goals, and help them reflect on some of the magic that originally brought them together."

"And then?"

"And then we have a way to see where their stories diverge. If she's looking for security and he wants to build a treehouse in Africa, they need to negotiate some serious compromises — or stop wasting time and move on. Or maybe he's an artist who doesn't think about his goals in terms of money. Maybe she wants the kids to be fed and the mortgage to be paid—these aren't unreasonable wishes—but she's telling her story in terms of 'not enough money,' and he's not able to focus on that as a goal because it's not meaningful to him. If they understand the *authentic* transformations they want to achieve, maybe they can rework and harmonize their stories. Storytelling offers a way to look under the hood to see what's causing all the crying and fighting."

"But trust me," said Kaitlin. "That problem of partnering up with an artist is a tough one. I've always focused on my writing, and I've lost a few good boyfriends along the way who thought my priorities were wacko."

"*The Care and Feeding of the Artist;* that massive book is a different cruise altogether," suggested Strider. "But Audrey is right. Who was your next patient?"

"The grieving woman," said Lenore.

"Right," Audrey took a few silent steps. "I think this one's a case of untangling stories—of separating them. This woman believes her story can't go on without her mother's participation. If I can get her to talk about her conflicts and goals, we can figure out which ones are hers and which ones were her mother's. If mom was a micromanager, it might be scary to wake up all that dormant self-determination, but I can see it wouldn't be too difficult to write a story about that."

"Just watch *Bambi*," suggested Kaitlin. "Disney is famous for killing off mom. Pinocchio and Peter Pan have no mothers, and there are plenty of orphans in other Disney stories."

"Those stories are all about growing up and taking charge of your destiny," said Strider. "That particular conflict grips everyone by the heart; it's made Disney a fortune. But I read that Walt Disney bought his parents a house. There was a gas leak and his parents got poisoned. His father made it out but his mother died. Some people think Walt felt responsible for her death and that's why we see that theme repeated so often in Disney stories."

"Interesting," Audrey mused, "and on the other hand, if Mom was her guiding light and best friend, my patient has to realize that all that guidance and wisdom and love now live within her. I'm imagining a story about a sailor who loves a lighthouse. He comes in and out through the rocks and becomes so familiar with the water that he no longer needs the lighthouse—but he doesn't know that. When a big storm comes and destroys the lighthouse, he's afraid his sailing days are over. But there's a ship out there in the storm that needs to get safely through the rocks to port. He sails out alone in the dark, and though he knows the lighthouse is gone, he can hear her bell in his head. He guides the ship home and discovers the light within himself."

"Did you make that up on the spot?" asked Lenore.

"Yes and no." Audrey looked sheepish. "Given that we were on top of the lighthouse this morning, that just seemed—well—obvious."

Strider put his hands above his head, danced in a circle, and grabbed Audrey up in a suffocating bear hug. "And the little girl who won't talk?"

"She has a monster under her bed," said Audrey slowly. "She has a monster under her bed and nobody will believe her. Terrible things happen to her at night but there are no marks. In the morning, she looks like a regular little girl. And her parents are under a spell; they can't see the monster. We—not I, but *we* as a society—need a story that teaches children how to fight real-life invisible monsters. My job is to be the one adult who acknowledges that they really exist. I'm the fairy godmother." A tear rolled down Audrey's cheek. "And that's *real magic* that saves real lives. If I can listen and connect and engage…"

"This storytelling stuff is big juju," said Strider. "I told you up front it's as big as the Universe and as deep as the soul."

"And all those poor people who have been turned into monsters. We need a story for them, too." Audrey stopped walking. "All of a sudden, I feel like I have this enormous perspective—this great power—and I hope I have the creative skill to write the stories I need to make my magic work."

Kaitlin put her arm around Audrey. "You've been thinking this way for how long—ten minutes? Give yourself a chance. Your lighthouse story popped out of nowhere. This is not an active, conscious process. Let your subconscious work this out. When you need stories, they'll appear. When you need to teach someone about stories, the lessons will be there."

Lenore took Audrey's hand. "I'm the scientist here—the skeptic. I'm the one who dropped a tropical geology lesson on Vincent's big 'sing-a-song-with-the-Universe' number, but I'm not a robot, either. There *is* a science to storytelling as much as there's something indescribable, and I just watched you use Strider's four elements to tackle some monumental problems. You wrote a beautiful story and shared some powerful, sensible ideas. I suspect that when you try this on patients, it won't be quite as cut and dried, but you're on a good path. Like Kaitlin says, 'Let this work itself out.' I don't think there's any other way to do it—but I think you're going to be one amazing therapist if you're not already."

Kaitlin turned, faced her companions, and placed a dramatic hand over her chest. "Once upon a time a crazy schooner captain and three hot ladies went for a walk on a tropical island. The conversation grew deep and interesting. The sun rose higher and the ladies got hotter … oh … what did you *think* I meant?"

Lenore and Audrey laughed. Strider smiled and shook his head.

"Suddenly the *hottest* one of the bunch decided it was time for them to all get out of their heads and enjoy their gorgeous surroundings. She interrupted their meeting of the minds under the pretense that she was going to tell a deep and meaningful story, then pointed down the street and said, 'Ice cream's on me. Let's go!'"

Questioning the King

While Vincent and Doug waded into the surf, Micky Tomm and Walter walked down Elbow Cay Beach. The northerly winds had subsided, leaving behind a soothing, cool, easterly wind and blue skies.

"So what do you think, Walt? Do you think this is a big setup? I mean, I don't care if it is; it's been fantastic, but Strider has *got* to be Mr. King."

"I keep wondering. That theory makes some sense, but our Strider doesn't seem like the type to affiliate himself with a happiness school—at least not a formal one. And I read some glowing reviews of the Happiness Congress program and none of them mentioned a boat."

Walter spread a dab of sunscreen on his nose. "True, but the Happiness Congress is held in a different place every year—usually in a remote natural setting. I'm not surprised that nautical themes are not…"

Micky Tomm reached for the sunscreen tube. "Strider seems to be permanently housed in his schooner. Can you picture him giving happiness workshops in Nepal or the Falklands or up in the Alaskan wilderness or at an oasis in the Sahara?"

"I'm just not sure," replied Walter. "Strider comes off as a bit of a small-town boy, but I've never met anyone who knows as much about everything as he does. He's not a show-off about it, but if you want to talk about Claude Debussy, he knows all the compositions. If you want to talk astronomy or ancient history or philosophy or coin collecting — or pretty much anything — he's a walking encyclopedia."

Walter continued. "Nobody has seen a picture of Mr. King. His book says he's a private person who limits public contact to a workshop once a year. He's declined some prestigious awards because he wasn't willing to appear at the ceremonies. Is it possible that the real Mr. King appoints a different stand-in every year — someone to take the seven people he selects off on a journey of discovery? 'King' could be a pen name for all we know."

"I thought about that," said Micky Tomm, "but we all read *The Happiness Book* or we wouldn't be here. The lessons we're getting from Strider are not remotely like the ones in the book. In fact, since I got shanghaied and taken to sea on the story ship, King's happiness ship is floating a little low in the water. There must be thousands of applicants for the Happiness Congress.

Questioning the King

I never expected to open my chocolate bar and find a golden ticket, but there it was—and for this I'm going to miss our company's biggest annual conference event. But if King sends me an apology letter and a rain check, I think I'll pass. My head is packed with enough material to keep it spinning for the rest of my life."

Walter reflected on Micky Tomm's words. "I almost had a speaking gig for IBM booked last weekend—20,000 employees and me up there on a Jumbotron screen in a stadium. It would have been the biggest speaking engagement I'd ever had, and on top of the speaking fee, I'm sure I could have sold two thousand books and DVDs. That's a lot of $20 bills! I'd been trying to catch that fish for years and was just about to sign the deal when King's letter came ... and here we are."

"Do you ever wonder why *we* were selected—out of all the people who would kneel down and worship at King's altar? I'm impressed by his book, but some of his fans are zealots. I've hardly heard his name mentioned by the people in our group."

Micky Tomm bent over to pick up a piece of sea glass. "If King is a private type, it makes sense that he wouldn't want to spend ten days with a bunch of drooling fanatics. I think he picked people from diverse backgrounds who could contribute to the discussion—and I think his choices were good ones. We're all different but compatible. I'll give him that even if he did go AWOL on us."

"But wouldn't it make a fantastic story? We all get stranded on an island and the guy who comes to rescue us turns out to be either King or one of his flunkies. We have a mind-blowing workshop—just like we expected—and at the end, he says, 'Guess what? This was all planned.'"

"That certainly would make a good story, but I'm good with it either way."

"So Micky, what are your thoughts about how you'll use all this storytelling stuff when you get back to what Strider calls 'the land of clocks and calendars?'"

"I'm a practical guy," said Micky Tomm. "I have way too much on my plate to spend time pondering my navel or the secrets of the Universe or what I am *not*. But I've come to see my job in a new way. Just as storytellers held important leadership positions in tribal cultures, I'm the chief storyteller at my company. I'm actually sort of a story manager. Our marketing department tells stories to doctors and patients about what our products do. I can think of a half-dozen ad campaigns I want to scrap as soon as I get back because they tell what the products *do,* but they don't tell patients that we understand their health problems and care about their comfort.

We're selling drugs instead of hope. Who wants to buy *anything* from a drug company? We need to become a comfort company. The knowledge that our products help people has always made me feel good, but that value needs to ripple through my organization.

Questioning the King

"We have finance people on one floor of the building and marketing people on another. I don't want to tell you how many lawyers are working the FDA compliance beat. And the research and development department is full of biochemists and geneticists who might as well be speaking Navajo when they explain what they're working on. It's like the blind men and the elephant; one feels the trunk and says the elephant is like a snake, the other feels its side and says it's like a wall, another touches a leg and says it's like a tree. All these people have different roles to play in a very large story that winds through our campus and out into the world, and all most of them see of it is their own piece. If I can teach them about storytelling, I think they'll be able to communicate better about their stake in the whole thing. And if I can create a mechanism through which doctors, patients, employees—*everyone*—can help create the story of what our enterprise is, I think we can deliver *meaning* for everyone. I don't think I can measure that on a spreadsheet, and I know I'm going to have to be sneaky about what I'm doing with some of the 'nuts and bolts' types. But I'll leave this trip knowing that if we make it our mission to deliver *meaning* to everyone we touch, inside and outside the organization, the rest of the stories—the ones about how the creative people in the marketing department hate the killjoys in the compliance department and how nobody cares if our anti-itch cream has 25% more active ingredients than our competitor's brand—the small stories will evolve as the values inside the company evolve. As chief storyteller, I'm ready to go make that happen. I like a challenge—and I like the idea that I can create authentic, meaningful stories that will help my *company* create an authentic, meaningful story.

"And y' know what, Walter? Last week, if some guy—*especially* some guy with zebra pants and a cowboy hat and a missing tooth—had walked into my office and starting babbling about storytelling, I'd have called security and had him escorted out!"

Walter laughed. "I thought about introducing Strider to the speaking business. I've seen a few speakers pull off the whole 'Take me as I am' game and get great bookings—but I can't picture him flying around the world and negotiating contracts with meeting planners. It's too bad, really, but I think he draws his power from his surroundings. A few cancelled flights and lost bags would send him screaming back to the islands."

"You're probably right. But what about you, Walter? How will you incorporate this storytelling stuff into your own speaking?"

"When I speak, I tell the story of how I got cancer and kept going to the gym, even when the chemo had me feeling like I wanted to die. I got better, went into remission, and then two years later, a spot showed up on my liver and I went back through the whole dog and pony show—and here I am in remission again, crossing my fingers that my next scan won't send me back down the chute for a third bull ride. I'm supposed to be cured, but who knows?

That's what they told me the first time. I keep checking. Every day's a gift.

"I tell audiences that story and I know how to look people in the eye and engage them. I've done this long enough to have the stagecraft down, and I usually get standing ovations; it feels good. But since I've been on this trip, I'm thinking I spend too much time on the me story and not enough time on the *them* story. A lot of speakers are guilty of that—especially the Everest climbers and life raft survivors and people who have great me stories.

"Most of the people I speak to don't literally have cancer, but sooner or later, some scary, unexpected event will pop up in their lives that can potentially be catastrophic—a divorce request that blindsides the wife, a bank account that gets sucked dry by an identity thief, a market crash, a business failure, a child who turns out to be a junkie. I'm a *very* engaging speaker, but I've let that be a substitute for being a very *connecting* speaker. I can get on stage and read the phone book on a Saturday night, and people will come hug me after the show and cry and tell me how I changed their lives. But on Monday morning, I wonder if any of what I say lingers in their heads. Are they high on the moment, or am I really changing their lives?

"Storytelling—not just telling my own story, but telling my *audience's* stories—will give me a tool that lets me dig deeper. I think all good speakers suffer from imposter syndrome—we all question ourselves and wonder if all the meeting planners and audience members aren't victims of some massive charade that we've only pulled off because we've bought into it ourselves. The big shepherd's crook is going to appear from stage left and…"

"I suspect all professionals suffer from that from time to time," assured Micky Tomm. "I know I do, and the ones who don't are narcissists—narcissism being the only disease where the sicker you are, the better you feel."

Walter laughed. "You should come to a speakers' convention! But maybe a small measure of self-doubt is healthy? Maybe it keeps us fresh?"

"Makes sense," said Micky Tomm. "In this case, I think it's healthy fallout that comes with the realization that we could have been doing our jobs better all this time—in spite of whatever success it's brought us."

"Thanks for that, Micky. I guess we can't make progress without a professional identity crisis once in a while—no conflict: no story. But I like the idea that I can use the four elements and the seven types of conflicts to tune my presentation to suit my audience. I can present my 'mind-body' message as part of a writing technique, as a way my audience members can create their own success stories. The whole 'If I can do it, you can do it' schtick is probably not very effective, and too many speakers fall back on it. *'I dropped out of high school and got into drugs and lost my business and my family and became a crack whore, but now I'm straight and got a doctoral degree and I'm standing in front of you getting paid big bucks to encourage you.'* Audience members get off on stories like that — and on my cancer survival stories — but I want to help them write their *own* success stories.

"There are a lot of 'catharsis speakers' out there who get on stage and work out their issues. Some of them are masterful speakers, and for all I know, it's therapeutic for them, but if I'm going to focus on delivering *meaning* and *value* to my audience members, I think storytelling is the ticket."

"The irony of that," said Micky Tomm, "is that we're deep in Strider's Essential Absurdities. For all this new conviction we've discovered, neither one of us has a clue how to define 'meaning' or 'value.'"

The two continued down the sand, listening to the sound of the surf crashing on the beach and feeling the caress of the wind on their faces.

"So," said Walter, "you never gave me your take on whether you think this trip was set up by King or if Strider actually *is* King."

"I've got a better story," said Micky Tomm. "What if King really flaked out? What if we really were stranded? It wouldn't have been the end of the world. We would have spent an uncomfortable night on the porch at Moraine Cay and gotten a lift off the island the next day. But what if we really did just *happen* to be on the island when Strider just *happened* to be anchored there on a boat big enough to accommodate everyone. What if one teacher dropped out and the Universe provided another one? We could have met a family on a sailing vacation or an old guy cruising around stretching out his Social Security check or some kid out on a walkabout on a little blue sailboat. *Anyone* could have hauled us to Green Turtle or back to Treasure Cay. But no, we met Strider and he turned out to be our Yoda — our unlikely teacher. He says he knows nothing about King. Based on my impressions of him, I think he's either an honest guy or one hell of an actor."

Meaningful Data

Lenore, Kaitlin, Audrey, and Strider walked through town with their ice cream, talking and laughing. Strider pointed out a sugar-apple tree and explained how the female papaya plant needed pollen from a male plant before it would grow fruit. He showed them how the gumelemi tree and the poisonwood tree grow side by side, and described how the bark of one could be used to ease the rash caused by the other.

Audrey looked at Kaitlin and Strider. "We won't be offended if you two hold hands."

Kaitlin's embarrassment was not diminished when Strider picked her up as if he meant to carry her across some imaginary threshold.

"You two have been eyeing each other this whole trip," chuckled Audrey. "I'm surprised you're not back on the boat 'baking bread.'"

"It's that obvious?" Kaitlin blubbered.

Lenore spoke up. "If it makes you feel any better, we don't have a problem with it. You're young and single and on vacation in this wonderland."

"Well, the connection may be obvious," Kaitlin confessed, "but we agreed to put the brakes on the island romance and use our time to engage in ways that didn't crowd the boat."

"I respect that," said Audrey. "I'm not sure if under the same circumstances, I'd be…"

Kaitlin grinned. "But if that cat's out of the bag, you ladies may have to put up with a little public hand-holding." She shifted her ice cream and took Strider's hand.

"Subject change," declared Strider.

"Oh, thank you, sweetheart," cooed Kaitlin in mock swoon.

"What's going on in that head of yours, Lenore?" Strider continued. "You like to sit back and observe. I don't know if you're quiet because you're used to having your observations go over most people's heads or maybe you're just reserved, but what brings a rocket scientist to the Bahamas for a Happiness Congress? You look like you're having fun, but are you finding what you were searching for?"

"You know," said Lenore, "we scientists aren't robots. We tell jokes and drink too much sometimes. We raise vegetable gardens and we gossip and have bad romances. Some of us drive impractical vehicles because we're vain or some salesman put the whammy on us. We send our kids to Sunday school to make paper Easter bunnies and cardboard menorahs and mailing tube nutcrackers for Christmas."

Meaningful Data

"So where's your conflict?" asked Strider. "What's unique about Lenore that lands her here? What is the transformation you came here looking for—and more important, are you finding it?"

Strider pointed to a low coral rock wall adjacent to the path where they could sit beneath a cluster of coconut palms.

"I love what I do," said Lenore, "but sometimes I feel stuck in the tower—the ivory tower. I go to work and I'm part of a community of people who swim in seas of mathematical expressions. We fill walls and blackboards and computer screens and books with this *poetry*—I don't know what else to call it—numbers and symbols and the relationships between them. Some of this stuff will absolutely blow your mind; it's world-changing stuff. And some of it makes no sense; it's as if all the numbers we use sometimes turn out to be approximations and not the rigid, unshifting constants we depend on.

"Take random numbers for instance. Let's pull numbers out of a box like they do in the lottery. If you graphed those values, you'd expect to find an even spread. Within the range of values, say one to a hundred, you'd expect the graph to look like a straight line. The odds of encountering any value on any given draw should be equal. But if you actually pull numbers and graph the results, about 30 percent of the numbers will begin with 1. Fewer of them will begin with 2, even fewer with 3, and so on, until only one number in twenty will begin with a 9. The more samples you take, the more this pattern emerges. So if I were to advise you on how to pick a winning lottery number based on *observation,* I'd tell you to pick more low numbers. But as an academic, I can't find any *logical* evidence to support that advice.

"Or how about this one: What's 11 x 11?"

"121 ... I think," replied Audrey.

"Good. Now what's 111 x 111?"

Audrey shrugged. "I'm out. Nothing in this head past the 12s."

"12,321. See the pattern? How about 1,111 x 1,111?"

"No idea."

"1,234,321 ... and so on. 111,111,111 x 111,111,111 = 12345678987654321.

"I could get into some really obscure stuff if I had a blackboard and enough coffee to keep you awake, but that's the problem. The farther out I go into the Universe, the farther away from earth I get. We discover amazing things every day that could change the world, but nobody understands them except a bunch of us geeks in lab coats—and half the time, we don't understand them. And then you get these bean counters who award funding or kill projects; they have no clue whether they're saving the world or dooming it."

"Do you understand how your car works?" asked Strider.

"Sure. I put gas in it and turn the key, the engine turns the fuel into heat which is converted to kinetic energy which…"

"You have no idea how your car works, do you? The combustion cycle? Valves and pistons and camshafts and all that?"

Lenore shook her head.

"But do you *need* to understand that to get to work or to the grocery store?"

"No."

"If you go to the car dealer, the salesman doesn't talk to you about fuel injection and double overhead cams, does he?"

"No."

"And can we assume he knows nothing about heat transference and the physics associated with the rapid oxidation of pressurized fuel?"

"I think that's a safe assumption," Lenore chuckled.

"Maybe if he did, you guys would end up going out for drinks, but why is that information not relevant to the criteria you use to select a vehicle?"

Lenore thought for a moment and smiled. "Because it's not meaningful."

"Yes! What do you care about when you choose a car?"

"Safety, style, fuel efficiency, price…"

"So if you work out the math for a lightweight battery or a high-efficiency solar panel, how do you sell that? How do you get the money folks to open up the bank vault so you can build your prototype?"

"Oh my God! I keep popping the hood and showing off the engine. I'm trying to win them over with data. I need to talk about…"

"The transformation!" said Kaitlin and Audrey in unison.

"So I need to figure out what the data mean to the people I need to convince to pay for it. The money people don't care how many dimensions the math is. They want to know that the reactor is going to produce less toxic waste. They want to know that the lightweight heat shield tiles on the new space shuttle—the one you're about to forget I ever mentioned—won't fly off. They want to know that we can prevent a meteor from hitting Los Angeles and causing a new ice age. They…"

"They want to know that your work is *meaningful to them*," said Strider. "So when you and your colleagues pitch your ideas and discoveries…"

"I've seen so many PowerPoint slides filled with graphs and charts and diagrams and mathematical formulas. We present these amazing projects—revolutionary stuff—and then we see them get shut down while some inconsequential piece of fluff gets staffed and funded. I've seen scientists crying in the break room—not only because their research got the axe—but because they knew they could have made a difference—fed people or kept them safe or…"

"I'll give you a sad tip," said Audrey. "All too often, 'meaningful' means 'it looks good on a spreadsheet.' I'm a mental health

Meaningful Data

professional; what I do makes an enormous difference in people's lives. But try to get an insurance company to pay for marriage counseling or cover a few sessions with a shrink so you can manage the pressures of a toxic work environment. Half the people who need me most won't come because they're afraid they'll be blacklisted as 'mentally ill.' Imagine if you couldn't go to the doctor when you had a skinned knee or the flu because your record would get flagged as 'prone to sickness.'"

"So how do you turn that around?" asked Lenore.

"I tell them that according to the University of Michigan, depression costs employers 44 *billion* dollars a year. I tell them that according to the World Health Organization, unless we make more treatment available, 12 *billion* working days will be lost to mental illness each year between now and 2030—that's *50 million years* of work. I give them data—but I give them data that is meaningful to them.

"The next thing you know, they're sponsoring depression-screening programs for the businesses they insure. And it's not because they suddenly got enlightened and started caring about people; it's no storybook transformation. Change happens because they're willing to spend millions to save billions—and then, maybe—just maybe—after it starts working and the productivity numbers go up and someone writes an online review about how their wonderful insurance company saved their marriage or gave them an alternative to jumping off a bridge, someone on the inside says, 'Hey, maybe we're doing some good.' Even if they don't come into it from a place of empathy, they end up paying for the change and they get to own the results. Deep down, all those paper pushers are human. They have marital problems and depression and they lose loved ones like the rest of us. When the work they do ends up helping someone, the connection happens—that brush with the Essential Absurdities."

"Now *that's* transforming data into meaning, Audrey." Strider put his hands together. "I love the evolution in that."

Lenore continued. "So the problem isn't with the data; it's with the wrong *kind* of data. And maybe the storytelling is a bit more complicated because there are two sets of stakeholders."

"What do you mean?" asked Kaitlin.

"The projects we do are meaningful to us scientists on many levels at once. If you're part of the science fraternity—if you speak geek—you get to put your math in front of other geeks and watch their eyes bug out. It's partially an ego trip, but it's also a connection thing—like when Strider and his sailing friends talk about jibs and halyards and boat stuff. We scientists need other people who understand the way we look at the Universe. And we're also mindful of the implications of our discoveries for humanity. This gives us a bridge to cross: we want the personal satisfaction of seeing our theoretical discoveries become tangible tools, and we also want to see them make a difference in people's lives.

"The people above us want the same things—to connect and make a difference—but they're looking at different stories—different conflicts. What will it cost to produce a prototype? What are the risks? What are the odds of success? Why this project and not that one? We need to tell the story of what we're doing in a way that empowers them to achieve transformation within the story of what *they're* doing."

"Which is what?" asked Kaitlin.

"They want to convince the suits that they picked the most promising projects. They want to keep their jobs by investing wisely. They care about the numbers because that's what they've been asked to oversee—and *then* they care about the transformation they're buying for the people downstream.

"Our stories need to bypass descriptions of chemical reactions and polymers and testing environments. These guys don't care what we put in the cake; they just want to know that it tastes good and that we can either make it cheap or fast or cook it without an oven. If it doesn't save time, money, or aggravation, it will never get a chance to save the world."

Strider crossed his arms behind his head and stretched. "So Lenore, given your current trajectory, how do we calculate your happiness coefficient?"

"I could still use a hunky boyfriend who wants to help me build a bridge between Einstein's relativity and Schrödinger's chemistry, but I think a lot of my angst has been caused by telling a story that isn't meaningful to the people I've been telling it to. And I think I'll be able to help some of my colleagues use storytelling skills to make some important projects see the light of day."

"Happy then?"

"Yes sir, Captain. Happy."

"I see only one place we can take that," said Kaitlin.

"Where's that?"

"This way," she pointed. "To the beach."

Darkness Before the Dawn

*A*fter spending another night in Hopetown Harbour under the watchful beam of the Elbow Cay Lighthouse, *The Metaphor* and its crew enjoyed a leisurely breakfast and slipped out into the sea of Abaco.

"You're an early riser," said Kaitlin. "Why are we leaving so much later than usual?"

"The farthest stop on our cruise will be Little Harbour. Between here and there, the shortest route is the shallow channel between Tilloo Cay and Lubber's Quarters. We want to pass through that channel when the tide is mostly full and still rising so we don't spend the night sitting on the bottom waiting for the tide to come back in again."

"What's the difference between high and low tide?"

"Not much; about three feet."

Strider engaged the self-steering vane, adjusted the sails, and allowed *The Metaphor* to steer her own southerly course between the two islands. "Congress is in session!" he declared, as he called all hands to their customary lounging spots.

"We've talked about ways to take stories *apart*—like the four elements and conflict categories—but as it seems I've successfully afflicted you all with my storytelling disease, let's talk about some ways we can put stories *together*."

"As a writer, I have some ideas," volunteered Kaitlin.

"Go ahead, love," encouraged Strider.

"As simple as it seems, it's important to set up the conflict early in the story. Readers—and probably listeners—are impatient. They want to know why they should stick around."

Walter nodded. "The same is definitely true for speaking."

"What I suspect is happening," said Audrey, "is that our subconscious story filters are checking for *authenticity;* they want to know if the story is metaphorically about *them*. If the narrative rambles on and nobody encounters a conflict, we go back to scanning the environment for things that need our attention."

Doug jumped in. "And this is why so many books and movies start with a flashback. If we see soldiers in a firefight at the beginning of the movie, it's much easier to return to all the politics that led up to the conflict. Start with the politics and nobody will pay attention. They need dots to connect."

"I love this," joked Strider. "All I have to do is prompt the conversation and my dear Happiness Congress steers on its own as straight and sure as this ship does with the steering vane engaged."

"Thanks to you," said Walter. "But to return to the topic: Speakers approach this in a variety of ways. Some lead with questions."

Walter put on his speaker's voice. "Have you ever found yourself in a situation where one moment you were flying high … and the next moment you were on the ground with no options, no Plan B, nowhere to go? Let me tell you about a day like that I had back in 2015.

"Another approach is a bit more practical." Walter took a breath and looked each of his colleagues in the eye. "Everything you know or *think* you know is a story. I'm here today to talk to you about stories, why they're important, and how you can use them to change lives and fortunes."

"That makes sense," said Lenore. "It's the topic paragraph of an essay. Tell them what you're going to talk about…"

"And what it means to them," added Vincent.

"And this is what kills a lot of academic papers," added Lenore. "I've had to read more than my share of them, but I'm only just beginning to understand *why* they're so painful. Not only do grad students think they need to impress their professors with pseudo-sophisticated language, they go on and on about their research and how it proves that a relationship exists between ABC and XYZ—without ever explaining the *impact* of that discovery."

Lenore thought for a moment. "And it's not just students; that's our whole academic culture!"

"No wonder students don't learn anything in schools," said Strider. "Students are too busy imitating people who don't know how to teach. Do you remember what I said to you about teaching the very first night you all came aboard?"

Kaitlin spoke up. "If you're not laughing, you're not learning!"

"What about sad stories?" asked Micky Tomm. "If I'm talking to my team about mortality statistics associated with immunosuppressant drugs, I can see how a little emotional boost will help them engage with the story—but I don't think it's appropriate to tell jokes about it."

"Of course not," said Strider, "but like you said, you can give the story its proper gravitas. Talk about the difficult choice people make between suffering from diseases that cause their immune system to treat cells in their own body as an infection, and inhibiting their immune system—which can save their lives as long as some other infection doesn't come along and kill them. That's the same scenario Walter used in his 'flying high—down on the ground' example. It's not so much about 'laughing' as it is about responding emotionally. If you don't provoke an emotional response, nobody will stay on board long enough to learn from you."

"How about a contextual model?" suggested Doug.

Darkness Before the Dawn

"You sound like Lenore," teased Audrey.

"Strider gave us a contextual model for storytelling. The characters in a story travel aboard a narrative boat that must navigate through the rocks of conflict to the safe port of transformation. The waters of authenticity must be deep enough to support the ship or the story will go aground—and since water is an archetype for consciousness, that's a perfect metaphor. And finally, there's magic—the invisible wind that pushes the story along. Can you picture that in your head? Could you draw a diagram of it?"

The happiness delegates exchanged nods of agreement.

"Then you can teach it."

"But we have to be careful," advised Strider. "These models are powerful devices. When the lobbyists start tinkering with them, school kids start learning that *dairy* is a food group."

"Never let the truth stand in the way of a good story," joked Vincent.

"That's the nature of 'the dark side of the force.'" Strider twisted the brim of his hat. "You can use a story as a Trojan horse to get lies into people's heads. Propagandists and advertisers know how to engage your subconscious; they understand what symbols to use to get past your story filters and plant messages deep inside you.

"But life doesn't always unfold in a nice, tidy rhythm like a novel does. After the treasure is recovered, the treasure hunter doesn't always end up wealthy for life; seventy percent of lottery winners go bankrupt. Real life heroes don't always make it to the scene on time; ask a paramedic. After the tragic misunderstanding and the big breakup, couples don't always get back together; ask *anybody*. If you want to teach or inspire, don't be afraid to change a few details around. I'm not saying you should force a happy ending on every story; I'm just suggesting that the loopbacks and pitfalls of real life can make the storytelling road too bumpy for listeners to travel on."

"But isn't that dishonest?" asked Lenore. "Are you saying it's okay to lie to an audience or a room full of students or a selection panel?"

"I heard a famous author tell a bunch of students that for a work to qualify as non-fiction, it must be absolutely true. Guess who got kicked out of that class?" Strider grinned. "But we already know that everything we see is past tense. We know that you and I can't see the same object from the same angle. If we all get together next year and write down what we remember about this cruise, we'll create very different 'true stories' about who said what and what islands we visited in what order. The longer we wait, the more we'll forget and the more details we'll invent without realizing it. The purpose of a story is to convey *meaning*, not truth; that's what journalism is for.

"Take our windsurfer maniac at Man-O-War Cay. Do any of you care why he was really out there?"

A silent pause confirmed Strider's suspicions.

"You know why you don't want to know?" asked Strider. "You're not interested because the real reason he was out there zooming through the coral heads probably won't compare to the stories you came up with on your own. Having already found so much meaning, you don't want to risk having the truth kill the magic."

"But where do you draw the line?" asked Micky Tomm.

"If you're sharing facts to inform, be as truthful as you can. That's journalism. But if you're telling stories to teach or inspire, then smooth the bumps, twist the timeline, or add or delete characters to make the narrative flow better. If you're writing a travelogue about cruising the Abacos and you made three voyages out of Marsh Harbour, why burden your reader with all that anchoring? Tell the story of one journey from Moraine Cay to Little Harbour. No harm will come from it, and the reader won't get jerked around—which means they'll have an easier time engaging with your story and converting it into meaning."

"I'm not sold," said Lenore.

"So let me tell you a few more details about my personal story," said Strider. "In the true version, I saw the schooner, got the inheritance, flew back to Oklahoma with Betty and signed a contract on a house. Then she went on a church retreat with her girlfriends and I found some pretense to fly back out to Kennebunk to look at the boat. I was almost ready to walk away when the owner came by and saw me staring at the hull. We started talking and he invited me aboard. She was sitting in a boat yard, so up the ladder we went. After chatting in the cabin for an hour, we went back down and I sprained my ankle when I missed the last rung of the ladder. I thanked him for the tour and was heading back to the airport when I received a romantic text message from Betty that was *definitely* not intended for me...."

"See how these details ruin the story? Now I'm giving you true but useless information. The sprained ankle is an irrelevant detail and I'm airing my dirty laundry—which makes me sound bitter. And by telling it this way, I'm challenging *you* to filter out the parts of the story that are meaningful."

"Every writer needs an editor," said Kaitlin.

"You said it, girl," replied Strider. "Which takes us out of my personal mud pit and back to good storytelling techniques. I don't care how good a storyteller you are; even professional editors hire professional editors. We are all too close to our own stories—stuck in the Universe we each personally create. If your goal is to engage and connect with others, doesn't it just make sense to try your story out on a professional 'other' before you let your broken heart bleed all over the stage?"

"Sure," said Vincent, "but why not just try your stories on friends and family members?"

"Do that, too," said Strider, "but show your work to someone who is experienced with the art of storytelling. If a friend came to you for story advice, would you give them better input now than you would have before you went off on this crazy sailing expedition?"

"Absolutely."

"I rest my case. Friends and family can be good representatives for the readers or audience members or sales prospects you'll be sharing your story with, but a good story whisperer will give you the tough love you need to make your stories powerful."

"That's why we have copywriting experts in our marketing department," said Micky Tomm.

"And now I'm wondering why we don't have editors working with our science geeks," added Lenore. "It makes complete sense."

"But it conflicts with the corporate culture story," suggested Strider, "the one that says that anyone with a Ph.D. must already be an articulate communicator. You and I know that half those people can hardly spell their name."

Lenore laughed.

"Imagine how powerful schools could be if every teacher was taught about storytelling and had a coach to work with."

"How about all those sales emails that end up in the trash because they sound like spam?" added Micky Tomm.

The Story Story

Strider adjusted the steering vane and let the ship fall off a few degrees. He made some sandwiches, brought out a few bottles of wine, and allowed the conversation to rest. Vincent crawled out on the bowsprit and shot some video of *The Metaphor*'s stem cutting through the water. A pod of bottlenose dolphins came by to play in the ship's wake. Kaitlin climbed the ratlines in the rigging and took some photographs of *The Metaphor*'s crew from up above. A few miles out of Little Harbour, Strider reconvened the Congress.

"Okay, so how about *tension* as a story factor we haven't talked about yet? Some people call it 'emotional arc.' Screenwriters create movie scripts according to a very well defined formula. Writers vary from it quite a bit, but we can steal some useful ideas.

"Walter suggested we set up the conflict early in the story. So, our character is walking along the street and he turns the corner. There's nothing ahead of him but stars and space. He almost falls off the edge, but he catches his balance and the conflict begins: *What happened to my world?* A strange flying vehicle pulls up and an unusual creature says, 'Get in; you've been chosen.' Two minutes into the movie, we know we want to see how Mr. Ordinary gets in and out of trouble, puts the earth back together, frees the attractive-but-oh-so-sarcastic girl from her evil alien captors, wins her heart, and resumes his life as Mr. Not-So-Ordinary."

Audrey laughed. "Do you make this stuff up on the spot? You should go to Hollywood."

Darkness Before the Dawn

"And crank out drivel? No thanks. I like the stories we're creating right here in the Abacos just fine, thank you.

"But what usually happens in stories like this is what I call 'the darkness before the dawn.' During the final battle scene, Mr. Ordinary is injured and bleeding. The evil alien overlord is busy monologuing and getting ready to end the hero's life. He approaches with his laser sword and gets ready to strike…

"And then the light goes out on the alien overlord's sword. As he drops it, we see him split in half and fall apart. How did this happen? It's the cute little alien monkey slave that Mr. Ordinary released from his evil master way back in scene 12. He never forgets a good deed and he's been watching from the shadows, waiting for his moment to save the day."

"How much for the merchandising rights, Strider?" asked Micky Tomm. "Every kid should get a free plastic Boppo the liberated alien monkey slave with every McMeal."

Strider laughed and continued. "Take it and run with it, Mick. Just don't tell me about it. Treat it like you would an open marriage."

Kaitlin shook her head.

"Characters start their sail through the rocks of conflict, but after a while, if we're not careful, the story gets boring. 'Hey, I avoided that rock.' 'Good, I missed another one.' 'Hmm, that was close.' A good story has twists and surprises. If it simply documents the safe passage of a character across the sea of conflict, it won't keep our interest. Ships get *stuck* on those rocks. Sometimes repairs need to be made before the journey can continue. Listeners and readers *invest* in a good story; there's a reason it's called *paying* attention. If the listener fears that investment is going to fail, they get tense; they want that happy ending; we all do. Give them a good scare.

"Walter, in your story, you've been doing chemotherapy for months. The numbers—the bad ones—are trending upward. You're trying to stay positive, but you know you're at a turning point. The doctor comes in and you're trying to read his face, but he's a poker player—one of those stone-faced doctors who disconnect because they lose half their patients no matter how good their work is. And then just as he's about to tell you the results of your last scan, a nurse comes in and pulls him out of the room for some emergency. You sweat for another half-hour. Thoughts race through your head. Half of you is ready to give up and half of you wants to keep fighting. Finally, after a thousand years, the doctor comes in…"

"Well we know what happens, and we probably knew what was going to happen when the movie started or the book or the speech started, but it doesn't matter. We are one hundred percent engaged and connected."

"But Strider, my doctor was magnificent. I still have dinner with him every few weeks. He was a hero in my story. I don't want to offend…"

"I suspect your heroic doctor wants to motivate people just like you do. Explain that you want to tell a dramatic, meaningful story and that your intention is not to vilify him. He'll be on board with it if he's as wonderful as you say he is."

"Strider's right," said Micky Tomm. "Pull your listeners into that tense situation and then deliver the good news right as all hope is lost."

"Bounce 'em off the bottom," said Kaitlin.

"Back to you, Walter," said Strider. "You're our speaker. What are the number one mistakes people make when speaking?"

"Eye contact is important."

"That sounds like a basic component of connection," agreed Audrey.

"Yes, I challenge myself to create a *relationship* with every person in the room. I try to make people feel *the speaker is talking to me.*

"Another important one is timing. Spoken language is a different art than written language. Strip it down to the basics and then … leave long … luxurious … pauses. Don't rush. Let your audience hang on your words. It takes a few seconds to translate a story into *meaning,* especially if you share something profound. Give your listener time to reflect."

Audrey raised her hand. "Allow the listener's subconscious to process what you have to say without forcing it to filter new information at the same time."

"That's why the first thing you do when you have a traffic accident is turn off the radio," added Strider. "Logically, it shouldn't make any difference, but at that moment you're dealing with emotions, rational decisions, questions about who might be hurt—including *you*—what a hassle it's going to be to wait for the police and file a report, what the insurance will cover, who's at fault. You don't have any bandwidth left to filter out the annoying announcer screaming about the amazing deals at Metro Toyota. Even if you're bleeding, the first thing you do is switch the radio off."

"Audiences do seem to engage during the pauses," reflected Walter.

"This idea of allowing people time to process information should affect the way we all talk and listen and teach," suggested Lenore.

"These are the 'missing' stories I spoke of," said Strider. "Students get taught to read and write, but they don't get taught how to tell stories, how to speak, how to listen, how to separate meaningful goals from distractions, how to honor what bubbles up from their subconscious even when it's irrational or contradictory. Considering that we're hardwired to crave connection and engagement, why aren't we teaching school children and professionals alike how to make that happen?"

"Who's supposed to teach this stuff?" asked Vincent.

Strider looked back from under the brim of his hat. "If a bunch of castaways stuck with an eccentric schooner captain on a boat in the Bahamas can bust into it, it can't be that difficult to access. We already know this stuff. That's why it feels 'true' when we hear it. The problem is that everyone's too stuck in their story to *realize* they're stuck in their story—and ironically, the only cure is better stories."

Strider disengaged the steering vane, rounded up into the wind, and dropped the foresail gently to the deck. Doug and Vincent gathered it up, tied off the sail, and put the sail cover over it. Kaitlin went down below to stow her beach towel and phone where they wouldn't interfere with anyone moving about the deck.

The Metaphor glided into the entrance of Little Harbour and hit the shallow sand bar in the channel with an ominous *crunch*. She stopped, twisted loose, and continued into the lagoon.

A bell began to ring down in the cabin. "Strider," called Kaitlin. "We've got water coming in!"

Catalyst

Strider quickly dropped the mainsail and wrapped a line around it, then started the engine. His voice was calm and slow, but the concern behind his calm was not well concealed. "Kaitlin, I need you up here. Can you steer while Doug and Vincent get the jib down? Pick up any open mooring ball and holler if you need a hand."

Kaitlin scrambled out the companionway hatch. Strider jumped down into the cabin and began to pull up floorboards. "Yep," he called out over the clatter of the diesel. "We have ourselves a leak about even with the foremast. Whatever we hit in the channel put a nasty crack in one of the planks. The pumps seem to be keeping up with the water, but we need to do something about it fast."

"Ship's moored up, captain," said Vincent a few minutes later. "How can we help?"

"First let me turn off that goddamned alarm bell. Give me a second, please." After a long moment, the alarm bell went silent.

Strider's unexpectedly smiling face appeared in the companionway. He held up a pair of wire cutters.

"There're two gray 5-gallon buckets in the lazarette with pieces of duck tape on them that used to say 'sawdust.' Can you grab those out of the locker for me and put them in one of the dinghies?"

"Yes, sir."

Strider rummaged in the locker opposite the head for a minute before producing two pairs of rubber gloves, a shrink-wrapped tube of a red rubbery substance, and a canvas bag. "Staff meeting in the cockpit right away, please!"

Everyone assembled quickly. Strider placed his hat over the compass, composed himself, and explained the situation. "We hit something hard and sharp on the sandbar that stretches across the entrance. We have a cracked plank, but we're not going to sink. If we do nothing at all, the pumps will keep up with the water as long as the battery lasts, and the battery will last three or four hours after the engine runs out of fuel. However, I'd rather sink than listen to the diesel for a week, so here's the plan: I'm going to dive down with some fine sawdust and let the waterflow draw it into the crack. As long as the crack is fine enough, the sawdust will get caught in it and the water will make it expand. Assuming we slow the leak down, I'll follow up with some underwater epoxy putty.

"Kaitlin, I'd like you to sit down in the cabin where the leak is. Place this block of wood against the hull and rap on it with this hammer so I can hear you under water. Don't make any noise until you see the leak slow down, but when you do, give me a series of taps that echoes the flow. When it's still flowing fast, I want to hear *taptaptaptaptap*. When it slows some more, give me *tap-tap-tap*. Once it slows down—assuming it does—to a minor drip—*tap ... tap ... tap*—you can stop and I'll know the sawdust has worked into the wood and expanded."

Strider unwrapped the red cylinder. "This is two-part epoxy putty," he explained. "It's red on the outside and gray on the inside." Strider took a pocketknife from its sheath on his rope belt and cut off two pieces. "Lenore and Walter, put these rubber gloves on and knead this stuff thoroughly so the gray and the red are *completely* mixed together. The gray is the hardener that acts on the red. It has an hour or so of working life before it stiffens up. Once we have the leak slowed down, I'll pack as much of this stuff in behind the sawdust as I can.

"Doug, can you sit in the dinghy and hand me sawdust or tools as I need them?"

Doug nodded.

"Micky Tomm, when I'm done with the epoxy putty, I want to tack a sheet of copper over the crack." Strider reached into the canvas bag. "Once I assess the damage, I'll give Doug some measurements. Use these shears to cut a piece of copper sheet off this roll. Goop one side of it up with this tube of caulking and we should be back in business.

"The rest of you should get in the second dinghy and go ashore. This is a special, beautiful place and there's no reason you should miss out on it just because…"

"No, Strider, we're staying here in case you need us. We…"

Strider waved his hand. "No need to let the meal get cold waiting for me to come to the table," he said. "I appreciate your loyalty, but there's no point. Go take a hike up the hill to the old lighthouse on the cliff, or have a drink at Pete's pub. Go! Enjoy! Captain's orders! We'll join you soon enough."

The first landing party was dispatched to the dock and repairs commenced. The frequency of Kaitlin's hammering stayed stubbornly fast at first, but the leak eventually began to slow. With a mask and snorkel and an underwater headlamp, Strider chiseled out a ten-inch sliver of fractured wood, packed in more sawdust, and followed it with epoxy. Kaitlin shut down the noisy engine, and Micky Tomm did an artful job cutting the copper patch. After an hour of diving under the boat to fix the copper in place with a border of small bronze nails, Strider ascended the boarding ladder and returned to the deck shivering and exhausted.

"Amazing work, Strider," Kaitlin said. "The leak's completely stopped as far as I can tell."

"One last thing … I almost forgot." Strider jumped into the dinghy and rowed over to the sandbar in the entrance channel. There he anchored, jumped overboard, and returned to the surface with a piece of heavy line in his hand. Soon after he climbed back aboard, the sound of chain rolling over the side of the dinghy reverberated through the harbour. A large anchor followed the last of it into the boat.

Strider returned to *The Metaphor* with his prize. "Why some dimwit left it on the sandbar is beyond me, but this is a nice, stainless steel anchor. It—and the stainless chain attached to it—are *very* expensive, and an excellent upgrade for the rusting, galvanized one I've been using. Some rich powerboater must have forgotten to tie it down and lost it overboard when they went blasting out the channel."

"What if they see it hanging on your bow?" asked Kaitlin.

"I hope they do," replied Strider. "Then I can talk to them about what it's going to cost to haul this boat out and pay the Man-O-War boatyard to replace that plank."

"You mean…?"

"This patch is probably fine for two or three months, but to fix it myself, I'd have to go back to Florida to find a do-it-yourself boatyard ... and that means crossing the Gulf Stream. I'm not taking this boat into deep water until she's properly repaired. Also, who better to do that job than the traditional wooden boat builders at Man-O-War Cay? They'll cut a plank from local Cuban mahogany and it'll be as good as the original. I just don't know how I'll afford it."

"Not any of our business," said Micky Tomm, "but how you make your living has been the subject of some quiet speculation this past week. You don't have to..."

Strider smiled gently and looked Micky Tomm in the eye. "That's okay. I have no secrets ... and I have no regular source of income, either. I explained to Kaitlin that I used to run occasional charters, but I have to be careful. This is not my country and I can't work here legally.

"But if you look up on top of that cliff, you'll see houses where there didn't used to be any — and where there *shouldn't* be any — but that's how it is. People sail in here, fall in love with the place, buy a piece of land, and start building their fantasy getaway houses. Before too long they'll be complaining about 'those horrible boaters' in the harbour and wondering why they can't have the whole place to themselves. It's a 'there goes the neighborhood' story no matter which side you're on. But a lot of Americans put down stakes here and they need people to caulk windows and hang ceiling fans and varnish floors. It'll take me three or four months to scrape the money together, but people know me here. There are worse places to work and worse people to work for." Strider shrugged.

"You know, Strider," said Micky Tomm. "You've been more than generous. I'd be honored to…"

"Thank you, Micky. I appreciate that more than you can know, but as soon as I had the setback—the leak—the cosmos gave me $4000 worth of anchor and chain. Maybe I'll sell it and maybe I'll use it, but at the risk of sounding like a superstitious old salt, I prefer to enjoy the irrational feeling that more good things are coming my way. I've got a hole in my ship, but in my experience, at least out here in these islands, I expect as much opportunity to pour in as seawater."

"Maybe my offer is that opportunity."

"Maybe, but I had a feeling back when I found you guys wandering on the beach at Moraine Cay. I decided not to charge you because I felt some larger good would come of it. I still feel that way. We've shared some wonderful moments. I don't want to sully that by exchanging money. There are other, more valuable forms of currency, and as far as that goes, I'm feeling pretty rich."

Micky Tomm shook his head. "I'm still not sure I understand."

"Let me reframe it. I just used two-part epoxy putty to patch the hole in my boat. When we mixed the red putty with the gray putty, we started a chemical reaction. The catalyst in one color acted on the chemicals in the other to make them start hardening. When you put the caulking on the back of the sheet of copper, you exposed the goop to the air. As long as that stuff was sealed up in the tube, it would have stayed sticky. Oxygen was the catalyst that sped up the reaction and caused it to start hardening.

"When we meet people—when we connect—we can interact in various ways. If your group had turned out to be a bunch of noisy college kids looking to drink on the beach, I would have rescued you for humanitarian reasons, accepted whatever tip you offered, and dropped you off at the Green Turtle Ferry Dock as quickly as I could. If you'd been a group of laid-back tourists who didn't need to get liquored up every day and just wanted to see the islands, I'd have offered you a schooner charter and tried to make some money in exchange for salvaging your trip. We might have had fun together, but cash would have been the catalyst that made that relationship happen. In your case, I felt you were all looking for something too big to name or understand—for a way to get closer to the Essential Absurdities. I'm no closer to holding the Mystery in my head than you are, but I wanted that shared interest—and not something material like money—to be the basis for our connection.

"Everyone wants to connect and engage so they can conduct more business. Connect and engage in the way most appropriate to each relationship. Do that successfully and the business stuff will somehow take care of itself. Watch that happen and you not only prosper, you get to marvel at the Mystery."

"Sounds great," said Doug, "but you still have a hole in your boat."

"We all do," said Strider, "and that's where great stories come from."

Dialects

With *The Metaphor* safely afloat, Strider cleaned up and accompanied the rest of his guests to shore. "This place," he explained, "has gotten a bit more civilized than it once was—or maybe less so, depending on how you define that. Now that the realtors have descended on it, I'm not so sure—but the first person to settle here was a sculpting professor from Smith College named Randolph Johnston who sailed here with his family in 1952. He established an art gallery and a bronze foundry—the busts in the sculpture garden in New Plymouth were all cast here—and his family continues to run the place. It's a perfect, natural harbour and quite an island art colony.

"Pete Johnston, Randolph's son, operates Pete's Pub down the beach from the bronze foundry, and up the hill is the old lighthouse. It's not grandiose like the one in Hopetown. It's just an old house built in 1899 that once had a beacon on it. The termites and the elements got to it, and the roof caved in decades ago. The government put up a solar powered electronic beacon next to the ruins—and that got wiped out by a hurricane—but it's worth a hike up there to see the view. Just below the light are two 'notches' in the coral. It's inspiring to watch the waves roll in there and smash against the cliffs at the bottom."

After dinner at Pete's Pub, the crew assembled on deck as had become their custom. The wind had fallen completely calm; not a ripple disturbed the water's surface. As the sky turned from purple to black, a dinghy came alongside *The Metaphor*. The young woman rowing it smiled silently, stowed her oars, and handed up a weathered wooden guitar case. A medium-sized white dog stepped across the seats to the bow and jumped nimbly under the rail to the deck.

"Everyone, this is Jane Geaux from the little yellow sailboat over there." Strider pointed across the lagoon. "Little Harbour's resident virtuoso. Vincent, tonight is your night; go get your instrument. I might even pull mine out from under the bunk. And the dog is Beethoven; you're going to love him."

Jane glided over the rail; she was obviously comfortable moving about on a boat. She looked each of the happiness delegates in the eye, pointed at her left palm where her name "Jane Geaux" was tattooed, placed her hands together again as if to offer a blessing, and then opened her hands as if to receive one from each person she greeted. Each of Strider's guests offered their name and she shook each of their hands.

She pointed at Beethoven, made a hugging sign to indicate that he was friendly, then put her fingers in her ears and shook her head.

"I think you've probably figured out that Jane is not a big talker," explained Strider, "but she's an amazing communicator."

"And Beethoven is deaf?" asked Audrey.

Jane nodded, then made a talking motion with her hand while waving it before everyone, signifying that the conversation should continue as it had before she arrived. She tapped on her ear to indicate she would listen.

"I know just what to talk about tonight," said Strider. "Here we are at an artists' colony, and we have three artists aboard, not counting Jane." Strider turned to Jane. "Kaitlin here is a very fine writer, Doug is an art teacher and a graphic designer, and Vincent is our musician."

Jane smiled and nodded.

"We've talked about the thinking behind stories, how to tell them, how to take them apart, how to move from data to storytelling…"

Jane stuck out her lower lip, pantomimed playing a sad violin, pointed to Strider, made more talking motions with her hand, and shook her head sympathetically.

The Happiness Congress laughed out loud. "And this is our *eighth* night aboard!" exclaimed Doug.

Strider shook his head and continued. "So we've talked about storytelling, but mostly about variants of its literal meaning—story *telling*. We communicate in so many other ways."

Beethoven began to circulate among the guests, looking for head scratches and handouts. Lenore looked uncomfortable. Jane tapped him to get his attention and called him away with a simple hand signal.

"As I was saying," said Strider, "if you want to see a true 'connection ballet,' catch this wonderful dance between a dog who doesn't hear and an owner who doesn't speak. Jane, can you show us some of Beethoven's super powers?"

Jane smiled with pride. From her seat on the deck, using hand gestures and facial expressions, she guided Beethoven through a series of circles, rollovers, and poses. When she was finished, she opened her arms to receive him. The dog stepped over to her and buried his head between her breasts.

Jane bowed her head as the guests applauded.

"So much of storytelling is non-verbal—as Jane and Beethoven so aptly demonstrate. Even animals read faces and hand gestures. We all do this naturally—though few of us are called by circumstance to polish it to such a high art.

"Doug, I've been watching you commune with your sketchbook this whole trip. Are you willing to share your art with us?"

Doug rose silently, climbed below deck, and returned with a black book. The Happiness Congress passed it around. Inside were swirling designs reminiscent of seashells. Ribbons of penciled color flowed across the pages with washes of turquoise and green watercolor.

"This is amazing work, Doug," said Micky Tomm.

"I'm impressed," said Walter.

"Even *I* like it," said Lenore, "and I usually don't *get* art—especially abstract stuff."

Jane placed a hand over her heart and nodded vigorously.

"Here we have these images," said Strider, "of nothing in particular. I see seashells… *maybe*… and maybe some geometric shapes that *could be* sails… and perhaps some water currents and sunset clouds, but I could be completely wrong; I might be projecting all of that."

Doug shrugged. "I have no idea what any of this is. I just pull out the paints and pencils and the rest is completely unconscious."

"And yet, everyone here has been immersed in the same symbolic stew for the past week. All of us—even Lenore who doesn't *get* art—got your art. You let your subconscious bubble up and guide your eye. What we have on the paper is clearly *authentic;* it's pure storytelling—even if it's abstract."

Doug thought for a moment. "I spoke a few days ago about how people pay much more for an original painting than they will for a poster print of the same piece. The story we discussed of the artist's *physical* relationship with the piece is compelling, but I think you're onto something deeper, Strider. People look for *authenticity* in art—and what they want to see is that the artist wasn't thinking about technique or how to make something that would look great in a billionaire's living room or sell a hundred copies at an art show. If the art looks like a product, if it looks like it was consciously intended to produce a business result, we won't value it as highly."

"Every piece of true art is a nude portrait of its creator's subconscious," said Strider.

"That's all fine and dandy," said Doug, "but not all art is abstract. What about artists like Christo and Jeanne-Claude who surrounded those islands in Miami with pink fabric and hung that curtain between two mountains in Colorado? What about Andy Warhol's soup cans and Duchamp's urinal? What about photographic art that aims to capture the literal?"

Strider raised an eyebrow. "Walter, you're missing your cue. Ask me the question."

"Strider." Walter spoke slowly and deliberately. "What the hell are you getting at?"

"Art—at least authentic art—brings some aspect of the subconscious world into the conscious world; otherwise we can call it 'crafts' or 'design,'" explained Strider. "Christo looked at those natural landscapes and in his mind's eye, he started painting on top of them. As I understand it, he made a lot of canvas paintings of those landscapes both before and after he painted *on* them. Christo understood—as did Duchamp and Warhol—that art will invariably connect with some people and not with others; the collective impression—the fact that some people love it and others don't—suggests that the Essential Absurdities are involved. And art photographers strive to capture extraordinary images that move us in unusual ways; they're just hunting for stories like any other artist hunts for stories. People love to debate about the immeasurable, unknowable nature of human expression. Ask a fourteen-year-old boy about art and he'll show you his black light 'skull-with-two-electric guitars-crossed-behind-it' poster. Ask an art teacher and you'll find they regard much of the stuff that gets popular acclaim as 'bubblegum.' One could argue that the more you understand about the mechanical processes through which art is realized, the better able you are to discern 'true artistic authenticity.' People have this notion of 'creative integrity,' but if the artist connects with the viewer, I think that's valid, even if the viewer is a philistine. It's not the art itself, but the *connection* that should be used as a yardstick."

"Still waiting," said Walter.

"We'll get there," replied Strider. "We always do."

Strider continued. "So you mentioned you're also into graphic design, Doug. What's the difference? You called it 'putting art to work.'"

"When I design a logo or typeset a page or design an ad, I have a specific message I'm trying to convey. My words and color choices and type choices may have their roots in subconscious or conscious associations, but my job is to communicate a message. I want people to feel a certain way about the content and I have factual data to communicate—something is on sale or XYZ product is superior. When I create fine art, I let the art create itself; when I *design* something, I want the viewer to feel nostalgic or that the company is professional, or that the product is natural or innovative."

"So let's look at the word 'design,'" suggested Strider. "What is a 'sign?'"

Doug pondered the question for a moment before answering. "A sign is an image with a meaning attached to it. A red octagon means 'stop,' but a sign could be a photograph or a word set in a certain typeface."

"Excellent," said Strider. "So what does the prefix 'de-' mean? Think of words like 'deconstruct' and 'decontaminate' and 'detoxify.'"

"It means 'to take apart,' 'to break down.'"

"So a de-signer is…?"

"Someone who understands the relationship between symbols and meanings," declared Doug. "A person who takes signs apart and works with their meanings can put messages together in strategic ways—which ties directly to storytelling!"

"So Walter, do you see the connection?"

"Yes! Art and design are *dialects* of storytelling—visual storytelling. Whether they're pure subconscious expression or evocative images that inspire connection and engagement, they work the same way as written or spoken storytelling."

Strider raised a finger. "Let's look at design from the perspective of conflict and transformation."

Micky Tomm stepped in. "A design—an ad or a logo or a campaign—is intended to produce a certain business result, a transformation. It tries to sell more products or show that someone's service is superior to their competitor's service. That competition and the need to get the word out are some of the conflicts."

"You're almost there," said Strider, "but that misconception ruins ninety-eight percent of the advertising we see. Even if you sell the benefits instead of the features, people can't connect with products or services. What *do* they connect with?"

"People!" said Audrey. "People connect with *people*. People engage with *people*—which means that an effective design connects viewers to the people behind a product or service. Stories are about *people*."

"And what part of storytelling are those people responsible for delivering?"

"Magic," said Walter. "Design *demonstrates* that the people behind the product are funny or innovative or sincere—that they're human and caring and worthy of having a relationship with—that they have the magic to deliver the desired transformation to their customers."

"So why not just *talk* about how wonderful the business is? Why not *tell* the story?" asked Strider.

"Because it takes too long," replied Audrey. "By the time you finish reading or listening, your subconscious has probably opened the garbage chute and dumped the message. Traditional storytelling works when people are already receptive to reading and listening—when they take a class or attend a lecture or take part in a conversation. But if you want to say, 'Hey you! I have a message for you,' design is the can-opener you need."

Doug closed his eyes and thought for a minute. "Which is why we designers are always taught, 'Show; don't tell.' You know, I've always thought of design as the process of building ads and logos and websites and other pieces of media. I've been teaching art at a public junior high school for years because businesses won't pay much for a brochure or a business card. But now I realize I've been selling the features instead of the benefits. It doesn't matter how many hours it takes me to create a logo. If that logo becomes the face of a business and it helps them build relationships with millions of customers…"

"Yes," said Kaitlin, "it's worth more than $99."

Doug's eyes lit up. "So I am a magician who creates the road to *transformation*. I help businesses understand what their stories are, and I help them tell those stories in ways that foster connection and engagement, and in ways that help them navigate through the conflicts they face."

"Can I offer you some advice — a story shift?" asked Micky Tomm.

"Sure," said Doug.

"My company doesn't hire 'graphic designers.' Most of the people who call themselves that are glorified software owners. We don't care about your skills with digital photo retouching or the fact that you bootlegged five thousand typefaces. Art schools churn out production monkeys by the millions, and they'll all work for nothing because they're strangled with student debt. Who we do hire are *marketing firms* — companies and consultants that have a track record of producing *results* — and most of the time, they have the same technical qualifications as the so-called 'designers.' Try a title change and multiply your rate by four."

"And here we have this idea of 'marketing,'" noted Strider. "Is there any difference between a 'mark' and a 'sign?'"

"I think about $75 an hour," laughed Doug.

"Okay, let's move on. I believe Doug has achieved transformation. Vincent, tune up."

Jane retrieved a weather-beaten old guitar from its case and began to tune up.

"What do you like to play?" asked Vincent.

Jane shrugged and indicated that Vincent should start and she'd follow.

"Let's warm up on a little blues," Vincent suggested. He began to play and Jane jumped in immediately with an artful solo.

"You're good," said Vincent, *"really* good."

Jane smiled and bowed her head.

When Jane finished her solo, she nodded to Vincent to take a turn. As he created his melody, she stayed underneath him, filling in the gaps between his phrases without ever stepping on top of him. The tempo never wavered. The happiness delegates compulsively tapped their feet.

Realizing he was in the presence of an accomplished player, Vincent switched to a ballad—"Round Midnight," by Thelonious Monk. Together they improvised and accompanied one another, leaving space, phrasing, weaving their melodies in and out of the harmony. At the end, on the song's final four bars, they looked each other in the eyes, and in perfect synchronization, they slowed the song down gradually and let the last chord ring.

"My guitar is definitely staying in the cabin tonight," declared Strider. "That was marvelous."

Vincent and Jane exchanged a warm hug until Beethoven decided he wanted in on the action. Everyone laughed. Beethoven rolled on his back and kicked his legs in the air with joy.

"Now take that apart, Vincent," said Strider. "What just happened in storytelling terms?"

"Jane and I share a common language—music."

Jane nodded enthusiastically.

"In this case, we both speak jazz—which means we know pieces from a standard repertoire that jazz musicians play everywhere in the world. Some of the tunes are old Broadway show tunes; others are old favorites by composers like Duke Ellington and Cole Porter."

"So give me conflict, transformation, authenticity, and magic," said Strider.

Doug contemplated the question. "The conflict," he began, "is that some of these songs have complicated chord changes; the keys change all over the place. When you improvise over them, you have to do more than just blow a bunch of notes. You need to play a melody that works with whatever sequence of chords is being played at any given moment, and you want to play a melody that's reminiscent of the song in some way. The soloist's goal is to 'play the tune, not just the changes.' Am I right, Jane?"

Jane raised a thumb of agreement.

"So we have this music which has a certain degree of harmonic sophistication to it, and we have a lot of freedom to substitute chords and change things around as long as we stay within certain intuitive boundaries; it still has to sound like the tune. Some music theory heads treat these songs like a video game; the chords come flying along and they 'shoot them down' with the right scale or arpeggio, but you can teach a computer to do that. Our challenge is to master the technical aspects of the tune without being mechanical or mathematical. It's a lot like when you speak, you can't be thinking, *I'm going to use an adjective followed by a noun followed by a verb.* If you want to communicate eloquently, you develop a certain facility with the language and you just go for it. So the challenge—the conflict—is to have a meaningful musical conversation that transcends the technical, mathematical, grammatical structure of the tune."

"I'm not a jazz aficionado," admitted Strider, "but I'm guessing that if jazz is a language, an authentic speaker would use certain melodic phrases and chord progressions that reflect some familiarity with the idiom. For example, a classical player might have the technique and the theory down, but…"

"Their improvised solo would reveal that they'd never listened to Charlie Parker and John Coltrane and Wes Montgomery and many others," said Doug. "It wouldn't be authentic."

"So the *magic* is your musicality—the combination of musical awareness and technique that allows you to speak the language," said Strider. "The transformation is?"

"It seems like it should be obvious," said Vincent, "but…"

"Even I can see it," said Lenore. "The transformation is that you sat down with a stranger—with someone you'd never played with before—with someone you can't have a spoken exchange with—and you had a meaningful conversation. You connected and engaged on a completely non-verbal level."

"And even though none of us appears to know much about jazz, you carried us with you," added Audrey. "We were all touched by your playing. Whatever was happening intellectually and technically was not part of our experience. We all engaged and there's no rational, scientific explanation I can think of that would explain that."

"Does this only work for jazz musicians," asked Walter, "or is there a way we can all tap into this?"

"I think I can answer that," said Vincent. "A musical group is just another kind of team. If everyone does their job, the work gets done and the *functional objective* gets met. But effective teams 'play music' together. They understand the language and they have the skills and insights; they communicate on a level that can't always be explained, and the work they produce is—as the saying goes—more than the sum of its parts."

The Story Story

Beethoven began to whine and paw Jane's leg. She pointed toward shore, packed up her guitar, and after a round of hugs, she boarded her dinghy and rowed her companion toward the beach to relieve himself.

Strider yawned. "Kaitlin, why don't you wrap up for us?"

"Okay, folks," she began. "Though it might surprise some of you to hear it, tonight's theme was—once again—storytelling."

"Damn, I'm getting predictable in my old age!" complained Strider.

"We started with art and design. On one side of the spectrum, we have expression driven by the subconscious—which we call 'fine art.' But we also have 'design,' which is a form of visual storytelling. A *de-signer* is someone who understands the relationship between symbols and meanings—which implies that an effective designer knows how to create visual messages that communicate authenticity, value, and magic. Given the sheer quantity of messages we're bombarded by in our environment and the sheer quantity of people who may know how to use graphic tools but have no knowledge of storytelling, true designers—marketers—have a powerful and important role to play in society and business.

"We also decided that Doug should use this story to quadruple his prices. I hope you all booked his services before our chat this evening.

"Then we listened to Vincent play music with Jane, and came to the realization that music, like art, is another dialect of storytelling. Musical connection is a potent metaphor for professional teamwork that doesn't just get the job done; it connects and engages—which makes me think that musical workshops—even simple ones that involve teaching people to play drums and sing harmony—could be useful in a professional environment. If the only thing participants get out of it is listening skills, the world might become a more civilized and productive place.

"To sum up, almost any form of human interaction from art to music to sex is probably a form of storytelling as long as its goal is to create a shared experience—a connection."

The Happiness Congress delegates lay back on the deck and watched the brilliant arm of the Milky Way stretch across the night sky. Hardly a word was spoken. All knew their time aboard *The Metaphor* was drawing to a close.

After some time, Strider put his finger to his lips. "Listen carefully," he whispered. "Hear that singing?"

The Happiness Congress nodded. A strange, wordless, melodic voice carried across the still water.

"There's no wind so the sound travels. That's Jane Geaux. She can't speak a word, but she sings in her sleep. It's the purest fine art you'll ever experience."

Blue Holes

The Happiness Congress spent the day exploring Little Harbour. They visited the bronze sculpture foundry, hiked the path through the scrub to the old lighthouse, swam and watched sea turtles in the lagoon, and explored the caves at its north side. One of Strider's friends owned a small powerboat. He led a snorkeling party to the blue hole in the Bight of Old Robinson—a "bottomless lake" fifty feet wide that lay beneath ten feet of water adjacent to the shore of Great Abaco.

That night, Strider felt it best to retire early. "Sometimes the best thing you can do for a good story is sleep on it. Reflect on it. Let it age. We have covered some distance—both physically and conceptually. Tomorrow, we'll leave on the rising tide and have a full day of sailing to get back to Marsh Harbour."

"What about Treasure Cay?" asked Lenore. "That's our airport."

"Most of the planes land at both airports, but if they won't switch for you, it's a short taxi ride. I might even be able to get a friend to haul you over there if her truck is working.

"But if it's all the same to you, when you fly home to work, I'll be doing the same thing. I need to get this ship back to Little Harbour so I can start hanging sheetrock and plastering walls and building steps and other fun stuff. Getting the resources together to haul this boat and replace that broken plank is going to take some doing. If I can drop you off at the Abaco Beach Resort, it'll save me some sailing time.

"Also, when you step out of this experience into a traditional tourist setting with a pool bar and a calypso band, you'll *marvel* at how different people can have vastly different experiences in the same place."

"I guess that's our story lesson for tonight?" asked Kaitlin.

"I recall a time when I got stuck out in the Gulf Stream in a gale on a small boat one very cold January night," said Strider. "The seas were big and sloppy—coming from every direction—and we watched a huge cruise ship pass way too close for comfort; I'm sure their radar couldn't see us in those big seas. I was wet and cold and tired and had lashed myself into the cockpit. When I looked up at the stern of the ship, I saw flashing colored lights and people *dancing*. How's *that* for experience contrast?"

Strider placed his hat over the compass and yawned. "Let me tell you the lesson in that; it's an important one. Other people will see and experience the world in ways you can't imagine. You might be fighting for survival in the same place and time that they're fighting to get to the bar for a third margarita, but their experience is no less valid or real. We can easily convince ourselves that the story of how we used a compass to navigate through an island wilderness is *better* than the story of how Mary and John spent a week getting hammered on a pair of chaise lounges at the hotel. We can point to the places we saw and the depth of our discussions and get snobby about what a waste it is to come here and nap by a swimming pool within sight of these clear waters. But if Mary and John get a break from their routines and go home rested, what is it to us? Most people don't go on vacation expecting to *invest* in their stories; they expect to *divest* themselves *from* their stories. The word 'vacation' refers to an emptying process. In fact, *you all* are the nut jobs who took ten days off work to fill up on experience."

"I think I've lost sight of exactly why I came out here," said Walter. "When I arrived, all I knew was that I was one of seven people selected by Houston Gibson King, Ph.D. to participate in a happiness workshop on a small island. I assumed I'd sit with some interesting people in front of a blackboard and maybe chant on the beach at night—I don't know. But after ending up here aboard *The Metaphor*, it's like I was swimming along and suddenly got sucked down into a blue hole, only to be ejected into some alien world."

"So, I finally get to turn the tables on you, Walter. What are you saying? How can we use that?"

Walter smiled. "I guess what I'm saying is that I put a lot into this experience and got a lot out of it. This has been life-changing. But if you'd asked me two weeks ago if I wanted to go drink Coronas by a hotel pool for ten days, I'd have been all over that. Today that seems like an utter waste of time. I can see how easy it would be to get judgmental about the ways people invest—or don't invest—in their stories."

"A little piece of the Mystery before I go down to my bunk:" offered Strider. "You—we all—were here at this place and time because this was the right time and place for us all to be. Nobody whined about the 'hardships' of living on board a boat—and they're very real compared to the way most of you probably live your day-to-day lives. Everyone here was *ready*. Maybe that's because Dr. King had good taste, and maybe that's just because the Universe thought it was right. When those people lounging by the pool are ready for whatever version of this *they're* ready for, they'll get sucked into the blue hole that's right for them and expelled into the alien world that's right for them."

Walter reflected on Strider's words.

"You don't have to save anyone," Strider continued. "You don't need to be the one abducting people and dropping them into your personal blue hole of salvation. Live a rich, happy, healthy, loving story of your own—which is the world's hardest and easiest thing to do. Those who are ready to find their own stories will find their own way. Maybe they'll even ask you for directions."

Micky Tomm spoke up. "A business mentor gave me some advice I've always appreciated. He told me never to hand anyone a business card unless they ask for one. In terms of our discussion, I think he meant that our stories, not our credentials, should be our calling cards."

"Be a lighthouse," said Audrey. "Let the ships do their own navigating. The ones headed for your port will see your light and pay attention."

"Listen to all the nautical metaphors," chuckled Strider. "I have wrecked you all; none of you will ever be popular at a party again." He turned and descended the steps to his bunk.

The Long, Strange Trip

*I*n the morning, Strider made coffee and got the ship under weigh early. By and by, the Happiness Congress arose and gathered in the cockpit. Strider turned the wheel over to Kaitlin while he cooked eggs and pancakes. The ship made steady progress under a light, easterly breeze.

Audrey looked at Strider with an uncomfortable expression. "Before we finish our journey together, I've got one more take on this whole Essential Absurdities thing—but I don't think you're going to like it much; I'm not sure any of us are. I know I don't."

"My dear Audrey." Strider paused and smiled. "Everything we've talked about is inferential—speculative. We didn't come here to find answers; we're here to get lost in the mystery. If you have something to add to the discussion, by all means…"

Audrey took a deep breath. "Well, as a psychologist I deal with a lot of mental illness, and a lot of mental illness is related to problems with brain chemistry. When I was working on my Ph.D., I studied with a neurologist who was convinced that everything we experience as meaningful—love, connection, peace, stress, the thrill of victory—what you call "The Essential Absurdities"—is nothing more than a series of hormone rushes in our brains. Dr. Pearse didn't see any part of human experience as speculative or mysterious. He saw it all as measurable, predictable, and explicable.

"We've been drilling deep into 'the power and magic of storytelling,' but part of me is worried that all we're doing is finding clever ways to induce hormone production in our brains. It *feels* so magnificent, but what if it's just a high? What if all we are is…?" Audrey stopped and ended with a shrug.

Strider smiled. "A series of chemical reactions? Micky Tomm, what's the conflict here?"

"Why not ask Audrey? I mean…"

"Because Audrey's the one having the conflict. What's easier: seeing your own conflicts or your friend's?"

"I get it." Micky Tomm nodded.

Audrey smiled her agreement.

Micky took a sip of coffee. "I think the conflict is an existential crisis. We've been having this amazing, powerful experience and producing all these deep revelations. What if this turned out to be a chemical hoax—some sort of movie or dream we'll wake up from? Wouldn't that just *suck?*"

The rest of the happiness delegates chuckled and nodded.

Strider raised the brim of his hat with a finger. "Lenore—transformation, please."

"I think the conflict is that the very idea of *meaning* is at stake." Lenore paused for a moment and closed her eyes to think. "If brain chemistry theory reduces human experience to a predictable set of rules and axioms, we're all robots—or hormone addicts. The hoped-for transformation is that we need to rescue the joy—no, not just the joy, but the whole spectrum—of human experience. We don't want to feel like we're mistaking some story we create out of protein chains for real life. We want to experience life fully without being skeptical of our perceptions. Wow! I'm getting pretty twisted up here, but that's what I'm coming up with."

"I think you nailed it," offered Kaitlin.

"Yeah," said Doug. "You got it."

"Good," said Strider. "All good stuff.

"So I'd say we're looking for some magic now—for a brisk wind to blow this ship home to the safe port of rich and full life experience. Audrey, why don't you explain—hopefully without having to draw befuddling diagrams of molecules—how some of this brain chemistry works."

Audrey assumed Kaitlin's customary speaking place behind the foremast. "What struck me was the idea that we are incredibly social beings. If we see someone smile, we smile. If we see someone yawn, we yawn. If someone tells us a story, especially a story that resonates with our own needs and feelings—with our own search for meaning—we *experience* that story. Think of storytelling as a way to transfer not just intellectual ideas and codified moral values, but actual experiences from one person to another.

"But what if the experience supposedly being transferred is just a particular combination of chemicals connected to a few choice word combinations? I don't like the idea that my deepest and most powerful experiences could theoretically be reproduced—or even created from scratch—in a laboratory."

"So sound this out," encouraged Strider. "Tell us how it works."

"A number of physiological and environmental factors affect human experience. Before we even get into brain chemistry, consider the effects of low or high blood sugar. Estrogen and progesterone levels fluctuate throughout a woman's monthly cycle and affect moods and outlook. Strider, you called yourself a 'human barometer'; the atmospheric pressure affects your energy and awareness levels. If you're too hot or too cold or suffering from a fever, those conditions can dramatically color your experiences. Add to these environmental factors some interesting hormones:

"Start with endorphins. These are the chemicals that mask pain. They can give you a 'runner's high' or a sense of satisfaction after a tough workout or passionate sexual activity. If you feel euphoria, that's largely the result of endorphins. Also interesting is that stress—not too much stress, but the right amount of physical or emotional stress—also produces endorphins.

"Then there's dopamine. When you 'feel good' after accomplishing a goal—whether that's coming back to the boat with a speared grouper or nailing a business presentation—that's dopamine at work. Dopamine does a lot of its job *before* we accomplish our goals. It encourages us to act, either to achieve something or to avoid some consequences. Dopamine makes us feel satisfied after a meal, excited when our team scores a goal, or super-up if we use drugs like amphetamines and cocaine that squeeze more dopamine out of our brain. The rush you feel when you do something daring like skydiving or sailing along with the boat heeled over—that's dopamine, too. The paradox with dopamine is the same as with endorphins; moments of stress are also associated with dopamine production. Roller coasters and carnival rides are stressful, but people who love them get off on the dopamine rush.

"Dopamine may explain why you sailed *The Metaphor* into Green Turtle Cay instead of turning on the motor, Strider. The risk and the challenge and the final accomplishment come with chemical rewards that wouldn't be received if the engine were running.

"Think of endorphins and dopamine as 'motivation hormones.' Successful people work their way toward big goals by rewarding themselves with the dopamine hits that come from achieving incremental small ones. Some people use stress as a motivator. I, for one, can't get much of anything done unless I have an approaching deadline. A brain scientist would say I use the deadline stress to trigger the dopamine that motivates me to get the job done."

Walter waved his hand and smiled.

Audrey turned to face him. "So, Walter, Mr. Skeptic, you want to know how this connects to storytelling. My neurology professor would say that when I tell you a story, when I present you with an authentic conflict, you experience a slight degree of stress. Intellectually, you understand that you're on the outside just listening to my story, but if you're engaged, part of your brain experiences stress and triggers small amounts of endorphins and dopamine. Because we're all hardwired for empathy, we respond chemically to *other* people's stories—and when we do, we imagine we've had this powerful, mystical transference of experience and 'energy.' Dr. Pearse would say you got high off my words and decided to validate that experience by labeling it 'meaningful.'

"Okay." Walter looked back at Audrey. "But what…?"

"Hold that thought if you will, Walter. I want to go through a few more chemicals. Kaitlin, are you taking notes?"

Kaitlin nodded.

"The next two hormones are serotonin and oxytocin.

"Serotonin is the 'Zen master' hormone. It produces feelings of peace and calm. It promotes feelings of gratitude toward people or spiritual forces you believe have supported or encouraged you. There's a drug called "Ecstasy" that causes your brain to release its full supply of serotonin. Users feel pretty depressed after the effects wear off, but they experience extreme peace and happiness while it's working. And remember, these experiences aren't caused by the actual chemicals in the drug; they're caused by an overdose of your own brain chemistry. When you're sitting on a mountaintop or hiking in the redwood forest or riding a wooden boat across a transparent turquoise sea, that rush of wonder and peace you feel—that's serotonin.

"Psychedelic drugs like LSD and 'magic mushrooms' work directly on the serotonin receptors in the brain—which is why users tell stories of 'timelessness and inner peace and oneness with the world.' In 1962, Harvard researchers gave divinity students psilocybin to see if the sacred setting combined with drugs would induce a mystical experience. Half of the twenty subjects were given a placebo. Nine of the students who received the drug went on to pursue ministry work as opposed to none of the placebo subjects. Most called the experiment one of the most important experiences of their lives, even if their drug trip was traumatic.

"On to happy hormone number four: When you share stories with a group of people at a workshop or on a sailing adventure, or survive a battle with fellow soldiers in a trench, when your church or your Rotary club or your family triggers that enormous sense of connection and community, the hormone responsible for that feeling is oxytocin. Head over heels in love? Oxytocin.

"Serotonin and oxytocin are the 'social hormones.' Our group has developed a special camaraderie during the short, intense time we've shared aboard *The Metaphor*. We've become a family of sorts, and we've all been affected by the magical setting, but Dr. Pearse would say we're all high on serotonin and oxytocin. The 'special experiences' and the 'special connections' are nothing more than chemical reactions that have evolved to help us survive and reproduce."

"That *is* kind of a bummer," agreed Walter. "We're having these transcendent experiences and sharing this amazing sense that being here together was somehow 'meant to be.' I'd hate to think all this philosophizing and storytelling and all the 'kumbaya' moments are just brain farts."

Vincent took a deep breath. "So when I play my guitar and Strider sails his boat and Lenore solves a math problem, when Walter gets a standing ovation and Doug makes a piece of art, the real meaning behind why we love what we do and get off on sharing it is all just *chemistry?*"

Strider smiled confidently and motioned for Audrey to continue. "I have just a few more.

"One, interestingly enough, is testosterone — and this applies to men and women; we ladies make it with our ovaries. Testosterone is linked to aggressive behavior and sexual attraction, but it's also linked to the thrill of victory. This notion of 'winning' is important to us. Subjects were invited to participate in a phony contest where they were asked to perform some set of physical actions. Winners were chosen at random, and then testosterone levels were measured after the supposed winners and losers were given the results. The winners all showed increased levels. So when you tell a story and your character overcomes the conflict, your listeners all get a testosterone boost. A story with multiple conflicts and multiple wins is just a multiple orgasm for the brain.

"The last one I'll bother with—and there are many more—is cortisol, the stress hormone which is triggered by adrenaline. If you're preparing to do something dangerous or unpleasant, your cortisol levels will be elevated. Students who are comfortable taking tests actually do better because the stress, or challenge, boosts their performance; the cortisol inspires a dopamine blast that helps them perform. Low anxiety students are pushed up into the 'sweet spot.' High-anxiety students are already stressed; the added stress of sitting down to take the exam pushes them over the threshold into a negative relationship between cortisol and performance. Again, we see this odd relationship between stress and performance. Stress—cortisol—is a dopamine trigger. People who suffer from depression, chronic worriers, and people who endure ongoing stressful circumstances like abusive relationships and toxic work environments—they drip cortisol all the time, which is extremely unhealthy. But mostly, cortisol is a sign that you're paying attention. We respond to conflict, both in life and in a story. How can we avoid a threat? How can we attain higher social status? How can we appease our appetite? How can we find a mate? If there's no conflict, there's no cortisol and we keep looking around for something worth focusing on.

So when you hear a story or ride a rollercoaster or skydive—where the odds are pretty good that you're going to end up in one piece—you experience stress, which gives you an adrenaline rush. Adrenaline produces cortisol. Cortisol produces dopamine. You might get a shot of endorphins to mask the pain if the story or experience mimics something really threatening. Listen to an exciting story with friends at a campfire and you'll get oxytocin and serotonin. And when the conflict is resolved, it's testosterone time. All the important parts of a story—conflict and transformation, magic and authenticity—can be linked to hormones.

Could it be that all we do with our lives—with our relationships and passions and jobs and the places we go and things we do—could it all just be an endless pursuit of chemical reward?"

Strider laughed gently. "That was marvelous, Audrey. Let me offer you some perspective.

"First, you're probably right, but you're seeing one tree in the whole forest. You've given us a fascinating new way to look at stories, but what good does it do to secrete a lot of cortisol over the notion that you're addicted to dopamine?"

"That sounds like a non-essential absurdity if ever there was one," joked Doug.

Audrey smiled weakly.

"Moreover, take the whole 'chemistry' perspective even further," continued Strider. "Your whole body—including your brain—is 93% oxygen, carbon, and hydrogen. Play games with that hydrogen and oxygen; you're 80% water. Look out at the stars and you don't qualify as a dust speck. Humans have been around for hardly a moment of this planet's history. And what tiny fraction of that instant of time do any of us get to spend here? If you want depressing perspectives on existence, you don't need to delve into anything as sophisticated as brain chemistry.

"And beyond that, so what? What if we *are* all chemical junkies? Even figuring that out and how it works only produces more chemical results. If your theory is true, it's an inescapable condition of being alive. But let me ask you: is it such a horrible prison?"

Audrey crossed her arms. "I just don't like the idea that this beautiful, transcendent, meaningful, shared experience might not be real—that all these good feelings might just be…"

"Go back to 'I am not that,'" suggested Strider. "Let's say the camaraderie we feel is just the result of us collectively being amped up on oxytocin. *Who* is it that has the elevated hormone levels? Who or what is it that's trying to decide whether or not the experience is meaningful? Maybe your brain is stewing in pleasure juice right now. Great! Whose brain? Yours. Who is you? It can't be *your* brain if *you're* observing *your* brain's condition.

"'Real' is one of the Essential Absurdities; you can't define it in any concrete way if you try. Your senses are limited. And any thoughts you have about the nature of reality can probably be reduced to brain chemistry anyway!"

"Okay, Strider," conceded Audrey. "Maybe it is a bit silly, but you seem kind of excited about this idea."

"Let me throw this one at Walter before he gets the jump on me. Walter, how can you use brain chemistry in your speeches? How can Kaitlin use it in her writing? Think about it for a minute if you need to."

Walter grabbed his chin with a thumb and forefinger and closed his eyes before replying. "I'm not sure, but what makes a story authentic is its ability to inspire a listener to feel that the story conflict is relevant to them. If you're telling a story and that story feels meaningful to me — if it speaks to some truth I'm trying to unlock or addresses some conflict I'm facing in my own life — or imagine facing — it will probably inspire a chemical reaction in my brain. I'll get a bigger rush of stress hormones and a bigger rush of dopamine. I'll feel connected to you as a speaker — like you 'get' me — and that will inspire an oxytocin rush. If your story teaches me to overcome conflict in my own life and I know what I need to do to take control, I'll feel more peaceful ... sorry, which hormone was that again?"

"Serotonin," said Audrey.

"Right," continued Walter, "and maybe there'll be a bigger testosterone blast when the storyteller's win becomes my win. I'll feel powerful and capable…

"But I'm not sure how to craft a story so it accomplishes that."

Kaitlin jumped in. "This is all new to me, but Walter, you started with authenticity, and I think intuitively you were onto something. If you're up there talking about yourself, the audience will tune you out. Why? No hormone rush. If you engage them—if you capture their attention with a story that's all about them—you'll know the chemicals are flowing because their eyes and ears will be directed at you. If you're a writer, you won't be there with your reader, but you hope they can't resist turning the page. They can't leave a powerful story or chapter unresolved because that would deprive them of that feelgood hormone blast that comes with resolution."

"Good," said Strider. "And this is a new perspective for me, too, but doesn't it make sense that a story could be too light or too heavy on conflict to produce the thrill that comes with a good dopamine rush? Could a resolution be too humdrum to deliver a good chemical reward? Maybe you could create a story that engages a group of listeners in a way that makes them feel bonded together because they've heard and understood it together while the rest of the world hasn't? Or maybe you could tell a story in a unique setting that creates that 'different world' experience.

Under the right environmental conditions, the oxytocin flows and the social bonds form. Then the community comfort and the pleasant setting deliver that peaceful serotonin high."

"I've been on executive retreats with small groups in beautiful settings," offered Micky Tomm. "Though the purposes of the workshops and the backgrounds of the attendees have been quite different from what they are in our Happiness Congress, the last night is always a tear-jerker. You feel like you're leaving a little haven full of life-changing friends, even though you met them all only a few days before."

"And maybe," offered Vincent, "that 'multiple voices' experience where you're of two minds at once — that 'quantum mechanics of consciousness' where the devil on one shoulder tells you to jump and the angel on the other tells you to hang on — maybe that's one part of your brain trying to cope with too much cortisol and another, entirely separate part of your brain responding to the adrenaline and the endorphins that help you survive."

"We could probably write a book on this," said Strider, "but I'll bet someone already has. It doesn't sound far-fetched that a storyteller could read up on some research into what kinds of words and scenarios are thought to produce what kinds of chemical responses in listeners' brains. And theoretically, if you observe the way people react to your stories and have a basic understanding of what dopamine and cortisol and serotonin and the other chemicals do, it won't matter whether or not you categorize what you see correctly. All you need to know is that stress, motivation, social bonding, and focus can be inspired by stories. See what words, hand gestures, images, notes, or mathematical formulas produce the strongest reactions in the people who you want to receive your messages."

"I love this," said Lenore. "My tribe speaks geek. Some of them aren't open to the 'spiritual side' of storytelling and the Essential Absurdities; they don't think that way. I see this as a quantifiable, empirical way to approach the 'science' of connection and engagement. If you want to say something is 'meaningful' and someone else wants to say it's 'a stimulus that provokes a dopamine secretion,' who cares? It sounds a little too academic—even for me—but if it gets the connection job done…"

Strider bowed and crossed his hands over his heart. "Now as long as you all are satisfied that the existential crisis has passed and the story of our warm fuzzies is valid, real, meaningful, and shared—at least sufficiently so that we can return to enjoying it—I vote we turn this over to Kaitlin for summary and completion."

"I second the motion," said Micky Tomm with a chuckle.

Audrey smiled and surrendered her position at the base of the foremast to Kaitlin.

"I think Audrey covered all the technical ground, so I'm going to keep my summary short and simple," said Kaitlin. "What I'm seeing is an interesting relationship between stress and happiness. A life without stress is boring—a flat line. By nature, we love challenges and we love to win. We're also chemically predisposed to empathize—to experience other people's stories and feelings as if they originated within ourselves. When people share their story conflicts, they produce a chemical response in the brains of their listeners that has emotional and even physiological effects. That stress then triggers a rush of excitement. We're paying attention. We want to find out what happens. We want the storyteller to win so we can experience that thrill of winning. Stories literally rewire our brains. They can make us feel confident and capable and powerful…"

"Or," interrupted Audrey, "they can do a lot of damage. If a person is constantly subjected to stories about their own valuelessness, they'll end up treading water in a miserable vat of cortisol. They'll lose their ability to make happy hormones in response to stories because the outcome is always negative. The conflict never gets overcome; they never get to win."

Kaitlin paused to let Audrey's warning about dark stories resonate and then continued. "I think I'll close with something we talked about the first night we came aboard *The Metaphor*: Sell the benefits, not the features. The idea of transformation—of being stronger or smarter or situated in a more advantageous locale—is biologically appealing to any sentient animal that wants to survive and thrive. Hence, when we imagine how good it will feel to achieve that, a piece of dopamine candy drops down the chute. We want more, and we want to overcome anything that stands in the way of achieving our transformation—but we're not there yet, so there's cortisol—stress—and that keeps us moving. We imagine transformation again and stay on-task. And when we relate to a storyteller, we feel a bond with them—more chemistry. If a community of people shares our conflicts and goals, we bond with them, too; that's another part of our survival mechanism. We ally ourselves with a tribe whose interests aren't competitive. And some of us imagine a heaven or paradise where there's no stress and time stops and we're one with the Universe—maybe because deep down, we know that's what we really are, even though we only get glimpses of it. There's that little shot of serotonin when we're in the right place at the right time with the right people … which brings us back to 'doh.'"

    Little was said for the rest of the day. All knew their time aboard *The Metaphor* was drawing to a close. Returning to the land of clocks and calendars would be no less a shock than that first swim in the cold Sea of Abaco at Moraine Cay.

No Man Is an Island

By afternoon, *The Metaphor* had cleared the tip of the big shoal that extends from Lubber's Quarters Cay across the Sea of Abaco toward the mainland to anchor near Boat Harbour Marina on the south side of Marsh Harbour.

"I'd love to buy everyone dinner at the hotel," offered Micky Tomm.

"Thank you, Mick. I appreciate it—we all do—but I think we should convene the Happiness Congress one last time."

Everyone nodded their agreement.

"I have some closing thoughts on storytelling," said Strider. "For whatever reasons, Dr. King picked a very diverse group of people to participate in this expedition. I know Walter still thinks King and I are the same person, but despite his attendance record, I'll give King his due as an HR director. But I'm starting to think there's one more level where we can connect around our stories. We need other people who understand stories—and who speak different dialects of storytelling—to help us tell our own.

"Take Walter for example. He could use someone like Doug to design the slides he uses in his presentations. Doug speaks the language of design. Walter—no offense intended—will probably create slides that meet the functional intention, but Doug will create slides that *connect*. Maybe Vincent can compose and record the theme music he uses when he walks on stage. Maybe Kaitlin can help with his writing style and word choice. Maybe Micky Tomm needs a speaker who understands the nuances of storytelling to help motivate his people. Maybe Audrey can reveal insights into the stories of the audiences Walter speaks to so he can tailor his talk to connect with them more deeply.

"I could go around the circle and point out who should rely on whom for what, but you are sitting in the presence of some unique resources. You're all prepared to have discussions within a special context about how to communicate and engage. Your talents and skills and diversity make you an unstoppable team. That doesn't mean you should quit your jobs and open up an ad agency—but by the very credible powers vested in me by myself, I confer upon each of you the official status of 'Master Storyteller.' Storytellers need other storytellers."

"No man is an island," quipped Vincent.

"But I get it," said Doug. "Kaitlin can write a book, but she needs an editor to help her polish it and she needs me to typeset it and design the cover. If she does it on her own…"

No Man Is an Island

"It could be great writing," agreed Kaitlin, "but it just won't achieve…"

"Excellence," said Strider. "It might even become a bestseller, but *you* will always know it could have been better. Excellence is perhaps one of the most essential of the absurdities. It's impossible to define, but we recognize it when we see it—and we know it when we produce it. I don't know if 'excellence' is synonymous with 'meaning,' but if not, they're closely related. The search for excellence is certainly meaningful."

Strider held up his wine glass and pulled the cord on the ship's bell.

"At different times during this trip, each of you has talked about how your new understanding of stories will make your lives and businesses different.

"Audrey, you spoke about working with your patients' stories.

"Micky Tomm, you talked about your employees' stories and your company's stories and about how you were coming to think of yourself as a 'story manager.'

"Vincent and Doug, you got in touch with creative, artistic stories that connect in ways that spoken or written language can't.

"Lenore, when we were eating ice cream on Green Turtle Cay, you had your revelation about wrapping data in a story so you could get important projects staffed and funded.

"Walter, you were our official ship's skeptic—which is an important and valuable role. You talked about refocusing and reframing the stories you share with your audiences when you speak, and we talked about the differences between storytelling—which is bound to meaning—and journalism—which is bound to fact.

"There's one person we haven't heard from yet: Kaitlin, our ship's secretary. You came on board and connected with the ship, with the sailing, with the terrain…"

"And with you, Strider. *Woo hoo!*" called Audrey.

Kaitlin turned red. Strider smiled warmly.

"This is our last night," said Strider. "If we were all characters in a strange novel, you'd be the only one who hadn't achieved transformation, Kaitlin."

"Yeah," teased Vincent. "Don't screw up our story."

Kaitlin closed her eyes and thought. The Happiness Congress silently gave her time to compose her thoughts.

"I don't think it makes sense to talk about my new storytelling awareness from a literal writer's perspective. Like you, I've found discussions of the four elements and the seven conflicts—and our adventures on the sea and out in the stars and deep inside the soul—to be life-changing and inspiring. Like you, I've been swimming in an impossible blue fantasy where I've had a chance to mainline rich colors and beautiful symbolism directly into my subconscious. As a writer of stories, most of what I've experienced and learned here will find 'surface-level' applications. My stories have always had conflict and transformation and magic and authenticity;

No Man Is an Island

I just never thought about them in those terms. How much they'll change is difficult to say. This may be disappointing, but I don't have a big revelation to share — some big epiphany that will send all of us seven dwarves back home to dance with Snow White in the cottage in the woods.

"My story — my conflict — is still unresolved, and though I wouldn't exchange the experiences I've had here — and with all of you — for anything, I'm returning to some interesting circumstances.

"Five years ago, I had an idea for a book. I sent it to a well-recommended agent, and he sat on it for a long time, kept me hanging, and then turned it down. No big deal; that's the writer's life. I got sidetracked with other things and then one night I got asked out on a movie date. I sat in disbelief as my story — with my same character names and settings — appeared on the screen. I probably wasn't much of a fun date that night. I called a copyright lawyer and showed him my manuscript and a copy of my query letter.

"I started thinking that maybe it was a good thing. A major motion picture studio had deep pockets and I had a rock-solid case. But by the time the lawyers went back and forth and played their games and stalled and called expert witnesses and cut deals, I ended up with about $20,000 — which translated into paying off my Subaru and covering my expenses to come here. I'm sure my lawyer is off skiing in Aspen or sitting in his skybox at a Seahawks game.

"The fallout from this is that because *I* got ripped off and *I* had the *audacity* to sue a multinational media conglomerate, I'm blacklisted. I can't get an agent to touch my work. Some of them are sympathetic, but they know they won't be able to sell my stories to a publisher. I'm going back to a writing career that's very much up in the air.

"And I love it here. Right now, the idea of exchanging this life for that one takes conflict to whole new level."

"So I'm sorry to be a bummer. I'm as transformed as anyone else here, but though I'm grateful for it, I've become painfully aware of how badly that needed to happen—and still does. I'm happy to be connected to all this and to you—and to you, Strider—but I think when I get back to my apartment tomorrow night and look at my apartment and my car and my computer, I'm going to feel just as far away from home as I did when I stepped off Charlie Albury's launch onto the dock at Moraine Cay.

"What about you, Strider?" Kaitlin changed the subject. "What's your big transformation? How does your story go?"

Strider took a long deep breath. "My dear, a man does not find himself alone in Paradise on a schooner named *The Metaphor* unless he has a few conflicts of his own. For now, my plan is to go to work, patch my ship, and keep sailing until I figure out what those conflicts are, and what port I want to drop anchor in. I'll look for water that's deep enough but not too deep—and hope for fair winds to push me on my journey. I'm as stuck in my story as anyone, but at least it's a good story. Getting stuck in a good story might be better than getting stuck in a bad one, but maybe 'stuck' is 'stuck.' Whether that turns out to make any difference remains to be seen."

Epilogue

Dear Strider,

It's been a time of adjustment for me - but things are better than expected. Maybe I'm getting my big transformation after all, though I suspect a life well lived involves a series of them. "Happily ever after" sounds boring.

As you suggested, the airlines had no problem picking us up at Marsh Harbour airport. We were all on the same outbound flight to Miami, so it was easy. The plane stopped at Treasure Cay on the way out to pick up one passenger. He sat next to me, and I happened to glance at his passport. It was none other than Houston Gibson King, Ph.D.

The Story Story

I started laughing like a maniac; I was sure I was going to pee my pants. But when I explained who we were, King turned out to be a gentleman. Turns out his in-bound flight had gotten cancelled and his cellphone went for a swim. He got in a day late and got stuck on Moraine Cay by himself - just him and enough food for eight people. He'd been lonely, but mostly he'd been beside himself wondering what had become of us. As far as anyone on shore knew, we were all camped out in the house on Moraine Cay. I think the experience challenged some of his definitions of happiness, but I suppose that's a challenge we all need from time to time.

We had a laugh on Walter who found out who the real Dr. King was. He actually lost a $100 bet with Micky Tomm, but Mick wouldn't accept the money. We ended up talking with Dr. King about stories during the flight and continued while we waited for our connections in Miami.

Epilogue

Two things came of that meeting:

First, Dr. King told me he wanted to learn more about the relationship between stories and happiness. He advised me to write about stories under a pen name and said he'd be happy to read my book and share it with his agent as long as it met the standards he felt certain it would.

I can hear you asking, "What book?" The manuscript you are holding - The Story Story - A Voyage Through the Islands of Connection and Engagement for Writers, Speakers, Professionals and Visionaries - is my response to our journey aboard The Metaphor and to Dr. King's challenge. I've been writing like a madwoman since the moment I got home; I think I've lost ten pounds! King has become a helpful friend and a much-needed high-level contact in the publishing business.

The second thing that happened is that Dr. King opened up his bag and pulled out a checkbook. He wrote us all refund checks right there on the plane with money added to cover expenses. He said he was relieved we had managed to salvage our trip, but that it could have been a disaster. He was so remorseful, I ended up feeling bad for him. The cost was nothing to him, and he knew it was the right thing to do. I got the Happiness Congress into a huddle and we decided we had all invested in our stories and preferred it that way. The enclosed envelope contains seven checks for $5000 - one from each of us - more than enough to haul and repair The Metaphor and get you back to your story.

    I have enough editing and copywriting work to keep me going while I wait for the universe to do what it will with my manuscript, but all that work is portable. Thanks to Dr. King covering my expenses for the first Bahamas trip, I propose a second one. I would so enjoy a chance to sit on

Epilogue

the deck of The Metaphor and get my work done with a good friend nearby and the sun on my cheeks.

Love,

Kaitlin

Itinerary

Day 1–Moraine Cay

Day 2–Moraine Cay to Green Turtle Cay

Day 3–Visit Green Turtle Cay

Day 4–Green Turtle to Marsh Harbour to Man-O-War Cay

Day 5–Visit Man-O-War Cay

Day 6–Man-O-War Cay to Hopetown

Day 7–Visit Hopetown

Day 8–Hopetown to Little Harbour

Day 9–Visit Little Harbour

Day 10–Sail to Marsh Harbour to drop off passengers

Author's Note

The voyages in this book are based on my own sailing experiences in the northern Bahamas during the late 1980s and early 1990s. The island settings are real. My voyages to the Bahamas and points beyond are recounted in my memoir, *The Blue Monk*.

The characters in *The Story Story* are clear individuals though I've described them in minimal detail. I hope you recognize yourself and people you know in them, and that I've given you latitude to paint your own pictures of them.

The Metaphor is loosely based on a 62-foot John Alden-designed schooner named *The Mayan* that once frequented the Abacos and the Florida Keys. David Crosby of the famous rock group owned this elegant ship, but though Mr. Crosby had his own adventures in the Abacos, our paths never knowingly crossed. *The Mayan* has been extensively restored and is now berthed in California.

Strider, the unlikely teacher, as eccentric as he is in the story, is an amalgam of two real, wonderful, colorful people I met on my travels aboard *The Blue Monk.* There really was a "Strider" who lived and sailed fearlessly aboard an engineless fiberglass sloop named *Mother Ocean*. And my friend, John "Strider" Nation, was another inspiration for the story's barefooted, zebra-pantsed, 'expert on everything' captain. John built his own 40-foot replica of a 1911 Nova Scotian fishing schooner and christened her *Zebra Dun* after an old cowboy song. In her cabin, anchored in the Bahamas, over coffee and pancakes, we two boat bums engaged in many of the discussions and explorations that led—almost thirty years later—to *The Story Story*. John also spent considerable time reading and discussing this manuscript with me prior to its publication. And of course you'll find some of me in Captain Strider, too.

As *The Story Story* suggests, we are *all* storytellers. Everything you know or think you know is a story. Use the ideas in this book to create stories that lead to meaningful transformations in the lives and businesses of your self and those you touch. Engage, connect, and succeed.

—Dave Bricker, November, 2017

Acknowledgments

A workshop by speaker and speaking coach Haley Foster inspired me to introduce my characters according to their individual passions and missions. Thank you, Haley, for one of this book's most valuable storytelling tips. Powerful introductions make powerful connections.

Truth is stranger than fiction. John Nation, I can still picture you aboard your schooner, pontificating about one thing or another, clad in zebra pants and sandals made from old tires. How wonderful it was to sit on deck in Man-O-War Cay, stare at the stars, carve experience from a block of timelessness, and revel in the Mystery. My friend, *The Story Story* would not have happened without you and those magic times and places.

Strider, like so many of "those people out there" in the Dinner Key Anchorage, you've sailed on, but your decision to show an 18-year-old kid what sailing in the Florida Keys was like inspired thousands of miles of adventure and ultimately, this book. Thank you.

The Story Story

George Walther, introducing me to the National Speakers Association was a gift I was not fully able to appreciate on first exposure, but that journey has proven every bit as adventurous and rewarding as setting sail in a small boat. Walter, the speaker in *The Story Story* is a tribute to you and the many friends I've made in that colorful community. Notable among those friends are Dr. Margarita Gurri, Caroline De Posada, Bruce Turkel, and Kelly Swanson. Your encouragement and ideas contributed directly to building a road I never imagined would lead to this book.

Tom McCaffery, you engaged me for a big pharma consulting project back in 2007 that I never would have thought could have turned into the adventure it did. By example, you taught me some valuable lessons about leadership. Though Micky Tomm is not a reflection of your personal and professional style, he's smart and cares about the impact of his work on people — as you do. His presence as a character in the book is my homage to you.

When I finish a manuscript (this being book #7), I always put out a call for test readers before sending the final draft along to my editor. Reading and critiquing an unpolished book is a task that requires time, focus, and willingness to dole out the honest feedback every author needs. Thank you to Felicity Howlett, Bud Maddock, Alberto Gross, David Weinstein, and Greg Glass

Acknowledgments

for finishing the manuscript, catching invisible typos, ferreting out clunky sentences, questioning idiosyncratic word choices, and challenging me to be a better writer. John Nation, you get additional kudos for being part of my reading team.

And as Kaitlin makes clear, every writer needs an editor. Thank you Steven Bauer for providing the tough love that turns manuscripts into books.

Because independent writers and publishers should be held to the same high standards as the mainstream publishing industry, I encourage you to post an honest and objective review of this book on Amazon.com or the online bookstore of your choice.

Thank you,

—Dave Bricker

www.ingramcontent.com/pod-product-compliance
Lightning Source LLC
Chambersburg PA
CBHW032032150426
43194CB00006B/243